Faulkner the Storyteller

Faulkner the Storyteller

BLAIR LABATT

THE UNIVERSITY OF ALABAMA PRESS
Tuscaloosa

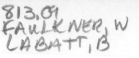

Copyright © 2005
The University of Alabama Press
Tuscaloosa, Alabama 35487-0380

Manufactured in the United States of America

Typeface: ACaslon

∞

The paper on which this book is printed meets the minimum requirements of American National Standard for Information Science–Permanence of Paper for Printed Library Materials, ANSI Z39.48-1984.

Library of Congress Cataloging-in-Publication Data

Labatt, Blair, 1947–
  Faulkner the storyteller / Blair Labatt.
    p. cm.
  Includes bibliographical references (p.) and index.
  ISBN 0-8173-1437-7 (cloth : alk. paper)   ISBN 0-8173-5350-x (alk. paper)
  1. Faulkner, William, 1897–1962—Stories, plots, etc. 2. Faulkner, William, 1897–1962—Technique. 3. Storytelling—Southern States. 4. Fiction—Technique. 5. Narration (Rhetoric) I. Title.
  PS3511.A86Z8735 2004
  813'.52—dc22

                                                                      2004010899

Contents

Abbreviations

AA   William Faulkner. *Absalom, Absalom!* New York: Random House, 1936; reprint, Modern Library, 1964.

AN   Henry James. *The Art of the Novel.* Ed. R. P. Blackmur. New York: Scribner, 1934.

CS   William Faulkner. *Collected Stories of William Faulkner.* New York: Random House, 1950.

H   William Faulkner. *The Hamlet.* New York: Random House, 1940.

LIA   William Faulkner. *Light in August.* New York: Harrison Smith and Robert Haas, 1932; reprint, Random House, 1966.

Lion   James B. Meriwether and Michael Millgate, eds. *Lion in the Garden: Interviews with William Faulkner, 1926–1962.* New York: Random House, 1968.

M   William Faulkner. *The Mansion.* New York: Random House, 1959.

S   William Faulkner. *Sartoris.* New York: Harcourt, Brace, 1929.

SF   William Faulkner. *The Sound and the Fury.* New York: Jonathan Cape and Harrison Smith, 1929; reprint, Random House, 1964.

T   William Faulkner. *The Town.* New York: Random House, 1957.

A cross-reference to pagination in the "corrected" texts appears in the appendix to this volume.

Acknowledgments

Upon completing a long-deliberated first book, the natural inclination is to want to thank everybody. Who knows when or if there may be a second chance? This is the privileged moment to record in print my gratitude to the friends, both in and out of academia, who have influenced both this book and its writer.

I particularly want to thank the special teachers who have shaped my reading life over many years: Tom Roche, Charles Fish, John Fleming, Bob Hollander, Jack Levenson, Christopher Tolkien, and John Bayley. Since we first experienced Princeton together, Ray Keck has been not only the closest of comrades but a never-ceasing fount of enthusiasm for learning, and a stimulus to look at unfamiliar works and new ways of seeing. I thank also John Brazil and the trustees of Trinity University for the use of the Coates Library. For their multifaceted friendship over many important times I am grateful to Bill McGrane, Duncan Osborne, Hoyt Duggan, Don Frost, Terry Oxford, Mike McCrory, Jim Johnson, Bruce Merrifield, and Weir Labatt.

No one has had a greater impact on me or deserves greater appreciation than Al Silva—colleague, adviser, critic, and the best of friends—not only for our many years together in the most fulfilling of careers but also for his encouragement in completing this book. I owe thanks also to hundreds of people in the common enterprise we build together, not only for making my professional life unfailingly stimulating but also for making it possible for me to be a covert "independent scholar." Of these I am especially indebted to Tony Canty; to Gary Beadle, for his magic software; and to Lynda Haner, for her unfailing patience, good humor, and diligence in preparing the manuscript.

In the broadest sense I want to thank Princeton University, where stimulus and abundance and recognition all came together in a magical time and place that created a lifetime vocation.

I am also the beneficiary of a lifetime of deep influences from my family: my mother, Gloria Bramlette Labatt, and my siblings Grace, Joe, and Fred Labatt; my three splendid children, Annie, Blair, and Grace, all of whom made their special contributions to this book; and above all, my wife, Barbara. Without her, nothing could have happened that has happened. At an Oxford High Table, Anthony Quinton once called her "a fairy princess among the ogres." Fortunately for all of us, she found her calling in devoting herself to the lesser lights at our lower table.

This book is dedicated to the memory of my personal cloud of witnesses, who were and will always remain sources of special inspiration to me:

Grace Jones Bramlette
Blair Plowman Labatt
Mary Lee Durham
Robert Bernard Martin
Laurence Bedwell Holland
Jane Watson Irwin

Introduction

What is this false ingenuousness, this business of "the storyteller"? Everyone knows a storyteller is some old coot who dresses up and sits in a rocking chair at the folklife festival, pretending to offer authentic old-time entertainment for the kids. The word might seem intended to recall the presumed false modesty with which William Faulkner presented himself as only a farmer, or only a carpenter, or only a teller of stories. But in fact the word has its uses. What I propose to do is think seriously about both stories and the ultimate "teller" in the work of one writer. The *fabula,* the syntax of events, is the aspect of narrative that most narratology deals with quickly if at all. My objective is to look at several such sequences and describe how they work. But beyond that, I want to ask how plot structures contribute to create the implied teller of the text. In an inspired aperçu, Paul Goodman writes: "In narrative works it is the narrator who convinces, and in principle we ought to be able to demonstrate this in the details of the work. A talking horse does not make sense, but Homer makes sense of Achilles' talking horse, and 'Homer' is a certain rhythm, diction, selection, and arrangement of episodes" (76). The question then becomes how a given plot acts with or against other continuities of a text—agency, imagery, the interplay of sequence and digression, and above all the voice(s) of an extradiegetic narrator—to make up the "Faulkner" of that text. A more conventional academic title would have been "Plot and Implied Author in Faulkner's Narrative." The word *storyteller,* however disreputable and old-fashioned, thus serviceably yokes my two concerns: the story and the implied teller.

"How easy it is to make up stories!" says the narrator of Diderot's *Jacques the Fatalist* (4). That, however, has not been my observation. The skeins of fabulation improvised by Diderot (and in this, as Malcolm Bradbury conveys in his novel *To the Hermitage,* Diderot is himself a postmodernist) bear more than a little resemblance to the annalistic and atavistic "story" that seemed so unsatisfying to E. M. Forster. I have undertaken to do a study in which I could find out very simply how one great writer makes things happen. I initially thought of something like Genette's *Narrative Discourse,* in which general reflection would move seamlessly into the particular, with the preponderance of the examples coming from one writer. Really, however, despite my delight in Genette's taxonomy and its terminological ingenuity (and his actually vast breadth of reference), the aspect of Genette's work that gives the most lasting pleasure is his remarkable ability not merely to describe the contents of Proust's work but to discriminate its differentiating characteristics, the things that make Proust Proust. For me, as well, a desire to learn about plot in general has led to an engagement with particular texts and with the uniqueness of one writer.

Talking of plots is still unpopular, even thankless. As N.J. Lowe says in beginning his splendid book, "'Plot' is an unloved word in narrative theory" (ix). Yes, a *fabula* exists, but it is of course a "back-formation" (O'Neill 40), a variable construct formulated by (each) reader from the discourse, apart from which it has no existence. This is a consensus not to be dissented from, and it can in practice be very condescending to the very notion of plot. Concern with plot can apparently be left to the practitioners (who, of course, have no status in theory).

Actually, in recent years there has been a fair amount of stimulating theoretical writing about plots: Thomas Pavel's use of problems and moves; Marie-Laure Ryan's comprehensive categorization of moves and of plot shapes; Emma Kafelnos's recasting and simplification of Propp's "functions"; Lubomir Dolezel's descriptions of agency in terms of imagined worlds; Lowe's replacement of the metaphor of "levels" with the concept of a reader's maintenance of a cognitive triptych of rules, of the *sjuzhet,* and of a gradually emerging *fabula.*

While Genette and Lowe work from the outside in, theorizing or categorizing and then testing their propositions against the great text, my instinct is to work from the inside out, from the texts to whatever comparisons or generalizations or excursions seem called for by the text. The urge to typology of plot, or even a poetics of plot, is not mine. I am naturally inclined to look for the pragmatic truth value, the "cash value" in actual texts. My idea has been to learn about plots not in the abstract but by finding out how a "great writer" (the phrase was once respectable) actually *makes* them. Instead of a general study, let alone a poetics, with examples from Faulkner, this became preeminently an empirical description of plots that attempted to give practical utility value to terminology, which assumed that the abstractions had no significance outside their unique working in unique texts.

Hanging over the head of anyone who writes about plot may be the ancient companion "plot summary," a term that calls up not just the type of critical writing Grandfather did, called "close readings," but something pejorative rooted deeply in everyone's personal history of reading—the most rudimentary, unsophisticated way of reading, the form of talking about books to be outgrown by the fifth grade—the mere plot summary, something like the chronological, annalistic sequence that led E. M. Forster to say, "Oh, dear, yes—a novel tells a story" (24).

People who write about plot do often seem to be looking behind them for the threat of that invective "plot summary."[1] There has certainly been on occasion a temptation to achieve some legitimizing sophistication by emulating a kind of scientific or at least linguistic notation. In fact, such notation can on occasion dramatize very effectively the cross purposes of the kind of plot that contains complicated new-comedy misunderstandings. Lowe is quite amusing in giving an example of this:

> [I]f the local function is "loves," the game state
> A(B) C(D) BD(C) / BC:A(C) BA:C(A) / C:B:C(D)
> describes a situation in which A loves B who instead loves C,
> who instead loves and is loved by D. But B and C both labour
> under the impression that A actually loves C, and B and A both
> think that C loves A. C, however, supposes that what B imagines
> is that C loves D—as is indeed the case. If this sounds an impos-
> sible brain-twister in its bare skeleton, it does not particularly
> strike us so in the form of *Twelfth Night* v.i.158–65; and New
> Comic plots are often far more convoluted than this. (52)

My approach will be much less pseudo-algebraic, as is Lowe's own. What the best writers on plot have fruitfully availed themselves of is not notation but metaphor. As Lowe notes of Thomas Pavel, what is useful in talking about plot is not mathematical game theory so much as the metaphors of game theory, the concept of "moves." The kind of paraphrase that helps to make distinctions between plots is one which can distinguish the material importance of different events and the relationship of events to the agents who are involved in them. For this neither algebraic notation nor pictorial diagrams are really necessary.[2]

It must be frustrating to anyone who covets a universal terminology to see even the best writers show so little interest in using or assimilating the words of their predecessors. Even the basic terms like plot and story, narrative, *sjuzhet*, and *fabula* have been grouped and categorized in seemingly every possible combination and permutation. Having created the methods they did, some of the best theorists, like Pavel, have abandoned their own innovations and gone on to other things. In a sense, every new writer finds him- or herself free from any obligatory set of definitions, let alone of methodology. I use a terminology at least in part compared and tested against those of the best theoretical writers like Genette and Lowe, but flexibly applied.

In my view the analysis of story must not stand alone, a paraphrase out of context. Story rightly discerned leads us back into the multifaceted text, to the ways story is joined to all that is not story—contemplations, pauses, excursions from the story—the "descriptive" material in the interstices of events. A willingness to look at the joints in the narrative in this way implicitly permits a discussion of craft, and thus reflects my concern with the perspective of the practitioner. Looking at the way things are put together encourages us as readers to make our own value judgments about whether and where the best choices have been made.

Further, story naturally calls us to think about the implications of story. The process of distinguishing the materiality of events, the different ways events are joined to each other, and the consequence of events leads to four possible outcomes. First, the process allows the description of the variety of kinds of events and stories used by a given writer, in this case William Faulkner. Second, it might lead us to ask in what ways the plots of Faulkner define "Faulkner." But that question brings in the related question of how or whether the plots cooperate with or conflict with other influences working to constitute "Faulkner," elements such as non-plot and the voice of the extradiegetic narrator. Finally, it becomes possible to ask in reasonable ways whether there is such a thing as a typical Faulkner plot, or at least whether a given plot is untypical. The last three matters I will raise in the final chapter. To raise these questions is to move beyond the stereotypical view of plot as insignificant, rudimentary, fodder for the unsophisticated. The best vindication of plot as good subject matter for a book like this thus comes not from theory but from all the things it gives one to do.

This is decidedly a book about Faulkner. There is a great deal to say about Faulkner's plotting, and Faulkner's plotting leads to many other things. The role of plotting and how it contributes to "imply" a "Faulkner" teller will hardly seem exhausted here. And yet I hope that the tone and context of my analysis is directed toward questions of general narratological importance. It should not be surprising that a great writer will completely take over a book of criticism and absorb all questions to himself, but that does not necessarily mean it makes the result narrowly what people call a book of "Faulkner criticism."

Yet in another sense I would like to think that this book sounds a note that will not be common in Faulkner criticism. Certainly a focus on the shape of plots departs from the common distrust of all formal analysis.[3] My method also does not make use of biographism, the use of biography to illuminate texts, what Lothar Honnighausen has called "the new biographical criticism" (*Masks and Metaphors* 58)—particularly in the quasi-Freudian form that sees Faulkner's writing as acting out primal scenes of personal distress.[4] Further, I do not pursue what Molly Hite, following Brian McHale, has called "postmodern text-processing strategies" (59). Donald Kartiganer describes with some sympathy this current critical practice of "reading against the text," a process that empowers the reader to "'rewrite' texts in order to give voice to characters and cultures . . . [that are] (almost) silent." Kartiganer observes that "'interrogation' can prod a text into performing the reversals that free it" ("Faulkner Criticism," 82–83). For me this argument bears a little too much resemblance to the old joke that if you torture the facts hard enough they will confess to anything.[5]

Certainly it is proper to entertain fugitive readings that find furtive or subterranean notes in the text or which find fault with the text either for dishonest omissions or internal incoherences. But it is important to know which is which, and it is important in hearing alternative notes to respect and accurately describe the proportions of the text. Few postmodern critics have adequately distinguished whether they are talking about novels the writer wanted to write, or novels they believe him to have written without understanding what he was doing, or simply novels they think he should have written. It is one thing to confront the intentionalities of the text, or to let the text bring forth its own strange blooms. What this kind of criticism often offers instead is the spectacle of the critic himself, cavorting in the hermeneutic gap.

Also, I will try to be somewhat skeptical about the relentless periodizing of Faulkner's career and even of specific texts. In 1991, Gary Lee Stonum wrote: "The view that Faulkner is quintessentially a modernist writer . . . seems to stand as the principal orthodoxy (or the principal achievement, if you like) of Faulkner studies as they enter the 90's" ("Modernism" 364). Philip Weinstein's modification of this orthodoxy is that Faulkner would "write himself out of modernism in the 1940s as decisively as he had written himself into it in the 1920s" (*Cambridge Companion* 11). This division makes it possible to describe a second phase in Faulkner's career with its own virtues—perhaps even describable as "postmodernism"—without necessarily abandoning the older orthodoxy that much of very late Faulkner is weakened by discursiveness, the public role-playing of a novelist sage, unenlightened views on civil rights, or perhaps just fatigue. Honnighausen, citing John Matthews and Kartiganer, has written of a critical tendency "to shift the focus from *The Sound and the Fury,* a favorite of the formalists, to *The Hamlet,* emphasizing its 'non-centeredness' . . . and its 'anarchy, indeed a madness built into the structure'" (*Masks and Metaphors* 66). The notion that Faulkner turns from modernism to fabulation in mid-career makes it important to describe exactly what kinds of *fabula* Faulkner does construct. But in my view even the amended orthodoxy is easy to overstate.

The proponents of postmodernism have come to value characterization that postulates a subjectivity which is "decentered," or a discontinuous series of performances, or a socially scripted set of obligations.[6] These are not at all three versions of the same thing, and except in an extreme form all should be thought of as traditional options in the novel form. If it is a postmodernist fable to see a passive and insecure child confused and victimized by socially imposed scripts, then *Great Expectations* is postmodern. Dickens knew about the yet-unformulated subject, or the subject scripted by external forces—the forces that make Pip metaphorically a Frankenstein's monster. But he also conveys the strangeness of personalities that may have no interiority at all. In Boswell's journals we see both a romantic distress over (and relishing of) the inconsistencies and complications of a decentered self *and* an eighteenth-century resolution to construct a better self through performative self-improvement;

both these sides of Boswell could be called postmodern. It is the modernist Fitzgerald who describes personality as composed of a series of gestures, the arch-modernist Lawrence who calls for a character which is not the "old stable ego of character" (Allott 289–90). The embattled subject of modernism can also be decentered, as Philip Weinstein shows concerning *Light in August* ("Postmodern Intimations"). The solipsistic individual, Prufrock or Quentin Compson, can be both intensely aware of his subjectivity and also unsure of what it is or what to do with it. He can be aware, too, of how entangled he is with the others whom he both is and is not separated from. No one could be more ensnarled than is Quentin in the toils of Compson.

All of this suggests that it may be problematic to establish unique attributes of character that will support a fine-tuned periodicity. To find a uniquely postmodern character we may look to the character who loses his identity entirely, Pynchon's vanishing Slothrop. But the vanishing of Slothrop might legitimately be thought of, not as a new postmodern subjectivity, but as a parody of paranoid insecurity, or even as simply a feckless way to terminate a story.

The application of the term "modernism" to Faulkner also has led to generalizations that tend to obscure the kinds of agency and event actually created in Faulkner's plots. There are many modernisms, even many modernist canons. Andre Bleikasten's pantheon is predominantly continental; David Lodge includes James and Conrad and sees the generation of Waugh and Antony Powell as already "post-modernist" (which is not, perhaps, the same as "postmodernist"). But the particular version of Faulkner's modernism that has had a status as critical orthodoxy is an attitude toward action and a philosophy of knowledge in which action seems meaningless and ineffective and knowledge is evanescent and always uncertain. The orthodox view has been that the modernist Faulkner's texts—and in this *Absalom, Absalom!* is paradigmatic—insist on events as by nature unknowable and indeterminate. Not only is any account of events not proven beyond a reasonable doubt, but such a standard is not even applicable because all doubt is reasonable. *Nothing* can be said to "fit." Faulkner has the aspect of the modernist, because event is hermeneutically and epistemologically indecipherable; but also perhaps of the postmodernist, because the text (of *Absalom, Absalom!* at any rate) offers the reader an open complicity in rescripting it, engaging it in ludic play.[7] The modernist Faulkner's attitude toward language is the devastating conviction of its ultimate inability to "say" what suffering humanity feels.[8]

As Philip Weinstein says, we must all be prepared to give up our own (naive) conceptions of Faulkner (*Faulkner's Subject* 8). "My" Faulkner, however, is not the modernist Faulkner, even where Stonum's modernist orthodoxy is amended to apply to only part of Faulkner's career. The disconnected modernist event moves in and out of Faulkner's work, but in general Faulkner's event structures do not represent "modernistic contestations of narrative" (Kroeber 3). The dominant form of plotting that I find in Faulkner is instead plotting with multiple characters engaged in sequences of moves that enact confrontation and conflict. It is eventful plotting. Epistemological questioning acts as a way of focusing the reader (and the characters) on arriving at an imaginative understanding of events undertaken by willful human agents. I place high value on these forms, both because of the intrinsic complexity (the variety of actors) and because in this case the complexity reflects significant and compelling assumptions about the nature of human actions. Faulkner's stories are based on the assumption of the existence of separate human people. The separateness of those people is what generates the plot. That is to say, Faulkner's stories deal with and reflect what Faulkner makes a basic condition of human life—the contrariety that works sometimes for good, sometimes for ill.

The modernist conviction of the failure of all language misses the point of Faulkner's language entirely. On the contrary, Faulkner ultimately enacts an attitude to language and to writing that is triumphant and authoritative. It is very easy to use his texts to support the ideas of the inability of words to say, the lack of faith in language, and the tone of despair. The problem is that the overall impact of the text reverses, contextualizes, and undercuts the explicit language that is easy to find and quote. The Faulkner out of love with language in fact amounts to a quotation out of context.

Faulkner's linkages are ultimately to a Victorian conception—a certainty in George Eliot, Trollope, and even Hardy—that character is destiny, or that in fiction character should be seen to be, if not a sufficient condition, then at least a necessary condition for what happens.[9] To put it somewhat differently, as Robert Caserio writes, "We may have in

Faulkner an American Dickens whose moral values will appear, as time passes, increasingly more like those of the nineteenth-century proponents of plot and less like the modernists' narrative antagonisms and experiments" (286). To say this is not to say that Faulkner is "not modernist but Victorian" but rather that Faulkner makes a fiction in which modernism is subsumed into some greater stability and poise and faith.

For Faulkner the statement made by plots is not that stories are easy, effortless improvisations of fabulation, but rather that good plots are significant, important, and highly wrought. They mark Faulkner—to use Henry James's characterization of Conrad—"as a votary of the way to do a thing that shall make it undergo most doing" ("The New Novel," *Future of the Novel* 279). Events are important expressions of identity, of will; as such they receive virtuoso "doing" from Faulkner.

I have made a selection of Faulknerian plots based both on the length of the texts and on the degree of complexity in the structure of events. Some of these texts—notably *The Town* and *The Mansion*—are not normally accorded the canonical status of the works of 1929–36. Nevertheless, in their planning and writing the Snopes novels span thirty years, Faulkner's entire career, and they have the virtue of showing the "same" characters in a variety of moves and events. They are instructive not simply because they all have the same characters but because they allow us to see Faulkner using these characters in very different kinds of event structures. Instead of repetitive structures, Faulkner gives us variety. A reading of his forms leads to the conviction that each individual plot achieves its unique working out.

If this is a "retro" Faulkner, then let him be brought back—along with, I entreat, the un-"corrected" texts and titles of his works as he published them and chose to leave them in his lifetime. This is an act of restoration to which Faulkner's readers are entitled. It would be of course desirable and valuable to have completely collated editions of the variants between all of Faulkner's texts and typescripts. Simply attributing all changes past the typescript stage to unwanted editorial imposition requires a leap of faith that is not only considerable but unscholarly. In a letter about Noel Polk's edition of *All The King's Men,* in which Polk changes the name of Willie Stark, Joyce Carol Oates writes: "That Noel Polk should make a project of 'restoring' a text in this way, and that this text should be published to compete with the author-approved text, is unconscionable, unethical, and indefensible" (54). What then should we say about "corrected" texts that not only compete with, but are permitted to replace and make unavailable, the entire oeuvre of a master writer?

Approaching this master writer through his plots illuminates the unique mixture of actions and contemplations that is "Faulkner." Christine Brooke-Rose writes, "If narrative 'syntax' isn't enough it is nevertheless essential" (291). I affirm with this study that plots are worth writing about, that they represent a window into the form of novels and also a way of understanding the unique attributes of a major novelist.

Faulkner the Storyteller

I

What Happens in Faulkner

Cause, Event, Effect

The contriving of doings has been perhaps the most underrated of all the achievements of novelists. If story is, as Henry James asserted, "just the spoiled child of art" (*AN* 315), it has been generally the neglected stepchild of commentary on art. Undoubtedly readers have suspected that the making of actions is the most mechanical of the writer's tasks. As Roland Barthes writes in *S/Z*, actions are the main armature of the readerly text (225). For Barthes and most other sophisticated readers, however, to read is to take that armature as a given and instead to focus on other sequences, other codes, especially where the readerly text offers its limited ambiguities; or, further, to call for writerly texts without armature and with unlimited polyvalence. The purpose of calling William Faulkner a "storyteller" is not to suggest that he has an affinity for some sort of primitive and garrulous oral narrative, but rather to recenter the fact that he is a writer interested in the making of stories, a writer to whom stories matter.

Faulkner shows a remarkable versatility in constructing events and series of events: plots of collision, and plots of gradually developing strategies; isolated actions, and parallel actions that give context to each other; events, and the tension-building periods of contemplation that make them notable. Faulkner is the maker of actions in which the desires and wills of human beings can stand at odds. Like James, he makes use of plots not as contrived mechanisms but as the very means of expressing characters and relations; his narratives detail the changes in situations shared by "communities of doom" (*AN* 293). He presents in narrative the infinite processes by which people do things to other people. Faulkner's story is implicitly an attempt to deal with the fundamental willfulness of people. Even though narratologists have often insisted on separating plot from agency, in Faulkner's case plot cannot be rightly expressed "in abstraction from the peculiar characters and mental processes of the agents" (R. S. Crane 619). In following the changes in relations among characters as expressed in plot structures, we recognize the kind of maker Faulkner is and the importance of his doings.

As a necessary preliminary, it will be important to deploy a vocabulary adequately flexible to permit the description of a *fabula* in terms of the consequences of events, the ways events are joined together, and the relative materiality of events. To distinguish between stories, we will have to assert the importance of a concept—event—while acknowledging its imprecision outside the context of each writer's rhetoric, or of local causes and effects. In *Aspects of the Novel*, E. M. Forster notoriously tends to devalue the features most characteristic of story makers. Forster's "story" is a "low atavistic form" in which events are arranged in their temporal sequence without any particular causation (26). It can only answer the question "and then?" (86). It can only help pass the time: "*Qua* story, it can only have one merit: that of making the audience want to know what happens next" (27). The higher form for Forster is "plot," in which causality is more important: "'The king died and then the queen died' is a story. 'The king died, and then the queen died of grief' is a plot. The time-sequence is preserved, but the sense of causality overshadows it" (86). A story satisfies the reader's curiosity; a plot satisfies curiosity and intelligence and memory (86).[1]

But in distinguishing the extremes of narrative as the narrative of sequence and the narrative of causation, Forster ignores the events themselves. At first he emphasizes the compatibility of plot and the "secret life" that is never expressed in events (83); later he develops the notion of a coercive plot that intermittently forces characters to make more overt contributions:

> [The characters] want to sit apart and brood or something, and
> the plot (whom I here visualize as a sort of higher government
> official) is concerned at their lack of public spirit: "This will not
> do," it seems to say. "Individualism is a most valuable quality; indeed my own position depends upon individuals; I have always
> admitted as much freely. Nevertheless there are certain limits, and
> those limits are being overstepped. Characters must not brood
> too long, they must not waste time running up and down ladders

in their own insides, they must contribute, or higher interests will be jeopardized." (85)

Obviously, the coercive part of the plot is not the causation but the events themselves, the element that "stories" and "plots" have in common. When Forster comes to discuss an obvious "contriver" (90) like George Meredith, he must forget the distinction between causation and temporality, and talk about the relation of character and "incident," in particular the changes which incident itself effects: "A Meredithian plot is not a temple to the tragic or even to the comic Muse, but rather resembles a series of kiosks most artfully placed among wooded slopes, which his people reach by their own impetus, and from which they emerge with altered aspect. Incident springs out of character, and having occurred it alters that character. People and events are closely connected, and he does it by means of these contrivances" (90–91). In this excursion from his own distinction, Forster comes to grips brilliantly with what he has hitherto ignored, the events that satisfy our curiosity as to what happens next. In his relation of character, events, and change, he opens up possibilities for a different way of comparing stories.

Perhaps the idea of causation is of only secondary importance in comparing narratives.[2] What is lacking in *Ulysses*, for example, is neither sequence nor causation but significant action, *change*. Joyce appeals to curiosity and the desire for explanation, but ultimately there is no action to explain, no sequence worth explaining. In *Ulysses* the presence of causation is a moot point; causation is not important because action is not finally important. Apparently a sequence can have perfectly clear causation as far as it goes and yet not go far enough to make a difference. But even with writers like Joyce we keep expecting something significant to happen, as Barbara Hardy notes:

> If the novel does not possess the form of the story then it is not a novel.
>
> Even defiant story-tellers like Sterne or Joyce or Robbe-Grillet have either had to retain its rudimentary features or have had to exploit the very form they were flouting. *Tristram Shandy* tantalizes conventional narrative expectations but only succeeds in its teasing satire by keeping within the limits of fiction and occasionally satisfying our need to know what happened next. We may

often be told what happened before instead of what happened afterwards, we may never know what happened in the end, but the whole ingenious structure is committed to the form of expectation and curiosity. (*Appropriate Form* 2)

Joyce can frustrate our curiosity about story only by first stimulating it. While we wait for something significant, we find ourselves fully occupied with keeping abreast of what turns out to be fairly small stakes—how each character has spent each hour. All writers may in some way provoke curiosity about what will happen or has happened, but not all really satisfy that curiosity. There are writers who are more or less successfully "defiant," who finally deny us significant events.

An interesting attempt to assert the basic difference between the plots where action matters and plots where "nothing happens" is made by Paul Goodman in *The Structure of Literature*. Goodman calls these two forms the "serious" plot and the "sentimental" or "novelistic" plot. He emphasizes, however, that the plots are often mixed, that sentimental plots in particular often include serious or tragic actions as a consequence of having finished their plots of sentiment:

"Seriousness" is taken as a relation between agents and actions, the relation of "being essentially involved." (26)

Novels of the sentimental kind are sequences of occasions for sentiment, leading to abiding attitudes or active commitments. Unlike serious poems, the actions of the persons do not essentially engage them; . . . the persons respond to the events rather than being completely in them. (127)

The ending is the character-fixation of the hero, such as it is. . . . In serious works we speak of "character change," as the character of Oedipus changes at the reversal. In such a change one abiding structure gives way to another related one, because from the beginning the character is seriously involved. In the novelistic "fixing of character," on the other hand, there is a sequence in relatively freely varying responses. (129)

In novels of sentiment the fixation of character may be followed by tragic scenes, as in *The Scarlet Letter* the fixing of the will of the Reverend Dimmesdale leads to the disclosure on the scaffold. (130)

The sentimental hero must have interests. . . . But—and this is very important to bear in mind—these interests taken as a whole do not give the hero's character, for he does not act them out to a finish or respond completely in the occasions that they bring about. (133)

We might well say that what Goodman calls the mixing of two forms of plots is really the mixing of plot and non-plot, or of events and contemplations. We might say that his "novelistic" plots, like the stories of Barbara Hardy's defiant storyteller, do not become completed stories until they become "serious" plots, or until the characters do act out their interests "to a finish." Nevertheless, whether we call these two extreme forms of stories, or the potential story and the completed story, or sentimental plots and serious plots, or contemplations and events, or non-plot and plot, the basic distinction allows us to follow the transitions and joints in the structure of novels, the changes in relations within the community of the novel.

What makes us feel that a significant event has begun and ended? What gives one event status with respect to the status quo? Forster's question "And then?" might be rephrased "What then?" in order to emphasize the new situation, the What. In reading stories, we do not simply want to assure ourselves that we have managed to consume another instant of time; we want to know that something has changed in that instant. The storyteller makes something happen; we know that it has happened because it makes a difference. And for it to make a difference there must be a field in which it *can* make a difference, people to whom change can matter. The real role of causation in narrative is to persuade us that events are significant, not random; our pragmatic gauge of the existence of event is in the event's ability to *be* caused, and to operate as a cause.

When we think of something as having happened, we usually think in terms of a disturbance to what is, by comparison, relatively stable. That stability we might call, with Boris Tomashevsky, the situation: "[The] interrelationship at any given moment is the *situation*. . . . A story may be thought of as a journey from one situation to another" (70). Tomashevsky defines event by interrelationship, so that what happens privately to one character must significantly affect that character's orientation to other characters if it is to be said to bring about a new situation. The importance in stories of other people may not be fully appreciated if we follow only the role of the protagonist, as does Norman Friedman, using the definition of Elder Olson: plot is "a group of two or more episodes effecting a completed process of change in the main character" ("Forms of the Plot" 150).[3]

Within each situation, ordinarily there is inherent a potential instability that makes change possible. Tzvetan Todorov successfully emphasizes this instability by using the metaphor of equilibrium:

> The minimal complete plot can be seen as the shift from one equilibrium to another. This term "equilibrium," which I am borrowing from genetic psychology, means the existence of a stable but not static relation between the members of a society; it is a social law, a rule of the game, a particular system of exchange. The two moments of equilibrium, similar and different, are separated by a period of imbalance, which is composed of a process of degeneration and a process of improvement. ("Structural Analysis" 75)

Whatever the terms by which we describe instability—"discord," "struggle," "hindrance" (Toliver 235 ff.), the old soldier "conflict" (Tomashevsky 71)—the basis of imbalance is separateness: nothing can happen if everyone wants the same thing in the same way. Cross-purposes are the lifeblood of stories.[4]

But in stories, the end of equilibrium must normally be precipitated by acts of will. Causation depends not only on people's emotions or desires but also on their actions. The bildungsroman often attempts an analogue to story that is private or inward, consisting only in the protagonist's change of heart. But the growth of maturity hardly seems measurable if it has no consequences. How often do we really believe an abstract resolution to do better? Change can only happen when people *do*—better or worse.[5] The writers of the bildungsroman have tried to persuade us otherwise, with resolutions or symbolic gestures. Depending on their efforts, however, we normally feel either that they have successfully contemplated a static situation or that they have simply plotted inadequately—not that they have really made things happen. That is to say, an intensification of desire within a stable structure of relations does not usually constitute an event in itself. Will is not wish, private opinion, or attitude, any of which can intensify forever and never make a difference. An assertion of will leaves a character richer or poorer, more or less likely to act again. Plot does not require intricate strategies from any one character, because intricacy can result simply from the complicated cross-purposes generated when each of several simple characters makes one assertion of will against everyone else. But this does not mean that there can be plot without the assertions that express separateness.[6]

Making distinctions between events is inevitable. Even within eventful stories this is a necessity, for all stories prepare for the significant with the less significant. "Delaying action" primes us for the central events (Shklovsky 49). One obvious borderline of events is the revolution in a character's private feelings, the provisional change of consciousness. If one person in a relation has really changed, the relation has in some sense changed, even if no one else has any way of knowing it. Yet usually we will not feel satisfied even by a character we believe until in some way the character manages to change the circumstances of the life he or she shares with the community of characters.

The word "will" may perhaps too broadly imply that the actor is fully characterized, has an implied interiority. It may fail to suggest the remarkably varied and personalized ways that writers have found to express agency in texts. Balzac, for instance, explicitly conceives actions in terms of will, conflict, and competition:

> And so, in private life, Nature works in a way which is considered the highest expression of Art in works of genius: its method of operation is self-interest, whose motive power is money. (*The Black Sheep* 310)

> "Are there opinions nowadays? Surely there are only conflicting interests," put in des Lupeaulx. (*A Harlot High and Low* 22)

> For some of the initiated, the seemingly unintelligible black book of competing interests is so precisely notated that they read it as though it were a novel, here and there amusing. (*Harlot* 18)

> It was one of those unknown but terrible battles in which all the strength and talent needed to establish a fortune expend themselves in hatred, petty irritations, marching and countermarching, ruses. (*Harlot* 138)

> The antagonism between all these people who reciprocally seek and evade each other constitutes an immense duel, eminently dramatic, sketched in these pages. (*Harlot* 444)

"You must think of people as tools to be used, to be taken up or dropped depending on whether or not they serve your purpose." (*Cousin Bette* 190)

In Faulkner, as in Balzac, there are lots of acts of will by lots of different people.

Balzac apparently found passive ("sentimental") characters so uninteresting that in his own paraphrase of *The Charterhouse of Parma* he essentially rewrote the book with Fabrizio as a subordinate character (Genette, *Palimpsests* 243). However, Balzac also conveys that in a complicated society the forces are if not impersonal then at least multi-personal. Societal structures are so complex and impenetrable that one cannot always move upon them by acts of will. The journalists of Paris represent a force that acts impersonally to reject the intrusion of Lucien in *Lost Illusions* (much as society rejects Becky Sharp in Thackeray). Rastignac's famous general challenge against society at the end of *Père Goriot* is ironic at least partly because Rastignac has no identifiable opponent and has no way to put his challenge into effect except by going out to dinner.

Bleak House is a demonstration of event that is unwilled. Dickens depicts a world of institutions that are ossified and fogbound, designed to resist event. Change happens because disease literally cannot be contained. The homeless Jo has no will except society's unchanging will that he keep "moving on." His action is not directed, not "teleological." But, inadvertently, he affects and infects Esther because disease knows no boundaries. The apparently coincidental bringing together of plotlines in fact makes a referential statement about the way the world really works. That is, apparently sealed-off social classes are connected despite everyone's intentions that they stay separate. Human beings are really not isolated, are ultimately part of one interconnected system whether we want it or not. In that sense, coincidence is meaning.

Even the intentional will suffers slippage as a cause of event. The infected will has been for centuries a rich source of theological confusion: "I do not understand my own actions. For I do not do what I want, but I do the very thing I hate. . . . I can will what is right, but I cannot do it. For I do not do the good I want, but the evil I do not want is what I do" (Romans 7:15, 18–19).

In modernist narrative, actions are often balked or impermanent. In *To the Lighthouse,* for example, the action sequences lead to important but evanescent tableaux: Mrs. Ramsay preparing and preparing for a moment when the dinner table is momentarily composed as art; Lily recomposing her picture years later as a response of love to Mrs. Ramsay. Other actions never realize themselves in event. Mr. Ramsay's constant striving to reach metaphorically from A to Z has sequence but no conclusion, no satisfaction, and no interaction with others' actions. Emotions build but break apart like waves before leading to a word. Paradoxically, in the interval between the acts, the real activity is that of nature and time.

In *The Sentimental Education,* which Paul Goodman rightly takes as the prototype of "sentimental" plots, Flaubert shows again and again how easily resolves can be forgotten or broken. In general, the less circumstances are affected by a change in the private attitude of a character— that is, the less reason other characters have to infer something new in the situation, whether simply in the attitude itself or in the circumstances —the less the situation can really be said to have changed. Another borderline of event is the minor assertion that actually does change the circumstances—but not very much. The sum of several such minor actions often makes a difference, even though we are not sure where the difference becomes substantial. But Flaubert also shows how easily such gestures can be taken back without even a gain in the abstract "education" of the bildungsroman. Usually we give to such gestures only provisional assent, since they may be parts of yet-uncompleted events but may also be only false starts.

But an action can take place on the fringe of daily behavior without being a proposal, a marriage, a confession, or a murder. The transmission of knowledge can be an event, and confrontations can act as catastrophes. James cautioned his readers that "It is an incident for a woman to stand up with her hand resting on a table and look out at you in a certain way; or if it be not an incident I think it will be hard to say what it is" ("Art of Fiction," *Future of the Novel* 16). It does not sound like an event, but it might be that too. In *The Golden Bowl,* James subverts the threatened catastrophe—the bowl is shattered and yet "nothing" is allowed to happen. However, in the phrase "Nothing is happening," ironically "nothing" becomes a positive quantity. Maggie gains the knowledge of her husband's betrayal; then, when a fortuitous entrance allows him to see the bowl shattered, the Prince learns that she has learned. These events alter the effect of a superficially static situation. Then two major confrontations between Maggie and Charlotte show Maggie asserting first independence, then control—all without an explicit acknowledgment between them of what is happening. But it should be noted that though James can make events out of a woman's look, he is not averse to including more overt acts as well. To a great deal of look-giving he always adds something like bloodletting—like the scene, earlier on in *The Golden Bowl*, where Charlotte prompts the Prince to overt physical betrayal.

In *Light in August*, Faulkner uses a combination of very different kinds of significant events. Faulkner often uses a structure in which a limited number of events of first importance are combined with an episodic chronicle that explains the backgrounds of event through the life history of a major participant: the whole Sutpen story in *Absalom, Absalom!* surrounds the murder of Charles Bon in this way—though without completely explaining Sutpen himself. *Light in August* is clustered around a murder, a birth, and another murder. Researches on the manuscript have demonstrated what we might have known already: the Hightower and Lena Grove story lines, each of which represents a separate beginning by Faulkner, both proved to be too static to support an entire plot (Fadiman). To a certain degree each of these stories is an explanation of the stability of a character, a stability that one major event, the birth of Lena's child, confirms in Lena, and surprisingly overturns—though only temporarily—in Hightower. Faulkner's solution to the static nature of his plot was the invention of the Joe Christmas story, which provides the two major deaths that bracket the birth. The novel essentially begins with the death of Joanna Burden, after which Faulkner introduces, in a long flashback, the chronicle of Joe's life, an expository meditation that attempts to establish as far as possible in what sense the event had to be. Faulkner chose to invent a narrative that contributed two climactic events rather than attempt to convince his audience that the static narratives were sufficiently interesting in themselves. The three obvious crises are given dominance in the novel.

And yet Faulkner emphasizes that there are significant changes that do not come in catastrophes: "the people who passed and looked at him could see no change: a small man you would not look at twice, that you would never believe he had done what he had done and felt what he had felt" (*LIA* 395). He does make use of the kind of events that literally consist of a look and a gesture. He describes at length the power of Lena's look, her "grave, unwinking, unbearable gaze" and the silent struggle between Lena and Burch, his own eyes "like two beasts about to break"

(406). Not only is Lena's action here a definite act of will, but it results in the willed and final sundering of the relation between Lena and her seducer: "It was as if she held him there and that she knew it. And that she released him by her own will, deliberately" (409). This moment of epiphany is not given the structural prominence of the birth, but it is a real turning point nonetheless.

If it is true that almost anything can be an event, it is also true that within each text events must be seen relative to each other. Events are not all of the same materiality. To find four "events" in a four-frame comic strip is to trivialize.[7] Some of the early attempts to build plot "grammars" made every sentence into an event and tried to decide how many events the minimal story would include. A more important activity in the reading of long narratives is to distinguish between events on the basis of their importance in the narrative. An account of a plot must distinguish which are the most material events within that narrative.

The attempts of Todorov and others to pursue an analogy or even a deep-structural equivalency between grammar structure and plot structures were flawed by their tendency to place focus on one protagonist. The emphasis on the subject of the sentence seemed as a practical matter to throw all the focus on one principal actor. It made it difficult to conceive major status for more than one character or source of agency. It also made it difficult to describe a plot in which independent actors do things simultaneously. Actually, this need not have been so. It is characteristic of narrative that even if things do happen simultaneously they are told sequentially. A compound sentence or even a subordinate clause is a reasonably good analogy for such a plot: "The reveler is hasting to his wine, the mourner burying his friend"; or "The son was living on pig scraps; meanwhile, the father was looking for him everywhere." Provided that plot is not reduced to a single paradigmatic sentence, it can be legitimately reduced to statements, sequentially rendered, in which the subject changes. This also reflects the fact that the significant actions are often made not independently or simultaneously but *in response to* the previous significant actions of other material actors. What is important is finding some way of reducing the actions to paraphrase and designating the successive subjects.

It seems important to recognize, however, that like the idea of plot "grammar," most ways of talking about plot turn out to be as much metaphor as science. Thomas Pavel's provocative idea of moves, for instance, is presented as "derived from game theory" (*Poetics of Plot* 14). However, as Lowe points out, Pavel does not really substantiate any theoretical basis for his concept in game theory (32). The important thing is selecting a metaphor that permits pragmatic distinctions between plots, that facilitates descriptions of essential elements. Game theory cannot be more than a source of metaphor and of terminology, because, to state the obvious, the description of literary structures (hypothetical or actual) is not a prediction of behavior and is not an optimization based on mathematical variables. It is a description of shapes someone has made up or might make up. But like game theory, literary criticism is solidly grounded in using the concepts of agents and moves.

The conception of a story as a series of independent or reactive or interactive moves has a metaphoric power in our language, resonating with images of games, of strategy, of seductions, of all forms of assertiveness and all kinds of change—change partial, change balked, change internal, change apparent, change real. The move of one may interfere with the move of another, or react to it, or ignore it, or be inhibited by it. In some stories there is only one mover; in some stories of constant motion there are actually no moves.

The following of plot moves also releases us from an overemphasis on endings. It is an oversimplification to make the end point the defining characteristic of all plots. It is possible for a writer to combine two plots, the ending of one of which by no means requires the ending of the other. In *Pride and Prejudice,* for instance, withheld *facts* are revealed, effecting Elizabeth Bennett's climactic change of heart ("Till this minute I never knew myself") by the end of the thirty-sixth of sixty-one chapters. Yet the marriage plot, concluding with the central change of fortune, requires many further converging actions and changes of attitude. Obviously, our suspense-interest in a great deal of the novel is directed to an end that is not the formal end of the novel's plot. In his own version of total plot relevance, James pays as much attention to the relations between events on the way to the climax as to the actual climax itself. We are required to be interested in the progress. The process of analysis in *The Ambassadors* stands by itself without the final, well-prepared surprise "crash." *The Golden Bowl* does arrive at a climax that is the object of our detective interest: what will be the final arrangement of the characters? Yet the climax depends on everything that has led up to it, not the other way round. Our desire to know what will happen in the end only encompasses, but does not negate, our immediate interest in the status of affairs at every given point and in the transition from one point to another. The end-plotting is only the end of the plotting, not something that in itself constitutes a plot. Also, while there are things in a story that point toward the end and prepare the closure (provisional or complete) of the ending, it should be remembered that the story is kept open until the end, holding out the possibility of some other end. The reader may know that there will be an end and that it is being prepared, but does not ordinarily know which end. Thus even the tightest plotting usually requires some plotting of the other end as well. We see in the best-made novels the necessity of duplicity, of openness up to the last minute. For all these reasons it is wrong to think of endings as inherently domineering and formally constrictive. What is more fruitful is weighing the particular way an ending completes or fails to complete a series of material moves that develops sequentially in a *fabula*.[8]

Conceiving a narrative as a game of moves is a fruitful metaphor. Lowe refines this metaphor to the image of a multi-player board game. In this game the narrative conveys to the reader its constitutive rules, creates a cooperative contract between the text and the reader. But this is not a game between reader and implied author.[9] The game is between the agents. The metaphor does not make sense without actors.[10] Both sentence grammars and the metaphor of moves foreground the role of actors and movers. That is, they differentiate the roles of characters and in so doing create hierarchies, or heroes. One most important distinction between events is the question of how many independent agents are acting in them and what kind of characters the text asks us to consider them to be.[11]

It is certainly true that complex plot predates a post-Enlightenment conception of character (Godzich xx). The pleasure of story can be seen as independent of any assumption about what people are like, based on formal properties alone. In Sidney's unfinished rewriting of the *Arcadia*, for example, the focus of the reader's attention is the seemingly unlimited process of expanding the plot by retardation, interruption, sidetracking. The shaping of plot, the formal property of deferral and postponement of resolution, is itself the subject of the plot. It has been common for theorists to unbundle the relation of character and story, to speak about agents or actants but not about character. Perhaps it is indicative, for example, that Genette cites frequent examples from works by Agatha

Christie, who creates agents but not characters. Lowe seeks a plot schema that is not character-centered. It might seem that the schema he does favor, using actants with goals (motivation), knowledge, and power, amounts to the same thing in practice (48). But what Lowe does not want is a schema that requires highly psychologized characters, which his classical plots do not necessarily have. Bakhtin makes the same point, saying that events in the Greek romance are not biographic events, because they do not change the shape of the lives of the characters (*Dialogic Imagination* 90).

If characters are not essentially involved in the plot—in other words, where there is plot without character—the measurement of event cannot be its effect on the community of characters in the plot. We have something of this effect in current "action" movies: "There was not much plot, only action." However, it is important to identify those plots that do change the shape of lives, in which character is more than a structural function of the plot. Because there are no developed characters, an Agatha Christie plot is much like the board game of *Clue*—a perfectly arbitrary and mechanical set of permutations of actor, weapon, and location ("Miss Scarlet . . . in the drawing room . . . with a wrench"). A sense of complex event virtually requires the essential involvement of characters.

Lowe comments that while we debate the significance of what happens, we normally do not dispute *what* happens. The problem is that the event and its significance cannot always be clearly distinguished, because we do not know the event until we know the actor. There is a one-vehicle accident in which the driver is killed. But is this event a heart attack, a drunk-driving incident, a suicide, or a murder? We do not know until we know the actor. Aeneas leaves Dido and departs for Italy. The event is meaningless, without significance, until we understand who Aeneas is—a cold-hearted seducer, a man driven inexorably by the gods against his will, or both. Is it really the same "event" interpreted in three different ways, or is the event itself incomplete without its realization in a text, for a reader, with a significant actor? Here it seems that significance defines event. This is also consistent with saying, as Bal and many others have, that the *fabula* has no existence except as it is realized in the text and reconstructed by the reader (Bal, *Narratology* 9). In Forster's famous aperçu, the assertion that plot requires causation ("Then the Queen died of grief") must be amended to add that plot requires significant event, causation, character, and a reader to make the connections among them.

The presence of characters rather than "actants" implies a referential conception of human behavior, human possibilities, and perhaps "human nature." As Robert Alter says, denying the referential aspect of character is "the kind of sophistication that becomes its own egregious naiveté" (*Pleasures of Reading* 53). The same should be said about the refusal to consider the interplay between plot and character. A description of the storytelling in novels would be diminished if it did not attempt to discern the impact of characterization on *fabula*.

Making distinctions between stories, describing the syntax of events represented by each *fabula*, requires a language of independent characters, of moves, and of the changes that come from material events. Talking about plot involves making distinctions between events, identifying where apparent causes have minimal effects, and following what happens when independent movers collide or engage in conflict with each other. What results will not be the reduction of plot to formulas but instead a sense of the nuanced variations in event that characterize a particular writer.

William Faulkner's own interest in story and character gives some sanction to the effort to examine the stories in his fictions. Of course we are speaking of another "Faulkner," one no longer at the writing desk, and one perfectly capable of whimsy and deception in self-characterization. But this Faulkner throughout his career asserted the importance to him of stories, and asserted it in ways that emphasize the inextricability in his mind of events and the people who perform them. As early as 1931 he was defending simple plot and character: "All exclusive of the story, Mr. Faulkner says, is dead weight. What is interesting in Dickens is not the way he takes things, but 'those people he wrote about and what they did'" (*Lion* 18). Even after receiving the Nobel Prize, he sought to foster an image of himself that did not accord with his new audience's conception of a "serious" writer. Faulkner wished to be thought of as a storyteller:

I think people try to find more in my work than I've put there. I like to tell stories, to create people and situations. But that's all. (Interview with Cynthia Grenier, 1955; *Lion* 220)

I'm a story-teller. I'm telling a story, introducing comic and tragic elements as I like. I'm telling a story—to be repeated and retold. I don't claim to be truthful. Fiction is fiction—not truth; it's make-believe. Thus I stack and lie at times, all for the purposes of the story—to entertain. (Interview with Simon Claxton, 1962; *Lion* 277)

Faulkner also encouraged his readers to see him as one for whom "message," the abstract values of the tale, was of secondary importance: "If one individual could write the authentic, credible, flesh-and-blood character and at the same time deliver the message, maybe he would, but I don't believe any writer is capable of doing both, that he's got to choose one of the two: either he is delivering a message or he's trying to create flesh-and-blood, living, suffering, anguishing human beings" (Gwynn and Blotner 47). Faulkner makes his own preferences clear when he goes on to give Balzac and Einstein as his exemplars of the two ends of writing. That is, it turns out that his writer of ideas is not a novelist at all. Faulkner clearly puts himself on the side of Balzac—and of people, "living, suffering, anguishing," acting.

Faulkner also continually implies that for him storytelling is not a rhetorical pose or a theoretical preference but an actual practice. Malcolm Cowley sensed that "the pattern or body of legend behind the novel [*The Sound and the Fury*]—and behind all his other books—was still developing" ("Introduction" 99). Faulkner clearly encourages that observation. The dedication to *The Town*—"To Phil Stone: He did half the laughing for thirty years"—reinforces the storyteller's bardic role and claims for the stories of the novel an oral and communal existence and growth independent of any specific versions that may have found literary form. Nor is this simply a late pose. In 1939 Faulkner treated Michel Mok to an anecdote involving Clarence Snopes and Montgomery Ward's French postcards, an anecdote that was never written by Faulkner (though the postcards themselves appeared eighteen years later in *The Town*) (*Lion* 40). The Faulkner-not-at-the-writing-desk foregrounds stories by demonstrating that his stories can in fact be told, that they have enough narrativity to sustain telling out loud. By following the events of Faulkner's writing, we in effect offer to determine the practical utility of the famous self-conception of the practitioner.

The texts of Faulkner also continuously invite a reading that follows sequentially the actions of characters and the changes in relations that follow those actions. The corpus of Faulkner's writing is filled with willed challenges, overt moves with known targets and adversaries. Furthermore, the shape of events is enclosed by a pervasive language of conflict and competition—gambits, designs, engagements, battles, winning, beating, echelons, moves.

> Because it was a full-scale action: no mere squabbling of outposts. It was all out, win or lose; logistics came into it, and terrain; faint thrust and parry, deception; but most of all patience, the long view. (*Reivers* 32)

> . . . Bon's mother already plotting and planting him since before he could remember for that day when he should be translated quick into so much rich and rotting dirt . . . (*AA* 300)

> . . . and so Lucas had beat him . . . (*Intruder* 17)

> Because it was over now. He had turned the other cheek and it had been accepted.
> He was free. (*Intruder* 27)

> He drew a long breath and expelled it while they faced each other through the bars, the bleared old man's eyes watching him, inscrutable and secret. They were not even urgent now and he thought peacefully *He's not only beat me, he never for one second had any doubt of it.* (*Intruder* 73)

> "'You see, I had a design in my mind. Whether it was a good or a bad design is beside the point; the question is, Where did I make the mistake in it, what did I do or misdo in it, whom or what injure by it to the extent which this would indicate. I had a design . . .'" (*AA* 263)

> . . . he had lost that move . . . (*AA* 332)

> "You might as well to quit," he said. "You cant beat him" (*H* 356)

> . . . moving up his echelons . . . (*T* 38)

> Now it was his move. He would have to say something, have to begin. (*Reivers* 48)

What is needed in reading any writer is a pragmatic recognition of differences, so that ultimately some sense can emerge of the variety, and the implications, of the stories which that writer makes. Apparent similarities traditionally presented as typical may turn out to represent real differences. In Faulkner's case, *The Sound and the Fury* and *Absalom, Absalom!* have come to be thought of as canonical modernist (or perhaps postmodern) texts. But the role of events in the two novels is very different. One is a drama about knowing events, the other a drama of events defused and disconnected.

The Sound and the Fury is a novel of drift, in which violent actions are present but not quite explicable. Things seem to happen, but ultimately we cannot say that any significant event has taken place. We cannot tell why this violence has taken place or that anybody cares. The acts are arbitrary, and they cannot break into any character's private version of what matters. The apparent turnings of the plot are many—a loss of virginity, a wedding, a suicide, a divorce, and finally a robbery. But the causes of these are so uncertain, and the effects are so inconsequential, that the novel almost completely frustrates the desire to see things happen.

The novel shows that a superfluity of causes can undo causation. Why does Caddy go bad? Mrs. Compson argues that it is simply in the blood: " . . . who can fight against bad blood[?] . . . " (*SF* 128). This is a form of fate, either a curse in Caddy's blood or a symptom of a decline in the blood of the entire Compson family.

> . . . Im bad anyway you cant help it
> theres a curse on us its not our fault is it our fault hush come on
> and go to bed now you cant make me theres a curse on us (*SF* 196)

But even fate can take many forms. It is positive sexual desire that appalls Quentin:

> did he make you then he made you do it . . . Caddy you hate him
> dont you dont you
>   she held my hand against her chest her heart thudding I
> turned and caught her arm
>   Caddy you hate him dont you
>   she moved my hand up against her throat her heart was hammering there
>   poor Quentin

yes I hate him I would die for him I've already died for him I
die for him over and over again everytime this goes (*SF* 187–88)

Faulkner does not reconcile the hate and the love, the sexual despair and
the sexual desire. From Caddy's "I hope we do get whipped" (*SF* 22) to
her hatred of rain (69), to her claim before the wedding that "*When they
touched me I died*" (185), we sense some unexplained despair that merely
uses sex as a vehicle: "*There was something terrible in me sometimes at night
I could see it grinning at me I could see it through them grinning at me through
their faces*" (138, cf. also 184). In neither the desire nor the despair is Caddy
indifferent to sex. That is a third explanation offered by Mr. Compson
(96, 143), and strangely supported by Faulkner in the Appendix, his own
later attempt to sort out the causation: "Doomed and knew it, accepted
the doom without either seeking or fleeing it. . . . Accepting the fact that
[Quentin] must value above all not her but the virginity of which she was
custodian and on which she placed no value whatever: the frail physical
stricture which to her was no more than a hangnail would have been"
(412). This explanation of Caddy's mind seems impossible to reconcile
with either of the other two.

But along with these explanations of Caddy's attitude toward sex there
are other causes and motivations. Caddy's authoritarian manner with her
brothers is explained by Mrs. Compson as vanity: "She couldn't bear for
any of you to do anything she couldn't. It was vanity in her, vanity and
false pride" (326). The contest with her brothers can be connected to her
sexuality in a vaguely Freudian way, in that there *is* apparently an incestuous attraction between Caddy and Quentin: " . . . I got pretty jealous I
says to myself who is this Quentin anyway . . . it never occurred to me it
was her brother she kept talking about she couldnt have talked about you
any more if you'd been the only man in the world husband wouldnt have
been in it . . . " (133). Desire, despair, vanity, sibling rivalry—we do not
doubt that somewhere in this complicated matrix of untraceable drives
there is more than sufficient cause to constitute a personal curse, whether
or not that curse is related to the decline of an entire family. But we
cannot, without some Freudian mechanism, sort out these causes and determine the sufficient cause. The causes seem to coexist. We cannot say,
for instance, that decline causes despair causes desire. All are simply there
together, and though we probably do believe that they explain, our belief

must be an act of faith not much more sophisticated than if we had believed from the first that Caddy was really under a curse.

A similar multiplication of several intermittently connected causes exists in the case of Quentin's suicide. The suicide follows Caddy's loss of virginity and consequent marriage and seems to reflect an obsessive sense of lost "purity" (143). This is connected to a sense of decline (impurity?) in his family as a whole. There is also Quentin's own love of death, which Faulkner emphasizes in the Appendix (411, 412). This is tenuously connected metaphorically to the decline of the family when Quentin thinks of "death as a man something like Grandfather a friend of his a kind of private and particular friend . . . Grandfather wore his uniform and we could hear the murmur of their voices from beyond the cedars they were always talking and Grandfather was always right" (218–19). This may or may not be related to his recurrent philosophical obsession with clocks and the passing of time. A more immediate source of dissatisfaction that does not necessarily depend on the decline of a family tradition is the inadequacy of Quentin's own parents:

> *My little sister had no. If I could say Mother. Mother* (117)

> When I was little there was a picture in one of our books, a dark place into which a single weak ray of light came slanting upon two faces lifted out of the shadow. *You know what I'd do if I were King? . . . I'd break that place open and drag them out and I'd whip them good* It was torn out, jagged out. I was glad. I'd have to turn back to it until the dungeon was Mother herself she and Father upward into weak light holding hands and us lost somewhere below even them without even a ray of light. (215)

Quentin's attitudes toward Caddy herself involve far more than a sense of lost purity. The incestuous love he wishes to feign is also real: "*If it could just be a hell beyond that: the clean flame the two of us more than dead. Then you will have only me then only me*" (144). This desire is also a rivalry, a contest:

> *I dont give a damn what you were doing*
> *You dont you don't I'll make you I'll make you give a damn. She hit*
> *my hands away I smeared mud on her with the other hand . . . I*

wiped mud from my legs smeared it on her wet hard turning body . . .
(170)

Mrs. Compson's explanation of the suicide is that "when her troubles began I knew that Quentin would feel that he had to do something just as bad" (326). This attitude toward Caddy, the wish to possess or to emulate her, motivates Quentin in ways directly opposite to the chivalric obsession with lost purity and family honor. For Quentin is also obsessed with his own *excessive* purity, his virginity: " . . . and I thought about how I'd thought about I could not be a virgin, with so many of them walking along in the shadows and whispering with their soft girlvoices lingering in the shadowy places and the words coming out and perfume and eyes you could feel not see, but if it was that simple to do it wouldnt be anything and if it wasnt anything, what was I . . . " (183). Yet obviously, this desire is only partially motivated by Caddy, for Quentin is himself responding to "girlvoices" in general. In seeking death Quentin is partially escaping his own virginity, but in a metaphorical sense he may be going to meet it in a new form, for according to Mr. Compson, virginity is "like death: only a state in which the others are left" (96). In the end all these factors are allowed to join together as contradictory but contributing motives for Quentin's ultimate assertion of his loneliness, his belief that "nobody knows what i know" (221). Too many things are involved for even Caddy's fall to take preeminence. So many causes are involved that none is really essential. All together make up a total malaise, not much more logical than the mechanism of conventional wasteland despair.

As these climactic actions show, an occurrence can be believable and yet inexplicable. Faulkner appears to emphasize a general uncertainty about why things happen. In addition to the multiplicity of named causes, there is the constant presence of superstition, the raising of the possibility of myriad causes that can never be traced or verified. Roskus attributes the general bad luck to the suppression of any mention of Caddy (37), to the changing of Benjy's name (35), and to the very fact of Benjy's idiocy (34). Dilsey rebukes Roskus for such talk, but she herself tells Caddy, *"Folks dont have no luck, changing names"* (71). A more ironic superstition is that of Mrs. Compson, who asks, "What reason did Quentin have? Under God's heaven what reason did he have? It cant be simply to flout and hurt me. Whoever God is, He would not permit that. I'm a lady" (374). Mrs. Compson looks back and sees only the selfishness of others, the mistreatment she herself has received from the Compson cabal. Seeing everywhere only the vanity of Compsons, the Compson scorn of Bascombs, she is able to create a myth in which everything can be explained by the wrongs she has suffered. In blaming the girl Quentin's supposed suicide on Caddy and Quentin, she speaks with a complacency that makes a massive irony against herself: "It's in the blood. Like uncle, like niece. Or mother. I dont know which would be worse. I dont seem to care" (374).

And yet there are indications that Faulkner was not satisfied by the multiplicity of causes, that he was himself attempting to understand his own material. In interviews he repeatedly said that something about the book was incomplete. While writing the Compson genealogy, he wrote Malcolm Cowley, "I should have done this when I wrote the book. Then the whole thing would have fallen into pattern like a jigsaw puzzle when the magician's wand touched it" (*Faulkner-Cowley File* 36). Later he wrote: "It is the book itself which is inconsistent: not the appendix. That is, at the age of 30 I did not know these people as at 45 I now do; that I was even wrong now and then in the very conclusions I drew from watching them, and the information in which I once believed" (90). In the Appendix, Faulkner attempted to exclude some of the causes he had allowed earlier, saying that Quentin "loved not his sister's body but some concept of Compson honor" (*SF* 411). Faulkner often uses the "not . . . but" construction to mean something else, but here he is apparently attempting to clarify his confusing plot, attempting a more rational explanation of character, circumstance, and effect.

But the plot is undermined by more than the fact that Caddy's fall and Quentin's suicide are the effects of undecipherable causes. The fall and the suicide are undeniable facts, even if they are seen as only givens in the plot. It is as causes in their own right that they most profoundly fragment the causation and are balked of significance as events. Caddy's fall, for instance, does lead partially to Quentin's suicide, but it is lost in the welter of other partial causes. Caddy believes also that her loss of virginity is the direct cause of her father's drinking: "*Father will be dead in a year they say if he doesnt stop drinking and he wont stop he cant stop since I since last summer*" (*SF* 154). It is true that Mr. Compson is shown drinking excessively after Caddy's loss of virginity, and Quentin attributes to him the argument that "*liquor teaches you to confuse the means with the end*. I am. Drink.

I was not" (216). But he is also seen drinking and voicing a similar cynicism long before, after the Patterson episode.

> "Bad health is the primary reason for all life. Created by disease, within putrefaction, into decay. Versh."
> "Sir." Versh said behind my chair.
> "Take the decanter and fill it." (53)

Caddy thinks of herself as the cause, but her father's drinking seems rather to express his general resignation than to show that he is affected by misfortune. His drinking is a sign of drift, not a reorientation. The drift of the family is beyond a specific cause. In this drift a true chain of cause and effect stands out starkly. Only Benjy has the simplicity to be moved by a definite cause. Caddy's disappearance obviously leads to Benjy's "attack" on the Burgess girl and to his consequent castration.

Caddy is a partial cause in all these matters, but the death of Quentin can hardly be called a cause at all. Obviously, the suicide is an assertion, though it seems more an expression of paralysis, an inability to act, than an attempt to affect the situation. It does affect the situation, but only in the most unavoidable way—Quentin disappears from the situation. In practice there is little sign that anyone is even slightly changed by his disappearance. Benjy never misses him. Mrs. Compson wonders what reason he might have had, but only by way of expressing an inability to explain the presumed suicide of the girl Quentin. She also uses him as a way of complimenting Jason: "Thank God if [Mr. Compson] had to be taken too, it is you left me and not Quentin" (249). Apparently only Caddy makes even the slightest gesture at Quentin's grave, and Jason is not even curious about it: "She looked at the flowers again. There must have been fifty dollars' worth. Somebody had put one bunch on Quentin's" (251). His death is without significance to the community, an act of paralysis that is only part of a general decline. Apparently even death is no event if no one else participates or cares. The repetition of Quentin's name in his niece is a seeming connection between generations that is in fact a bitter irony. It is a mere repetition, mechanical and unthinking, of a family name; it is a fossilized memory.

Each Compson is self-righteously sensitive to mistreatment, but it looks very much as though they are not really in relation with each other at all. Their sensitivity has become a universal malaise; so preoccupied have they become with themselves that they are no longer vulnerable to each other at all. When egoism goes to that extreme, it becomes nearly impossible for a story to take place.

Faulkner told Henry Nash Smith in 1931 that "It was not until the book was finished that I realized I had in it the anecdote of the girl who ran away with the man from the traveling show" (*Lion* 31). The arrival of the girl Quentin is the obvious effect of Caddy's sad history. Mrs. Compson, already completely given over to self-pity, is scarcely swayed in her commitment to decline. In this sense even this event is defused of consequence. Jason, on the other hand, wishes to make an event of Caddy's misconduct by using it to change his life. He claims repeatedly that the failure of her marriage has cost him his future (though on occasion he is willing to suggest that the fabled bank job was itself only another lie). More importantly, he uses the girl's money for his own enrichment. He cannot yet spend the money, but it represents at least potentially a complete change in his life. The girl herself is largely only an opportunity for theft, though there is the suggestion that in her own person she increases his sexual frustration. In the end she insists on becoming a person by making her own act of will, which constitutes the last "anecdote." The final irony, however, is that by attempting an event of her own the girl Quentin deprives her mother's life of its last potential significance to anyone in the remaining population of the novel. One event undercuts another. The money is gone, and because of the means by which he has gotten it Jason cannot even report the crime. Except for yet another inward intensification of Jason's frustrations, no one will be affected in the slightest by either Quentin's coming or her going.

Each event in turn is thus denied effect. Coupled with the multiplicity of causes, the novel must leave the impression of random acts of violence, largely uncaused and inconsequential. In effect, *The Sound and the Fury* seems made of arbitrary acts. As Donald Kartiganer has aptly put it, "The primary motivation of the work—although rarely achieved and never sustained—is the quest of one fragment to move into the life of another, to shatter the private prison and stand at least momentarily in relationship itself. . . . It is a series of voices or actions echoing, however dissonantly, a single not quite realized event" ("Faulkner's Quest for Form" 613–14). Kartiganer notes the relation of Quentin to Sartre's similarly named Roquentin, who says, "There are no beginnings. . . . Neither is there an end."[12] The reader is left with the same frustrated desire for event as Quentin, who can make of his frustration only a disconnected conditional clause: "If things just finished themselves" (*SF* 97). Things do not finish themselves.[13] Technically speaking, nothing happens; we are reduced to following what we can, and contemplating what we cannot follow. Clearly, Dilsey's stoicism reinforces our sense of incapacity for finding the source of decline or for saying what difference any single quasi-event has made. As Forster would say, we can only arrange these quasi-events in their temporal sequence; we can only say, with Dilsey, that we have seen the first and the last.

As readers we construct our *fabula* retrospectively. Looking back, we see that the *fabula* of *The Sound and the Fury* is a sequence in which three of the principal characters—Caddy, Quentin, and the younger Quentin—zero themselves out of the action. They literally withdraw, negative themselves. What is important and different about Dilsey is that, whatever minimal value there may be to enduring, she does not subtract herself.

The following of vague connections through time is a strategy Faulkner also uses in *Go Down, Moses,* though with very different effect. The novel makes us think about the way the present is created by, caused by the past—even though the events themselves are spread over the years with the apparent effect of making the book loose in structure. This is especially true in the novel's juxtaposition and comparison of three McCaslins: Old Carothers, Lucas Beauchamp, and Ike. Lucas continually thinks himself better than Ike, who relinquished his birthright. Ike is said to carry with him still the Carothers he repudiates, to be most like him in repudiating him. Lucas is a patriarchal figure like the Carothers he apes, but with first a comic and then an admirable effect; he tries to manipulate others, notably Aunt Molly, but fails—and he does so, it appears, only in an attempt to be a man. Through these similar characters, the novel emphasizes how important genealogy really is in telescoping the apparent diffuseness of time, the apparent lack of connection between things. Carothers is not only perpetuated in his descendants but is also the *cause* of their characters—though they never simply repeat him. Unlike *The Sound and the Fury,* where one event erases another as time and the characters drift onward toward death, *Go Down, Moses* offers a time in which the life of the past is a living component of all the characters do in the present. And yet the basic structure, in the wide spacing of central events, is almost exactly the same.

The Sound and the Fury, then, represents in Faulkner's career an extreme and uncharacteristic case, a plot where apparently significant events ironically undercut each other, cancel each other out, leaving the reader with a sense of strain and paralysis. Faulkner here apparently shows the Joycean influence in more than stream of consciousness alone, for in his own way, perhaps against his intention, he achieves the modernist desire to dispense with plot. But he does so by disconnecting apparent events, not by avoiding significant action altogether; by raising and frustrating conventional expectations, not by attempting a compelling contemplation of an obviously stable situation. Even here Faulkner tells a story, though he untells it in the end.

In *Absalom, Absalom!*, on the other hand, the following and deducing of cause and effect is the very means of telling the story. The novel is structured anecdotally; that is, it is built around one major event, the murder of Charles Bon. Faulkner adjusts the order of telling to emphasize the centrality of one event. Yet the murder itself takes only a few pages to tell. Quentin's detective quest for more explanation is a recognition that the event is incomplete without an understanding of both its causes and its consequences. The process of telling and retelling until a sufficient cause is found emphasizes the connection between storytelling and detection. It is as though Faulkner were asking us to think about the questions: What constitutes an event? When is an event thoroughly an event? The book is "about" narration because narration is about things happening, events.

Absalom, Absalom! has become the proof text for readers with a postmodern relish for epistemological uncertainty, or even for ludic improvisation about the infinite scriptability of experience. John Matthews articulates this attitude best: "Storytelling for Faulkner is serious play, and its significance arises not in the capture of truth but in the rituals of pursuit, exchange, collaboration, and invention. That language plays suggests there may be no actuality or truth behind the text's words that can be fully presented" (16).[14] In this version of *Absalom* the emphasis is on the hermeneutic gaps, and perhaps ultimately all is gap. But a critical appreciation and even exaltation in uncertainty and the unknowable is actually consistent with a simultaneous recognition of the text's desire to explain what can be explained in the way in which it makes the most sense. In *Absalom* there is a marriage of ambiguity, uncertainty, and subjectivity on the one hand and an inspiriting drive to probability, explanation, and a sense of knowledge on the other. Where the peripheries remain subject to the infinite play of speculation, the text drives toward a best solution of one central event. It is a solution that by no means explains everything—not evil, not the South, or why people live there, or why they live at all—but it is a solution that comes with a cathartic release, a sense of completion, a fulfilling sense of having refused to accept all apparent explanations, of having pushed on until (like Ratliff in another context) we know that we have gone "far enough."

There is obviously in *Absalom, Absalom!* something that needs explaining as well as an impulse to explain it. The novel moves through several discrete theories, attempts to tell who the characters are and what events have taken place. The first, most irrational fiction is Rosa's fairy tale, essentially a "theory" that a man-demon has tried to force his way to respectability in a normal town—something that could only happen by "fatality and curse" (21). In chapters 2–4 Mr. Compson begins to correct that theory by offering one of his own, the notion that "fateful mischance" has governed the fall of Sutpen's family (78). Mr. Compson does attempt to come to some more specific and rational explanation of the murder, the event that caused the failure of Sutpen's design to perpetuate his success. He offers the theory that Henry would be mortally offended by the fact of the ceremony in Bon's morganatic marriage to his octoroon mistress (109). Mr. Compson wants "to reconstruct causes which lead up to the actions of men and women," and he would like to believe in the simplicity of motive: "We find ourselves now and then reduced to the belief, the only possible belief, that they stemmed from some of the old virtues . . . the thief who steals not for greed but for love, the murderer who kills not out of lust but pity" (121). Yet his most compelling cry is his expression of the frustration of this desire to explain: "It's just incredible. It just does not explain. Or perhaps that's it: they dont explain and we are not supposed to know" (100).

The central event meanwhile is revealed bit by bit, and so it returns again and again to the center of our attention. At the end of chapter 3 Wash Jones is riding up shouting for Rosa (87); at the end of chapter 4 he is telling her the news: "Henry has done shot that durn French feller. Kilt him dead as a beef" (133). In chapter 5 Rosa brings the narrative back to her own suffering, her own involvement in burying Bon's body after the murder and in acting as "all polymath love's androgynous advocate" (146) in the "summer of wistaria" (143) four years before that. But here

Quentin himself feels compelled to go back to what Rosa cannot know, the fact of the murder itself, and the incredible words between Henry and Judith afterward: "But Quentin was not listening, because there was also something which he too could not pass—that door, the running feet on the stairs beyond it almost a continuation of the faint shot" (172).

In going back to the door, Quentin takes his first step toward an active attempt to share his father's impulse to explain, to find what has not yet been said. Joseph Reed feels that Rosa's story is designed "to frustrate the reader in pursuing his stock responses. . . . [She] assumes that we already know the main outline and she maddeningly embroiders details" (149–50). But this is precisely what the detective is always faced with. Miss Rosa assumes that Quentin knows the whole story because she assumes that she has *told* the whole story. Quentin's involvement in the act of detection is first in not believing or not caring about the story as she tells it, and then in realizing that there must be more to the story than either she or his father has been able to give him. The quasi-event he has been told about is not the full event.

In the final four chapters, Shreve and Quentin make their own attempts to explain the entire Sutpen story. Chapter 6 deals with the consequences of the central murder: Sutpen's death in trying to father another son; Judith's attempt to care for Charles Bon's mulatto son; and finally the consequence that Quentin himself has experienced, the fact that "some one was hiding out there" (*AA* 216). Chapter 7 goes back to the cause, Sutpen himself, and develops a theory of General Compson's that corrects Miss Rosa's: "Sutpen's trouble was innocence" (220). In following that innocence through Sutpen's life, Quentin and Shreve begin to unveil facts about the cause of the murder. In chapter 8 the tellers finally return to the central murder itself, once again making conjectures that might explain why Henry would kill his friend. At first they theorize that Henry must have known Bon was his brother, but they are forced to believe that actually Henry would have accepted this as he would the octoroon "wife." They must move beyond incest to find the probable cause: "*So it's the miscegenation, not the incest, which you cant bear*" (356). Surely it is wrong to say that this "comes as a distinct nonrevelation. We as readers already know this in the way Quentin and Shreve do, by having arrived at it, absorbed it, and become more interested in other things" (Reed 167). Clearly there are grounds of efficacy involved in these conjectures, and we identify with Quentin and Shreve because they go all the way toward explaining a central problem that other, incomplete tellers have not been able to explain. It involves a great expenditure of energy to reach the point where the final conjecture can be made, and the discharge of energy on finding a sufficient cause is tremendous, a source of both pain and jubilation. The main event of *Absalom, Absalom!* has finally been brought within the range of our intelligence. The revelation of the motive is a variant of Faulkner's favorite "not . . . but" construction, which might be applied to the relation of the other, successively corrected theories as well: not the ceremony, but the incest; not the incest, but the miscegenation; not the demon, but the innocent. Causes are thus assigned to a strict hierarchy grammatically. But Faulkner's "not . . . but" really means "both . . . and"; incest is not denied as a contributing cause but only as a sufficient cause. What we have arrived at is a multiple motivation, but not that of *The Sound and the Fury*. The secondary causes do not undercut the major cause, as in *The Sound and the Fury*—rather, they support it and build on it.

One cause, however, is preeminent, and Faulkner makes a strong attempt to link the whole social structure of the South to the assumptions behind that one cause. When Henry sees Charles not as his brother but as a Negro, he is repeating his father's own authoritarian rejection, Sutpen's willingness to use power in order to deny human claims. Sutpen's whole design has been initiated because he was turned away from a door; as Quentin notes, Charles Bon himself is in exactly the position of the innocent young Sutpen: "And sure enough and after fifty years the forlorn nameless and homeless lost child came to knock at it" (*AA* 267). In turning Bon away, Sutpen confirms the inhumanity of his position as authoritarian manipulator of his created world, the fatal flaw in his power to say "the *Be Sutpen's Hundred* like the oldentime *Be Light*" (9). It is the same power, the power to say "Go there," that causes the actual defeat of the South in the Civil War: " . . . battles lost not alone because of superior numbers and failing ammunition and stores, but because of generals who should not have been generals, who were generals not through training in contemporary methods or aptitude for learning them, but by the divine right to say 'Go there' conferred upon them by an absolute caste system" (345). Sutpen's (and Henry's) confusion of power and rectitude is clearly connected to the generals' confusion of power and competence. The world of the South reflects and supports Quentin and Shreve's deductions of the motive for the murder of Bon. The fact that miscegenation, not incest, is cause for murder is, we can see, a sign not only of the specific oppression of black people but of the universal abuse of all human beings whom power can control. The murder is the acting out both of Sutpen's specific rejection of Charles and also of the racial caste system; it is a special abuse within a more universal abuse of power by Sutpen and his society. That is why the fact that the mystery is "solved" can never be merely pacifying, a source of flattery to rational deduction. For logic forces Quentin and Shreve to look at *themselves* and at the whole fabric of southern society, and to shoulder the tremendous burden of the guilt of man. The act of telling has a painful impact on the teller.

The completion of the central event is the completion of the novel's structure. The cause that fits the effect appears only in the final, most elaborate conjectural embellishment. The motive is finally right. But that does not mean that Quentin and Shreve have been able to tie everything down pat, or that they want to. For the process of separating the relevant facts from the irrelevant, Faulkner requires a wealth of extraneous mate-rial. This plenitude suits the eclectic assemblage he apparently used in writing the novel: "[I began with] the idea of a man who wanted sons and got sons who destroyed him. The other characters I had to get out of the attic to tell the story of Sutpen" (Gwynn and Blotner 73). The phrase "out of the attic" refers to the prior and separate origin of the secondary ma-terial; it might well describe also material that is secondary structurally in the finished work, no matter what the origin. In this sense, even the end of *Absalom, Absalom!* is full of attic material. Faulkner is content to say as narrator that the image of Sutpen's first wife is far from verifiable, but adequate to its function: "the slight dowdy woman . . . whom Shreve and Quentin had likewise invented and which was likewise probably true enough" (*AA* 335). Another nonessential part of Shreve's story is the scheming New Orleans lawyer, whom Faulkner himself forgot, and whom we can see Faulkner virtually reinventing during the Virginia interviews: "There probably was a lawyer. I don't remember that book, but yes, yes, there was a lawyer. That sounds too logical in Mississippi terms. Yes, he was—there was a little lawyer there" (Gwynn and Blotner 77). Faulkner manages to have both plot and non-plot, both the necessary facts and a liberating freedom from fact. The transparent improvisations continue.

Nor does rational cause and effect in itself explain the central charac-ter. Quentin and Shreve's rationality can explain the murder, but it does not quite connect the murder to Sutpen. Apparently it can do no more than work vainly at developing the theories of others about Sutpen himself: "Quentin's Mississippi shade who in life had acted and reacted to the minimum of logic and morality, who dying had escaped it completely, who dead remained not only indifferent but impervious to it, somehow a thousand times more potent and alive" (*AA* 280). Yet Faulkner said in interviews that despite the failure of Quentin's rationality, eventually Sutpen is more or less explained:

> But taken all together, the truth is in what they saw though nobody saw the truth intact. . . . But the old man was himself a little too big for people no greater in stature than Quentin and Miss Rosa and Mr. Compson to see all at once. . . . It was, as you say, thirteen ways of looking at a blackbird. But the truth, I would like to think, comes out, that when the reader has read all these thirteen different ways of looking at the blackbird, the reader has his own fourteenth image of that blackbird which I would like to think is the truth. (Gwynn and Blotner 273–74)

Nonetheless, Faulkner still manages to combine the storyteller's urge to explain with an encompassing ambiguity, an abiding sense of the unexplainable. The murder is caused by Sutpen's peculiarly innocent abuse of power, but what causes *that* madness? "Miscegenation, not incest" makes sense as a motive, given the entire social context of the murder, but what explains the entire social context? We know, finally, only how the world works, not why it is as it is.

> "You cant understand it. You would have to be born there."
> "Would I then?" Quentin did not answer. "Do you understand it?"
> "I dont know," Quentin said. "Yes, of course I understand it." They breathed in the darkness. After a moment Quentin said: "I dont know."
> "Yes. You dont know. . . . "
>
> " . . . Do you?"
> "No," Quentin said peacefully. (*AA* 361–62)

The successful detection of events coexists with a deeper paralysis before the inexplicable. Like all great mysteries, *Absalom, Absalom!* solves the story of a man without solving the problem of evil, the story of Man.

Absalom, Absalom! and *The Sound and the Fury* are very different novels in the way they use events, and in their sense of agency. Even Quentin Compson is a different character in both. In *The Sound and the Fury,* every assertion except his last one is balked, ineffectual. In *Absalom, Absalom!,* on the other hand, Quentin not only engages—along with Shreve —in an imaginative and intellectual act of incredible emotive force, but he asserts himself in a very material physical way. He goes "out there" (*AA* 274). The novel may foreground the dominant agency of Sutpen and the ambiguous and terrible conflict of Henry Sutpen and Charles Bon. But Quentin plays his part too. The Quentin trembling and sweating on his bed after his encounter with Henry Sutpen is a different person from the trembling ineffective boy disarmed by Dalton Ames. In this sense the intertextual Quentin posited by some readers is very questionable.

If *The Sound and the Fury* and *Absalom, Absalom!* are both modernist, they are modernism's twin poles. Richard Moreland appropriately describes his sense of Faulkner's modernism with an allusion to the modernism of T. S. Eliot; modernism is a representation of modern life "as a 'heap of broken images'" (5). In *The Sound and the Fury,* cause is sundered from effect, effect inadequate to cause. The plot does not signify "nothing," but neither does it signify enough. It is in fact a heap of broken images. It is "these fragments I have shored against my ruins" (*The Waste Land* 1.431). On the other hand, as Joseph Urgo has written, "There is tremendous faith in *Absalom, Absalom!,* faith in human creativity and intellectual power, faith in the capacity of human beings to negotiate some kind of peaceful coexistence with their time, their place, and their conditions" ("Postvomiting" 141). Urgo has seen *Absalom, Absalom!* and *Pylon* as modernism and its postmodern double, the reaction of nausea at the difficulty of sustaining harmony and belief in truth.

> *Absalom, Absalom!* may well be the grand narrative of twentieth-century American literature, the ultimate modernist project. But nearly everything that *Absalom, Absalom!* represents in the way of imaginative re-creation, characterization, faith in narrative reason, and authorial knowledge is undone in *Pylon.* (132)

Postmodern culture rejects what Quentin and Shreve worked all night in order to reinsert into the Sutpen story: linearity, plausibility, the logic of cause and effect, "the best of thought" . . . and "the best of ratiocination." (133)

The contrast of *Absalom* and *Pylon* is a valuable one. But it might be better to say that *Pylon* is, like *The Sound and the Fury,* a truly modernist work. Its characters are isolated, not engaged in meaningful interaction. Actions are balked, ineffective. The entire environment of the novel is expressed in the language of literary modernism, the imagery of Prufrock and the wasteland. In the unreal city of New Valois, nausea is a classic response to modern life.

In *Absalom, Absalom!* Faulkner might be said to have raised all the appropriate modernist uncertainties about what we know and how we know it, reservations that act to retard knowledge. But having raised the epistemological questions, he allows the plotting to move on, allows the event to be completed through Quentin and Shreve's act of narration. If Faulkner moves beyond modernist uncertainties here (used though they are in the service of the suspense of the plot), he moves not toward play but toward completion, teleologically structured shape. That completion can be described as accomplished through creativity, an existential leap of faith, empathy, or a Freudian transference (Kreiswirth, "Intertextuality"). What finally matters is not whether completion is empirically arrived at but whether the narrative authenticates itself as narrative.

~

The modernist desire not to tell a story often takes the form of narratives like *The Sound and the Fury,* in which causation has been dismantled, leaving only noncohering actions. The postmodern innovation has been to burlesque event by obviously including too much action. After "modernistic contestations of narrative" (Kroeber 3) come postmodern parodies, improvisations, excesses of unresolved fabulation. Both modernist inertia and postmodern narratives of the arbitrary act are paradoxically very like the atavistic form that Forster labels "only" story, actions without causation, arranged in their temporal sequence. Obviously, not all texts ask to be followed as stories, though perhaps they can frustrate our curiosity about the story only by first stimulating it. We can appreciate on their own terms narratives that seem intentionally lacking in significant event.

But we are often surprised into believing as story what we have been resigned to appreciate only on some other ground. The nature of what is believable as change differs from novel to novel. Reorientations that some writers persuade us to accept as decisive would hardly be noticed in busier novels. A writer can claim the importance of a relatively minor assertion, can show the gradual growth of an assertion (or even of a failure of assertion, as in Edith Wharton's study of habituation, "The Other Two"), or can show on the other hand that a violent event is really no event at all. Often it becomes meaningless to try to say at what precise point a situation has changed, let alone just which gesture or assertion has been the essence of the event, the real source of change. The term "event" is a guideline for our necessarily empirical experience of the effects of particular novels. Our emphasis on the characters who participate in communities, and on the community situations that precede and follow events, allows us to follow in a novel the skeletal structure of significant changes and its relation to all the other instants a novel records.

Each story is a new assemblage, and it requires its readers to follow in a new way. It has become somewhat conventional to allude to Faulkner as an assembler of parts. Faulkner makes novels by combining short stories; Faulkner makes novels by juxtaposing chunks of material—these observations are commonplaces among Faulkner's critics. Michael Millgate generalizes irreproachably about a "characteristic feature of Faulkner's creative method": "To . . . an initial image other material rapidly accreted, and in the process of writing a new novel Faulkner was very likely to absorb into it, perhaps in completely transmuted form, a good deal of diverse material which already existed in his memory or his imagination, or actually on paper—perhaps even published" (*Achievement* 161). The assumptions of such a way of looking at novels are discussed more explicitly in the famous interchange between James and Stevenson in "The Art of Fiction" and "A Humble Remonstrance."

> I cannot imagine composition existing in a series of blocks, nor conceive, in any novel worth discussing at all, of a passage of description that is not in its intention narrative, a passage of dialogue that is not in its intention descriptive, a touch of truth of any sort that does not partake of the nature of incident, or an incident that derives its interest from any other source than the gen-

eral and only source of the success of a work of art—that of being illustrative. A novel is a living thing, all one and continuous, like any other organism, and in proportion as it lives will it be found, I think, that in each of the parts there is something of each of the other parts. (James, *Future of the Novel* 15)

James's remarks are in great part rhetorical, dedicated to promulgating an attitude toward the novel, an organic metaphor. Yet James's fiction falls as strikingly as any into manifest blocks, as James seems aware when in his later Prefaces he differentiates between scene and preparation for scene (*AN* 322–34). Undoubtedly these are in some sense unified in the consciousness of characters, but the reader is nonetheless struck by the dichotomy—even in the sheer appearance of the print.

In his reply to James's manifesto, Stevenson does not deny that the highest art may achieve the appearance of continuity. He manages to compliment James while advocating the opposite method of analysis. Stevenson approaches the work of art as yet unwritten. He emphasizes discontinuities, the varieties of available combinations and ingredients, and the need for techniques of assemblage. His method implies that for the laborer and craftsman, there must always be allocations of materials.

The true artist will vary his method and change the point of attack. (919)

[Mr. James] spoke of the finished picture and its worth when done; I, of the brushes, the palette, and the north light. He uttered his views in the tone and for the ear of good society; I, with the emphasis and technicalities of the obtrusive student. But the point, I may reply, is not merely to amuse the public, but to offer helpful advice to the young writer. And the young writer will not so much be helped by genial pictures of what an art may aspire to at its highest, as by a true idea of what it must be on the lowest terms. (923)

Stevenson's less mystical approach seems to agree with Faulkner's experience: "Unless a book follows a simple direct line such as a story of adventure, it becomes a series of pieces. It's a good deal like dressing a showcase window. It takes a certain amount of judgment and taste to arrange the different pieces in the most effective place in juxtaposition to one another" (Gwynn and Blotner 45).

The willingness to talk about blocks of material is not unrelated to genetic criticism, in that it is a recognition of the necessity of craft in the writing of narrative. The writer is his own first reader, and he does his own assembling and revising on the basis of the effectiveness of his writing on *him:* "It seemed to me that was the most effective place to put that" (Gwynn and Blotner 45). Faulkner also described the sense of failure in similar terms: "It don't make me feel good enough, to use Hemingway's phrase. That's a condition that probably I can't put into words, but if I ever do strike it, I will know it" (Gwynn and Blotner 62). To follow the structure of stories is to be willing to see not the unity but the parts; we allow ourselves to see the jointures, the places where Faulkner has been working. Our willingness to see and evaluate the joints in the narrative is analogous to the original act of assemblage, without the presumption of guessing in what order the pieces were first conceived. The reader as vicarious craftsman takes on the burden of making his or her own judgments on the effectiveness of each part of the whole. The reader must be as willing as the writer to say "Not Proven." As R. S. Crane writes, "We are not likely to feel strongly the emotional effect of a work in which the worse rather than the better alternatives among these different expedients are consistently chosen or chosen in crucial scenes" (623).

We have emphasized so far the total picture the reader puts together of the story as well as the different ways the writer can emphasize or deconstruct the coherence of the most prominent events. But it is necessary also to follow the gradual way in which the reader collects the pieces of the story, accommodating material that is static, contemplative, or irrelevant to the story structure altogether. A plot is generated through time, and a full sense of the variations of its pace and of the growth of its antagonisms requires us to follow the story chronologically. We need to follow "step by step" the essential motion forward, and the causation that links events, and the pacing between events, in order to see how they work, and how well they work.

Faulkner's making of stories is an art of immense variety. *The Sound and the Fury* and *Absalom, Absalom!* represent extreme cases in Faulkner's uses of story structures: a novel of anti-story, in which all events are undercut and dismantled; and a novel structured by the telling of one central anecdote, completed only with the deduction of complex causes. But throughout his career Faulkner shows his great inventiveness at telling stories, making sequences of cause and effect. He makes something happen in both his shortest stories and his longest—the Snopes novel cycle. The succeeding chapters, then, examine stories, long and short, made of different kinds of sequences of events. In his short stories, for instance, Faulkner may do without event completely, or divert our attention from the action; but quite often he accepts the challenge to compress a rapid sequence of reorientations into the short form. The novels may exhibit long and complicated series of strategies, or a simpler collision and recoil, or even a near-anecdotal reliance on a surprise ending. After describing the variety of Faulkner's plotting, it will be appropriate to pose the question of how that variety acts to define "Faulkner," and how an implied "Faulkner" reciprocally affects the plots he tells.

2
Short Plots

Among the uncelebrated tales in Faulkner's *Collected Stories*, and also among those stories retold in the novels, there is an underappreciated wealth of Faulknerian craftsmanship. Faulkner demonstrates in these tales his versatility in inventing anecdotes, events, and narrative intricacies. The actions of his independent characters at odds form short plots which resist the conventional wisdom that the short story is too short to trace significant changes, that instead it must contemplate or reveal character.

To some degree we can find in the stories analogues and parallels to the strategies of the novels to be discussed in other chapters. In a few stories Faulkner deemphasizes or even excludes events. "That Will Be Fine" has a plot, but the text opens an ironic distance between the event and the character who participates in it, creating in a plotted narrative some of the disorientation of event in more overtly modernist narrative. Somewhat as in parts of *The Hamlet*, Faulkner focuses the narrative on the mechanics of finance. The action simply is not at the center of the reader's attention. "My Grandmother Millard," on the other hand, looks forward to *The Town* in its multiplication of actors, its moves and coun-termoves. The continual and complex reorientation of characters makes it difficult to say where one event ends and another begins. "Mountain Victory," like *The Mansion*, is built on a restraint from event, a narrative of waiting, and a climax generated by a concealed convergence of several independent wills. "Mountain Victory" at first appears to be all ending, but in fact deceptively conceals its really intricate conflict of human wills.[1]

Perhaps as much as any other short-story writer, Faulkner successfully violates the prescriptions made in all good faith by other practitioners of the art. Prescriptive critics of short stories have usually disapproved of too great a complexity of event. "Any young writer will only waste his time and court base temptation by poking about for ingenious situations, or composing clever plots," says Sean O'Faolain (189). Frank O'Connor writes that "the crisis of the short story *is* the short story" (105). But O'Connor means a crisis situation, not the resolution of that crisis in event. O'Connor and O'Faolain do not want the story *only* to relay the crisis event itself. In fact, O'Faolain argues that formal "climax" *within* the story is best sacrificed to a "deeper verisimilitude": "Situation is much more fructive than anecdote and . . . construction plus situation can supply all the plot we need" (181). O'Connor is concerned lest a story be dependent on its "point": "The point of a short story belongs to the basic anecdote—the brothel closed 'Because of First Communion'—and as far as the literary critic is concerned had better be smothered at birth. You do not exhaust 'The Tellier House' when you have made the point that the most pious people at the First Communion service are prostitutes. You don't even begin to touch it, because the surface of a great short story is like a sponge; it sucks up hundreds of impressions that have nothing whatever to do with the anecdote" (66–67). O'Faolain praises a story by Ernst Ahlgren because "The anecdote here is so innocent that when we apply our simple test of restating it in a sentence we find that it vanishes completely" (180). O'Faolain has defined anecdotes to mean tricks, or at least subjects paraphrasable as single statements. He counsels that "Not until a writer has been a long time at his craft does he really harden his heart towards anecdotes" (173).

O'Faolain and O'Connor seem to be advising against both intricate plots and simpler anecdotes—the plots because they are too complicated, the anecdotes because they are too obvious and unrewarding. The experience of Henry James, however, would suggest a less restrictive view of the possibilities of the short form. James, in the prefaces to his own stories, finds that the short form can incorporate not only simple anecdotes but also the greater complications usually thought of as belonging to nouvelles. He tries to categorize the anecdotes structurally on the basis of their focus (one protagonist) and their length (brief), but he finds his distinctions continually frustrated by the surprising agility of his own tales. The short stories in volume 16 of the New York Edition, for instance, turn out to be "novels intensely compressed"; they "could but conceal the fact that they *were* 'nouvelles'; they could but masquerade as little anecdotes" (*AN* 235). Though these stories, such as "The Middle Years," take the "form" (length) of the "concise anecdote," their actual "subject treated would perhaps seem one comparatively demanding 'developments'

—if indeed, amid these mysteries, distinctions were so absolute" (232). In the preface to "The Reverberator," in volume 13, James attempts to distinguish anecdotes on the basis of their focus, the assumption being that a story focused on one person would tend *usually* to be short: "The anecdote consists, ever, of something that has oddly happened to some one, and the first of its duties is to point directly to the person whom it so distinguishes. He may be you or I or any one else, but a condition of our interest—perhaps the principal one—is that the anecdote shall know him, and shall accordingly speak of him, as its subject. . . . The anecdote has always a question to answer—of whom necessarily is it told?" (181). Thus "The Reverberator" may appear "quite in the light of an exemplary anecdote" (180), even though it is as long as a short novel. The difficulty with this distinction is that on application to the immediate example James is unable to determine of whom the story is told, "whereby," as he engagingly concedes, "anecdotic grace does break down" (182). He smooths over the inconsistency with his pleasure that the story can be seen as a "little rounded drama" (180) where "What 'happens' . . . happens thus to every one concerned, exactly as in much more prodigious recitals" (182). In the circumlocutions of his pleasure, James must simply beg the definitional question he has raised about the nature of anecdotic grace.

Faulkner's stories seem as resistant to formal classification as James's, especially in their combination of narrative complexity and the short form. His stories are often, as James would say, "all narrative" (*Notebooks* 74). More importantly, what happens does often happen, as James says, "to every one concerned." Faulkner feels free to flout the warning that short stories are better off without plot.

"That Evening Sun" is structured on the interplay of selfishnesses and willfulnesses of a set of characters. The interplay of characters is brought to a point of tension by an impending murder, but the murder is not necessary for the characters to have something to say to each other. In "That Evening Sun," in fact, murder not only fails to propel character into action but is exploited as an ironic and horrible counterpoint to the inward-turned selfishness of the Compson family. Nancy is doomed to participate in an event, but the Compsons have no intention of participating with her or of changing their attitudes toward her. The parents disbelieve in the event itself; the children believe in something final, but they look beyond the event itself to inquire who will be Nancy's replacement. Nancy is thus a servant who is there or a servant who is not there, but she is not a person in danger, or one whom it is the Compsons' duty to protect, calm, or console. It is possible to argue that the murder is never a danger (since, the argument goes, Faulkner shows Nancy still alive in *Requiem for a Nun*); this argument shifts the focus of the story from Nancy to the figure of the father, paralyzed between querulous bickering on one hand and irrational fear on the other. If there were no event, only Nancy's fear, the father would become a much more sympathetic figure. Our belief or disbelief in the event thus does radically affect our understanding of each character's relation to the facts. But whether or not the murder is an impending fact, it is not an event that does or will change the characters' orientation to each other.

"That Will Be Fine," like "That Evening Sun," focuses attention on a character more than on what happens to that character. Clearly, in "That Will Be Fine" a complex situation and a violent action are involved: Uncle Rodney steals from his employer and forges a check in an effort to cover a previous embezzlement; his family searches for the stolen bonds, thinking he is safely incarcerated in the servant's cabin; but he escapes with the aid of his young nephew and is shot while trying to leave town with a lady friend (and, more importantly, her jewels). Yet this summary of the action fails to account for the "point" of the story. The entire direction of our interest is neither Uncle Rodney nor some ironic perception of the distance between the action and Georgie's understanding of the action. The interest is Georgie himself; except for their value as counterpoint, the incidents of action could well have been left out. We are not to be concerned with Uncle Rodney except as he manifests or repeats himself in the boy.

In "That Will Be Fine," unlike "That Evening Sun," the murder is more than impending, but Georgie, the central character, is no less disengaged than was the Compson family. Georgie almost ignores the actual incident. Our attention is not directed through the naïf to the situation, as it is in "Two Soldiers" and numerous other Faulkner stories. In "That Will Be Fine," instead of taking Georgie's revelation of the world at face value, we feel that it is not "the world" but Georgie who is unveiled, not the situation unwittingly explained by Georgie but rather Georgie explained by everyone and everything. To be sure, there is a dramatic situation to be conveyed, as well as dramatic action to be performed. But for a naïf Georgie shows unusual reticences in his description of the situation; it is largely through others that we get the exposition. Though

Georgie tells about the absence of Mandy, the cook, and about the nailing up of Mandy's windows, we are not told the actual situation until Rodney tells (through Georgie) with Brer Rabbit glee "about how papa and Uncle Fred had nailed him up in the house to keep him when that was exactly what he wanted" (276).[2] That is, Georgie does not tell all he knows, though here his reticence is more endemic than intentional, and he willingly repeats the fuller explanations he hears from others. He gives the impression not only that he has known all along but that he is unimpressed. Other naïfs can be relied upon to relay their awareness of novelty, their enthusiasm for those things for which they lack conventional language but which they make new for us by attentive observation and simple enthusiasm, the will to communicate.

The spuriousness of Georgie's naïveté is revealed by his relation to events. Georgie is precocious in his aptitude for identifying a sheriff and for giving the answer that will please Rodney, though perhaps not the rest of the family. (He tells the sheriff that Rodney has gone, though perhaps the family has promised the authorities to keep him at home until the bonds are found.) "So he couldn't fool me either," he says, prefiguring Lump Snopes's praise for Flem (278). Given that precocity, Georgie's failure to prevent the murder is strange. He sticks to the letter of Rodney's instructions, explaining away the unusual circumstances: "Only I didn't know Uncle Rodney ever did business with men. But maybe after he began to work in the Compress Association he had to. And then he had told me I would not know them anyway, so maybe that was what he meant" (283). But he might be expected to discern a trap from the lady "fighting and slobbering sure enough" or from the man's instructions to tell Rodney "*She* says to come and help carry it" (283, emphasis added). When he unquestioningly repeats those words, Rodney questions him closely, and this time he definitely edits the truth, saying the words not as a memorized message but as a statement of fact that he knows to be untrue:

> "What?" Uncle Rodney said. "She said he's not there?"
> "No, sir. She said for you to come and help carry it. For me to say that twice." Then I said, "Where's my twenty quarters?" (284)

The implication must be that Georgie intentionally simplifies the situation, since when he is given a second opportunity to tell about the man he does not do so. He seems to be more intent on the economic question than on the situation of even Uncle Rodney. There is no honor among these thieves. The reason for his lie is mysterious, but it cannot be explained by naïveté. For Georgie, as for the reader, other matters take precedence over story.

For much of the story, Faulkner has contrived that past action or present situation should gain as large a proportion of our attention as the actual narrative events that are taking place. The reader's *detection* is channeled toward an investigation of what the situation is at the expense of his investigation of what events are taking place. Faulkner requires a convention of obfuscation to make the exposition more difficult than the forward action. Pronoun antecedents are as confusing as at the beginning of *Intruder in the Dust*, where the obfuscation is more plausible in a stream-of-consciousness narration that does not pretend to be spoken aloud to an audience. "We could hear the water running into the tub." Who is we? It takes a slow and patient reader to consider both "mamma" and "Grandpa" in the first paragraph but wait for "Rosie" well down the page:

> We could hear the water running into the tub. We looked at the presents scattered over the bed where mamma had wrapped them in the colored paper, with our names on them so Grandpa could tell who they belonged to easy when he would take them off the tree. There was a present for everybody except Grandpa because mamma said that Grandpa is too old to get presents any more.
>
> "This one is yours," I said.
>
> "Sho now," Rosie said. "You come on and get in that tub like your mamma tell you." (265)

"We" is two persons, Georgie and Rosie, whereas "our" is everyone except Grandpa. Mamma wrapped the presents; Grandpa will open them. At first glance either or both could be part of "we." All the characters' names are flung into play, and the reader's interest is provoked to sort them out in the absence of logical and conventional exposition. Of course this exposition might be explained mimetically (i.e., a seven-year-old boy does not know he needs to explain who he is), but that would not account for the full working of the device in the reader, its role in making a game of directing our attention toward the exposition.

All the time, our attention is also focused on the economic side of

Georgie. Before we even hear of Uncle Rodney, we are in the midst of the negotiations that define this materialistic little man. Like the child Jason Compson in "That Evening Sun," but without the frustrations or the failures, Georgie is already the insidious and garrulous materialist, his eye not on Uncle Rodney but on the main chance:

> "I know what's in it," I said. "I could tell you if I wanted to."
> Rosie looked at her present. "I reckon I kin wait twell hit be handed to me at the right time," she said.
> "I'll tell you what's in it for a nickel," I said.
> Rosie looked at her present. "I ain't got no nickel," she said. "But I will have Christmas morning when Mr. Rodney give me that dime."
> "You'll know what's in it anyway then and you won't pay me," I said. "Go and ask mamma to lend you a nickel."
> Then Rosie grabbed me by the arm. "You come on and get in that tub," she said. "You and money! If you ain't rich time you twenty-one, hit will be because the law done abolished money or done abolished you." (265)

This kind of byplay returns again and again; the reader is delighted with comic routines for their own sake. Often the routine is capped by a return to the previous stage of such negotiations.

> "Jesus?" [Rosie] hollered. "Jesus? You let your mamma hear you cussing and I bound you'll wait. You talk to me about a nickel! For a nickel I'd tell her just what you said."
> "If you'll pay me a nickel I'll tell her myself," I said.
> "Get into that bed!" Rosie hollered. "A seven-year-old boy, cussing!"
> "If you will promise not to tell her, I'll tell you what's in your present and you can pay me the nickel Christmas morning," I said. (266)

We take as comic the boy's offer to tattle on himself for money, but he tops himself when by way of a concession and in the form of pleading for mercy, he nonetheless still finds a way to propose the nickel profit for himself.

But such moments are only routines after all. The economic motif is put to much more interesting uses. Through the story Georgie's continual calculation of his profits amounts to structure that is very much like a narrative being told, but without any reliance on the apparently central episode. Georgie's calculations parallel and overlap the adventures of Uncle Rodney. It is as a by-product of Georgie's estimation of a potential fee, for instance, that we learn that (much like Maury Bascomb in *The Sound and the Fury*) Uncle Rodney has been "doing business with Mrs. Tucker" the previous summer (266). A large part of Georgie's exposition deals with the nickels he has earned the previous summer, the quarter he earned last Christmas for helping Rodney "prize open" Grandpa's desk, and the dime present he has bought for Rodney in the hopes of getting another quarter. This economic material is like the exposition of the "main" incidents in that Rodney's troubles stem from the time that his "generosity, or whatever mamma wanted to call it, was at least five hundred dollars shorter than his pocket book" (267). But though we come to learn Rodney's net deficit (it is $2,500), Georgie *never* reveals his own net worth. He hopes to move up from a quarter to a half-dollar, though when it seems Rodney has disappeared he good-humoredly accepts the situation: "Only at first I thought maybe it wouldn't be a quarter even, it wouldn't be nothing this time, so at first all I had to think about was that anyway it would be Christmas and that would be something anyway" (275). But things are better than that, and he soon has a chance to earn ten quarters by helping Rodney escape. Then comes a strange number that emphasizes the hiddenness of Georgie but perhaps reveals his awareness as well: " . . . and I thought how maybe I could go on downtown when I got through working for Uncle Rodney and buy a present for Grandpa with a dime out of the ten quarters and give it to him tomorrow and maybe, because nobody else had given him a present, Grandpa might give me a quarter too instead of the dime tomorrow, and that would be twenty-one quarters, except for the dime, and that would be fine sure enough. But I didn't have time to do that" (278). Within three lines the ten quarters have inexplicably inflated to twenty (plus the one from Grandpa that Georgie is hoping to add to them). Either this is a clumsy anticipation on Faulkner's part of a portion of the story that will not come for a page yet, or it is an inadvertence on Georgie's part that reveals the boy already planning the inflationary pressures he will bring to bear on Uncle Rodney. Two pages later, when Georgie demands his ten quarters immediately, Uncle Rodney tries to buy him off with the revelation that "this was a twenty-quarter job" (280). Georgie's anticipation of the exact figure Rodney names is perhaps too uncanny to be absolutely convincing, but it proves his keenness of observation and also calls into question his loyalty.

At the end of the story Georgie is creatively pursuing his characteristic assumption, shown in the banter with Rosie at the story's beginning, that a profit once conceived should never be conceded. Though he has not followed up his idea of giving a dime present in hopes of getting a quarter, he thinks of a new way to get the same profit: " . . . thinking about how maybe I could tell Grandpa that I had wanted to buy him a present and so maybe he might give me fifteen cents instead of a dime anyway" (285). The ongoing financial history and growth prospectus here coincide in bitter irony with the "main" incident, for it is at this very moment that "they started shooting firecrackers back at the house where Uncle Rodney had gone." In this history there is no time to be aware of grief. Ironically, even Uncle Rodney figures finally as an element in an economic equation. The story ends with yet another increment in the profit making: "But I didn't stop. We could get the ladder and get the possum and give it to Grandpa along with the side of meat and it wouldn't cost even a dime and then maybe Grandpa might even give me a quarter too, and then when I got the twenty quarters from Uncle Rodney I would have twenty-one quarters and that will be fine" (287–88). Georgie does not, of course, know who the "side of beef" is (286). It is chilling to find suddenly that Georgie could be so wise about everything but this last, that somewhere at the core he is a naïf after all. It may in fact be too late to believe it. So wise has Georgie been that we must wonder how he could fail to understand what the news is when "folks began to come out of the houses and holler at one another" (285). His conception of the "side of beef" as a Christmas present for Grandpa is not pathetic but sardonic; his willingness to let Rodney's corpse figure in his calculations, however unintentional, can only be a grim reflection on himself. Faulkner does not spare Georgie, for all his seven years. Georgie does not know that Rodney is dead, but we are under no illusion that he will spare time to miss his favorite uncle anymore than he has taken time to warn him. If there is anything pitiful it is that one so young could be so unaware of the consequences of his greed, not that Georgie is "really" only a little boy after all.

Georgie's balance sheet may lead us eventually to statements about the implications of such a mind, but our immediate response must be an engagement with the cumulative facts of the history—from nickels and a quarter (in the past) to potential half-dollar to ten quarters to twenty quarters to twenty-one quarters less a dime to twenty-one scot-free quarters. This kind of economic structure has a developing and complicating effect quite unlike that of a series of images or thematic or philosophical conjectures. Such variation and development as such matters show affect the reader in a way that is different in kind from purely narrative effects. Image patterns and philosophical concerns require abstraction; they ask the reader to formulate something in the nature of abstract statements about the rhetorical effect or the theoretical significance of the narrative. There is in "That Will Be Fine" an example of this kind of effect, the repeated mention of the Christmas firecracker: "Then I could hear the firecrackers plain from downtown, and the moon was shining now but I could still see the Roman candles and the skyrockets running up the sky" (279). Georgie mentions the firecrackers six times in eight pages. There is some ambiguity in the preparation of the image, some doubt as to whether it is a token of gaiety or an omen of disaster. But the constant repetition seems a little gratuitous until Georgie mistakes gunfire for firecrackers in the seventh mention: "All of a sudden they started shooting firecrackers back at the house where Uncle Rodney had gone. Only they just shot five of them fast, and when they didn't shoot any more I thought that maybe in a minute they would shoot the skyrockets and Roman candles too. But they didn't. They just shot the five firecrackers right quick and then stopped, and I stood by the buggy and then folks began to come out of the houses and holler at one another" (285). The device of the firecrackers, so insistent and marginally relevant before, now seems to have become functional in a rather contrived, even predictable fashion. Had we known that Faulkner would use the naturalist's niggardly economy of effects, the firecrackers might have seemed not irrelevant but obvious, like Hedda Gabler's pistols. Unlike the dynamic function of money in the story, the device of the firecrackers is an effect repeated without variation, or with only one variation. It is both static and a gimmick at the same time. The two effects differ not only in adroitness but in importance. It might be said that the firecracker imagery is a very minor structure *used* by the story, while the history of the Georgian economy is the major structure, is the story. "That Will Be Fine" demonstrates that it is quite possible that a short story should have no central event, or that despite having one it should not rely on it. "That Will Be Fine" might be called an anecdotal story in which the anecdote itself is deemphasized.

"My Grandmother Millard and General Bedford Forrest and The Battle of Harrykin Creek" shows that a complex story need not be a handicap. This story especially ignores the prescriptions of Sean O'Faolain. "My Grandmother Millard" is a story whose ingenuity goes far beyond its trick ending. Despite its complex narrative, it nevertheless seems the kind of structure O'Faolain disapproves of in much simpler "anecdotes": "The anecdote is a finished thing in itself, and . . . all that seems necessary is to get it down on paper at once. . . . It is generally a husk, as far as its effects on the soil of the mind is concerned. . . . Good talkers, good raconteurs rarely make good writers" (O'Faolain 173).

Faulkner controls the elaborate narrative of "My Grandmother Millard" by assimilating most of the individual incidents and actions to the central chain of cause and effect. He thus prevents the impression of undeveloped narrative. The joints in the story are not exploited but concealed, and the story affects the reader in such a way as to support Faulkner's image of his processes of invention: "Even in the same breath, almost like lightning, it begins to take a shape" (Gwynn and Blotner 48). The entire chain of cause and effect might have been generated out of the figure of the grandmother, or the picture of self-stereotyping chivalric lovers, or the comic distortion of the great events of the Civil War, or any number of individual effects such as the burying of the silver, the attack on the outhouse, the strumming of the dulcimer, or Philip's misplaced zeal in battle. The original idea is well concealed. Faulkner appears to be finding the characters to perform the original actions and, simultaneously, more actions for them to perform. But of course not all of these things happen at the same time or take positions of equal importance in the structure of the story. As the story develops in time, the reader is engaged in remembering, in forming a map of the complex interactions.

The story begins with matters well away from the central events connected with Cousin Philip. Faulkner focuses attention first of all on the burying of the silver, characteristically throwing the reader into the event without exposition, with the usual obfuscatory use of pronouns: "It would be right after supper, before we had left the table" (667). Faulkner avoids the stereotype in this archetypal southern ritual by forcing the reader to puzzle out what is happening. The action, lengthily and minutely detailed in a sentence that uses the word "and" fourteen times, seems to dissolve into its component actions, focusing attention not on the archetype but on such details as "her hands raised and about eight inches apart and her neck bowed so she could watch the clock-face over her spectacles" and then "just the single light loud pop of her palms when the hand came to the nearest hour-mark" (668). Sounds and gestures are made to have an integrity and importance of their own.

Then, by free association, the unnamed narrator (who must be Bayard Sartoris) quickly tells an anecdote not directly related to the rest of the action, the story of Lucius's desire for freedom. Bayard has mentioned that Granny would not let Philadelphia (Lucius's wife) help bury the silver "because of Lucius" (even though she requires Lucius himself to take part). Granny tells Philadelphia, "I want all of you free folks to watch what the rest of us that aint free have to do to keep that way" (669). This requires an explanation of Lucius: "That began about eight months ago" (669). Faulkner frequently uses the Sternean device of being continually delayed by more exposition of the past, or of discovering that he has gotten ahead of the story. The anecdote (669–70) has to do with the meaning of freedom, a theme explored directly in *Go Down, Moses*. "Freedom" is not rigorously evaluated in "My Grandmother Millard"; instead, Granny appears to give it a debunking that is of a piece with the story's general treatment of such ordinarily serious matters as war. The anecdote about Lucius, however, is primarily a vehicle for exploring the relations between characters, and particularly the crusty individualism of the grandmother. Whereas Tom Sawyer's Aunt Polly rarely looks through her spectacles at anything so small as a boy, Grandmother Millard never looks through hers at anything (669). She is an original.

The action does not proceed without delays. The second section begins by saying that the first section was irrelevant to the main story: "And then when the time came to really bury the silver, it was too late" (672). Part 1 was a rehearsal; part 2 is the hopelessly complicated actuality, the "battle" of Harrykin Creek. Yet instead of going directly to the action, part 2 begins by telling the ending ("Cousin Melisandre and Cousin Philip were finally married") and by taking an excursion in which Colonel Sartoris discourses on freedom and Bayard attests to his father's accuracy by telling a compressed anecdote about General Early at the time of the Spanish-American War. Finally, then, the story proper begins in the second paragraph of part 2 (673). Faulkner also manages significant delays from that action, the actual battle, to develop the character of Ab Snopes, not really a central figure of the story, and to detail the anecdote of Miz Compson in the privy, which is well integrated but not indispensable.

Yet that is not to say that anything is wasted. As the story is generated through time, characters, vignettes, tableaux, and serious actions are all drawn effortlessly together and attached to its sequences of cause and effect. The narrative material is all put to use. Ab Snopes, for instance, exemplifies a class whose duplicity the grandmother will tolerate if directed against Yankees, but whose deferences to her are allowed to be only infinitesimally abridged even in war. Ab also exists in the story to call out that uprightly tyrannical authority which Granny demonstrates when she proves to him that some southern ladies will not be taken advantage of in the evaluation of horses or the taking of spoils. That is, Ab Snopes reveals important qualities in the central character.

At first reading there is so much activity, such a wealth of people doing so many different things, that the story seems one of baroque complexity. On further inspection, the central movement is extremely simple—an anecdote, in fact. The perennially zealous young officer is fixed in motion. He also is unfortunately named Backhouse. These are givens. These givens, and the placement of the maiden in a literal outhouse at the time of the military encounters in the backyard, set up a situational problem. This problem arises through no conscious move of Philip's—his valor in war (driving off the raiding party) inadvertently exposes (literally) the "beautiful girl" in the outhouse. The young officer completes the problem by making a conventional falling-in-love move, expressing that move by more furious energy that actually disorders and makes chaotic the General's planned military action. His move, disobeying orders out of excessive love-ridden chivalric zeal, is not a move in the game either but an irritant, a distraction, to the real players—the General and the Grandmother. The solution to the problem is a simple unilateral response of concerted action—a joint move—by the General and the Grandmother. This comic move comes in the form of what is called in *The Town* a "joked up piece of paper." With Melisandre frozen in the potty or in the library with the dulcimer, and Philip frozen in his romanticism, Granny and the General are the pragmatists who change not events but the way of naming them. Intertwined in the welter of nonsense in the story, the central anecdote only simulates intricacy.

The previous relation between General Bedford Forrest and Grand-

mother Millard helps connect love and war. The real southern lady, with
only the illusions she chooses to have, must commandeer the real general,
whose chivalry she in no way reveres, to restore the stability of ordinary
war and peace. Significantly, Granny is always one step ahead of the military man. When she sends for "that boy," Lucius returns to report "He
say 'whut boy'" (689). But, as Bayard succinctly notes, "General Forrest
found out what boy."

> "Well, Miss Rosie," he said. "I—"
>   "Don't call me Rosie," Granny said. "Can't you even say Rosa?"
>   "Yessum," he said. But he couldn't. At least, he never did. "I
> reckon we both have had about enough of this. That boy—" . . .
>
> He said "fit" for fought just as he said "druv" for drove and "drug"
> for dragged. But maybe when you fought battles like he did, even
> Granny didn't mind how you talked. (691–92)

General Bedford Forrest traces the failure of the sure victory through
the extended chain of cause and effect back to Melisandre:

> " . . . a girl, one single lone young female girl that ain't got any-
> thing under the sun against him except that, since it was his mis-
> fortune to save her from a passel of raiding enemy in a situation
> that everybody but her is trying to forget, she can't seem to bear
> to hear his last name. Yet because of that, every battle I plan from
> now on will be at the mercy of a twenty-two-year-old shavetail—
> excuse me again. . . . " (693–94)

One further twist is the undercutting of this entire chain of cause and
effect with the fact that this young girl is no young Granny, not even a
moderately sensible girl, and surely not a Faulknerian monument of passivity. She is, as Granny is ultimately provoked to say, "that damn bride"
(697). When Melisandre demands the "banjo," Granny protests that
Melisandre does not know how to play the dulcimer. And Bayard observes that "Granny was surely right; she just never said but half of it"
(687): "[A]nd I thought how if I was General Forrest I would go back and
get Cousin Philip and make him sit in the library until about supper-time
while Cousin Melisandre played the dulcimer and sang. Then he could

take Cousin Philip on back and then he could finish the war without worrying" (694–95). Bayard's solution is another excursion from the central matter. It is a comic improvisation, a moment of fantasy. But it does masquerade as a solution (and is in fact far more sensible than the actual solution), and consequently it too becomes connected to the plot, fused to the central action. All potential causes and consequences become "relevant."

The actual denouement of "My Grandmother Millard" is not perhaps the most convincing part of the story. In retrospect we can see how Faulkner has prepared for it. Ab Snopes is made to use the words "back house" (676), though Bayard's expression is "outhouse" (675). When Melisandre first hears Philip's name and goes into hysterics, Bayard suggests, "Why don't you change your name?" (682). Philip's reply is proud and chivalric, but he is made to leave a conditional clause that the sensible people can use to his disadvantage (as the devil uses a similar vow in "The Franklin's Tale"):

> "My Grandfather was at King's Mountain, with Marion all through Carolina. My uncle was defeated for Governor of Tennessee by a corrupt and traitorous cabal of tavern-keepers and Republican Abolitionists, and my father died at Chapultepec. After that, the name they bore is not mine to change." . . . Then he stopped laughing, or whatever it was. . . . "Unless I lose it in battle," he said.
>
> "You can't very well do that sitting here," Granny said. (682)

The problem is that we have difficulty remembering the conditional "unless" twenty pages later, and Faulkner never recalls it to our attention. Also, despite the fact that we perceive these characters in comic situations and with comic self-distortions, we are always led to believe they are distortions well bolstered by theory, justified by ideals. Given the ideal premises, all their behavior is understandable. But convention has not prepared us to see these characters as merely ridiculous. Cousin Philip is a hyperserious young officer, and nothing is more serious about him than his good name. The metaphorical "loss" of a name can mean to him only loss of life or loss of honor. Can we really believe he would be persuaded to take the words literally and allow himself to be comically declared dead in battle so that his name could be changed? It seems a different sort of comedy altogether. Unless, that is, we accept as dominant that other component of Philip's character, reverence for the General. It is clearly Faulkner's intention that Philip should be proud to be declared dead and resurrected by General Bedford Forrest. Faulkner also wants us to see Philip as able to accept with comic recognition the disparity between the rules, the letter of the law, and the distortions and practical accommodations forced from men by circumstance. As General Bedford Forrest is trying "to run a military command according to certain fixed and inviolable rules, no matter how foolish the business looks to superior outside folks" (and, implicitly, to himself as well), so Philip must frame Forrest's ridiculous decree and hang it on his mantel (696). He must take pride in what he knows is foolishness. If this seems over Philip's head and beyond his capacities, it means that Faulkner has not found a denouement that does justice to the rest of the plot. But though the denouement is not so adroit as what precedes it, it does not invalidate what precedes it. In this ornate story, the end depends on the middle. Even if we were to disavow the present end completely, the middle would continue to wait for a better one.

As anticlimax the story returns to its prologue. The silver has been necessary for the wedding, of course, so Faulkner can make a smooth transition to its reburial. It is appropriate that we be given, almost as an encore, the little episode of Cousin Melisandre and the silver: " . . . and even Cousin Melisandre polished a little of it although Louvinia could pick out the ones she polished without hardly looking and hand them to Philadelphia to polish again" (698). But after all this nonsense, it is back to training-as-usual. The rehearsals must go on by the book even though the real war has been so exhausting and undisciplined. And yet, we find, even Granny has been worn down a little by this carnival: "She didn't even look at Louvinia either. 'Put the clock in too,' she said. 'I don't think we'll bother to time ourselves tonight'" (699). The story is thus made formally symmetrical, but with comic variation at the end.

In short stories there is always some temptation to cap the climax with a better punch line, to make the joke more complex. Many stories have a last corollary episode. This episode is usually not another major event. In James's notebook sketch for the story "The Marriages," for instance, it is instead the lady's refusal of an invitation to more action: "I am very sorry —but I have just become engaged to Mr. So-and-So!" (*Notebooks* 70). In the written story, this episode reveals, in a summary not only concise but abrupt, a totally new point of view or explanation of all the preceding events: "She had never believed me—it was too absurd; she had only, at the time, disliked me. She found me utterly false . . . and she told papa that she thought I was horrid. She said that she could never live with such a girl, and as I would certainly never marry I must be sent away; in short she quite loathed me. Papa defended me, he refused to sacrifice me, and this led practically to their rupture. Papa gave her up, as it were, for me. . . . Mrs. Churchley can never come back—she is going to marry Lord Dovedale" ("The Marriages" 70). The corollary episode is a Last Word, an occasion for a verbal riposte that either summarizes the action or puts it unexpectedly in perspective. Such an appropriate last word happens when Faulkner emerges from the complexity of "My Grandmother Millard" with the focus once more on the central figure, resolutely but weariedly getting back to business.

Thus Faulkner demonstrates his ability to draw various strands together and make a wide relevance in his short stories. The central anecdote is accomplished with a few simple moves, but Faulkner is continually doing things *around* the anecdote. "My Grandmother Millard" is an example of a memorable intricacy, a story so complex and a fusion so complicated that its material is in no way used up in one telling. Backfilling through memory, we are engaged in mapping the strategies of characters, the symmetries of events. Yet for all the affective force of such complex tales as "My Grandmother Millard," O'Faolain's strictures against plot imply that such structures are too complicated to be significant, that they ought to be only a temporary vehicle for the writer and not the central focus of our interest, that they ought to be the means to some more lasting profundity. Intricacies of plot do not *remain* available to the memory as do moods and abstractions. We cannot remember the sequence of strategies by opposing characters in *The Egoist,* the comic reversals of Fielding or Eudora Welty, the economics of Faulkner. Faulkner himself, questioned about the fine points of his stories, showed a disarming ability to forget some of his own subtleties: "I have to go back and look at it to unravel what the person was doing. I remember the character, though" (Gwynn and Blotner 49). Faulkner might seem to be saying that character is more *important* than plot because more easily remembered. Eudora Welty explicitly discounts the importance of some narrative ins and outs:

Indeed, for the writer, the practical problems of narrative are on the whole minutiae. (But . . . they are "giant minutiae.") We could call these in combination the problem of How the Old Woman Got Home.

We get her there, only in the next story to have to get her there again. . . . No writer, I daresay, remembers for long the exact count of the children, or where in the sky the three-quarter moon had to be by nine on a June evening. All has vanished. Yet to his dying day he may carry around the memory of whatever feeling compelled that story, and with it the feeling that came of trying to do what he could about writing it. And I think that as readers we have the same kind of forgetting, the same kind of remembering, and the same reasons for both. (*Three Papers* 26–27)

But of course sometimes the facts are of more central interest than the three-quarter moon, and what the Old Woman did on her way home may be important. Welty concedes that almost all plots could be said to have plots of "life versus death," or the errand of search, and that therefore "We must distinguish plots not by their skeletons but by their full bodies" (30). The Old Woman surely is part of the full body, even if we do forget her. Perhaps, then, we should not assume that our memories long after reading the story are really grounds for discriminations. We should perhaps view it as a positive advantage not to remember, for our forgetting gives the story back its power to surprise and to engage us in deciphering and constructing. Though simple anecdotes, as O'Connor and O'Faolain suggest, may be essentially used up with one reading, we find that more complex plots must always be re-spun in the reading. In the rare case of the intricacy that we *can* remember, our memories are still kept perpetually active in recalling the interplay of the writer's keen inventions, which we must reproduce in making the story our own for verbal retelling. We feel compelled to share our mastery of the intricacy with others. "My Grandmother Millard" is perhaps the rare story that remains as more than a mood or an abstraction, the kind of story for which memory finds a place.

Narrative complexity does not commonly come in the form of the furious and various action, with the large cast, of "My Grandmother Millard." In each story Faulkner makes a new synthesis of event and character, of the dynamic and the static relationship. The story "Mountain Victory" climaxes with a murder, as does "That Will Be Fine"; it is anecdotal in that its one central occurrence is its climax, the rest of the story being all preparation for one event. But "Mountain Victory" is deceptively simple. Up to the climax, the machinations do not have the busyness of "My Grandmother Millard." But the believability of the one central event depends on a subtler complexity, the separate wills of the characters. The characters are not known to be involved in strategies against each other; on the contrary, they conceal their independence through their very refusal to commit themselves until the catastrophe. The unrevealed wills of the characters give the story the one really insuperable element of all complex plots. In thus reducing the elements of plot to a tension long hidden in inaction, the story demonstrates that plots are built ultimately on the complex intractability of people.

The event in "Mountain Victory" is simple: a gentleman Confederate soldier returning home from the war is killed by mountain people in Tennessee. The only definite intermediary action is that the southerner's former slave gets drunk and delays the travelers' departure until morning. Otherwise, potentially decisive actions are pointedly not allowed to happen: the daughter of the mountaineers wants to give herself to Weddel, but he shows no interest; the son offers to go away with him, but he refuses that offer as well. Yet the ending is not only not gratuitous, it seems inevitable. Weddel is a man in a dilemma in which, to remain alive, he must control all the variables. He cannot, because the variables are real, separate people. His death could come about in innumerable ways; one is enough.

The story is built on conflicts. The word "victory" in the title is obviously in large part ironic in this tale where nothing material is gained by anyone, yet at the same time the language emphasizes that both Vatch and Weddel are seeking metaphysical victories through their inflexibility. Vatch hears the rebels yelling in his dreams; he seeks to conquer fear through murder. Weddel shows some restraint with Vatch: "I think I know how you feel. . . . I expect I felt that way once. But it's hard to keep on feeling any way for four years. Even feeling at all" (758). But he will not completely stifle his wit. Earlier, when Vatch has suggested Weddel would recognize Yankee bullets better behind his back, Weddel says, "If he [Vatch] was in the army for as long as one year, he has run too, once. Perhaps oftener, if he faced the Army of Northern Virginia" (751). The

word "too" takes the edge off his arrogance, yet he has nonetheless in-
stinctively found Vatch's unhealed sore. There is no doubt that the story
depicts a psychic battleground.

The interactions between people are in part generated and accelerated
by important commitments made by two characters, the girl and Jubal.
Their decisive acts early in the story catalyze the antagonisms of Vatch,
Weddel, the father, and Hule. These two characters are not unpredictable
like the rest. Their respective stances or positions of decisiveness and
drunkenness lead to the denouement in which the other characters' wits
must engage each other. Jubal's drunkenness, it is implied, actually results
from a certain predictability in him whenever a bottle is available. He is,
then, as a character, a fixed commodity, a vehicle of the plot. Yet Faulkner
does find means to suggest an inwardness to such characters. The gestures with which Jubal responds to the alcohol suggest, at least from his
point of view, an unexpectedness about this unforeseen earthen jug: "He
said, 'Whuf!' shaking his head with a violent, shuddering motion" (753);
"Again he said, 'Whuf!' and drew his back hand across his mouth" (757).
The four-letter ejaculation adequately converts Jubal from a mere plot
vehicle to a man beset by uncooperative circumstance.

Similarly, Faulkner manages to convey the girl's point of view by the
expansion of trivial (even stereotyped) details into an expression of the
very mystery and romance that make her convert herself into a fixed
quantity. Weddel's bizarre name takes on a sort of incantatory power for
her. Weddel's otherworldliness, which the narrator describes as arrogance, is shown to become for her a mark of splendor "like a creature
from another world with other air to breathe and another kind of blood
to warm the veins. 'Soshay Weddel,' she breathed" (749). Her sense of
despair and foreignness again fixes on a significant detail until it does
indeed express immense separation and compulsion: "The Negro could
hear her breathing. Then she was not looking at him at all, though she
had not yet even blinked nor turned her head. 'I dont reckon he'd have
any time for a girl that didn't have any shoes,' she said. She went to the
wall and stooped again to the crack" (757). The conversion of a complex
self into an object seems bizarrely necessary when it is not large conceptions but minute details that make one rapt. The girl has become immov-
able through an irrevocable commitment. She, like Jubal, remains an un-
swayable.

The other characters maintain the tension by not making their intentions and positions obvious. From the point of view of each other and the reader, they are unpredictables. Faulkner refuses to romanticize Weddel; inflexibility is an inseparable part of him. We recognize this as arrogance, without seeing how he could substantially modify his rectitude. He cannot very well either leave Jubal behind or take away the boy and girl. But he does not seem to think of Hule as a serious factor: "He could hear the boy's breathing, fast, young, swift with excitement perhaps. Weddel did not pause to speculate, nor at the faintly hysterical tone of the boy's voice: 'I'll help you'" (765). Nor does he seem to take seriously the offer the boy makes of himself and his sister. His replies to the boy's worship seem curt beyond all understanding, and he seems willing to settle for explanations that could only be rhetorically confusing to the boy:

> "No. I never saw her but once. I might not even know her if I saw her again."
> "She says different. I dont believe you. You are lying."
> "No," Weddel said.
> "Is it because you are afraid to?"
> "Yes. That's it."
> "Of Vatch?"
> "Not Vatch. I'm just afraid. I think my luck has given out. I know that it has lasted too long; I am afraid that I shall find that I have forgot how to be afraid." (769)

Similarly, though he does not take offense as we might expect at being called black, his sardonic reply can hardly be called diplomatic: "'So it's my face and not my uniform,' the stranger said. 'And you fought four years to free us, I understand'" (751). In fact, Faulkner continually emphasizes the arrogance in his expression: "the half Gallic half Mongol face thin and worn like a bronze casting, with eyes like those of the dead, in which only vision has ceased and not sight" (762); "his face worn, almost gaunt, stamped with a kind of indomitable weariness and yet arrogant too" (749). Clearly, he is one whom it is possible to sentimentalize, yet Faulkner lets us see the most extreme instance of his self-sacrificing benignity through the eyes of the girl, who conspicuously can see only one side of him: "She was looking at the cloak when Vatch grasped her by the shoulder, but it was at Weddel that she looked. 'You cut hit out and gave hit to that nigra to wrap his feet in,' she said" (762). Weddel, on the other hand, sees himself as a man, like the freed slaves, "burdened with freedom" (760). Jubal, he says, does not know that his master is free. That freedom Weddel sees ironically, for he is in fact not free to leave Jubal or to dissolve his obligations. If his condition is called freedom, it is nonetheless a burden. In addition, Weddel knows himself to be fighting for a victory over his spiritual torpor: "'And so I am running away,' Weddel said. 'When I get home I shall not be very proud of this. Yes, I will. It means that I am still alive. Still alive, since I still know fear and desire'" (772); "I was concerned. I had thought that it was exhausted; that I had lost the privilege of being afraid. But I have not. And so I am happy. Quite happy" (766). The combination of kindness and arrogance, romance and cruelty, makes Weddel not simply a hero coping with variability in others but himself an eccentric element in this dance of death.

Early in the story Faulkner gives us to believe that we are to witness an inevitable act: "The voices came, not yet raised yet forever irreconcilable and already doomed, the one blind victim, the other blind executioner" (750). It is an instance of a rhetoric that gives insufficient credit to the freedom of the deed. The story itself progresses by detailing the pairings and separations that dramatize instability and augmenting tension between the partially inscrutable characters in this community of doom. Catastrophe is flirted with but averted again and again. The story begins (parts 1 and 2) with the confrontation between the major groups, Weddel opposed to the three mountain men. The girl, eventually to be the object of contention, lingers in the periphery of this confrontation, an outsider. Then Weddel's group (Weddel and Jubal) reconvenes and exhibits its own lack of unanimity in assessing the situation (part 3). Weddel knows it is dangerous and takes his pistol; Jubal is incensed at their lack of dignity. We sense now that Jubal's unreliability is shortly to be proven. In fact, he begins to get drunk in the next scene (part 4), a pairing of the two characters who will be catalysts and fixed quantities in what follows. There, Jubal and the girl are conspicuously speaking different tongues, Jubal failing (but not by much) to catch the drift of the girl's questions about Weddel in his preoccupation with "dat ere light-drinking kahysene" (757). Meanwhile, the second confrontation is taking place at dinner, where Weddel flaunts his aristocracy and Vatch tells his story about his killing of a wounded southern major (part 5). The eruption of the girl into the confrontation terminates this scene but precipitates what follows, drawing the father into Vatch's antagonism. The dispersal of the characters leads to scenes where both the father and Weddel find themselves frustrated at the fixedness of their subordinates, the girl and Jubal. Neither can prevent this double acceleration of what has heretofore seemed only potentially a disastrous situation. The scene between father and daughter (part 6) is a pairing, however, while Jubal himself is seen alone (part 7). That is, the essential equality between these two short scenes is concealed by an incomplete parallelism. The pace of the story rests with the ominous fixed frame of an incapacitated individual: " . . . sprawling above the jug, gaining his feet at last, stooped, swaying, drooling, with that expression of outraged consternation on his face. Then he fell headlong to the floor, overturning the jug" (763–64). Unlike the father, there is no way for Weddel to struggle with this, so the next scene (part 8) shows him already in the middle of the third confrontation, already having accepted this little doom. The father and Hule help Weddel move the drunken Jubal, but the father insists that Weddel should leave immediately: "Leave him here. Leave him one horse, and you ride on. He is nothing but a nigra" (765). Significantly, this ensemble takes place without Vatch, whose absence is both mysterious and ominous. His position has been fully asserted, but his behavior now becomes desperately unpredictable. The father, on the other hand, has now been drawn to the fore of the opposition. The boy, Hule, also becomes a factor, though his "faintly hysterical tone" (765) is still somewhat ambiguous. After this confrontation comes the long night, and the two successive desperate pairings in which first Hule (part 9) and then the father (part 10) try to stave off the last confrontation in their own ways. Hule offers himself and his sister and tries to promise death if Weddel does not accept. It is an attempt at explanation to which somehow Weddel cannot respond. The father, less able to help the situation, can only reiterate his warning, can only affirm the irretrievability of the course of events if dawn comes. The focus in the last sections is on Weddel's arrogant rectitude, his own attempt to avert violence. But as these last pairings and separations demonstrate, Weddel can be fully in control only of himself. The others are somewhere else, equally alive, and Weddel goes into the fourth, the inevitable confrontation essentially alone. In that last scene (part 11), and specifically in death, he is only one of many. At the moment of his death the point of view is not his but that of a disengaged observer.

It is only in the final ensemble that events reach stability, and then only through mass murder. Within that last scene we are most aware of sepa-

rate wills working to shape events in opposite directions. The offer of
Hule, evolving as it does from his interrupted meeting with Weddel at
night to his appearance as Weddel is leaving in the morning, encourages
on the reader's part the expectation of a total realignment of allegiances
like that enacted by the girl earlier. The girl's realignment has accelerated
the basic friction; the boy's proves to be only apparent and incomplete, a
source of spurious hope. In part II, Hule offers to lead Weddel away by
another path to the left of the laurel copse. As Weddel summarizes the
situation, he cannot stay where he is but must choose between three
things: "That's what throws a man off—that extra alternative. Just when
he has come to realize that living consists in choosing wrongly between
two alternatives, to have to choose among three" (773–74). His is an effective statement of perplexity in a complex situation, but it is difficult to
be sure which three alternatives he perceives. They may be going straight
ahead, going to the left, and going back in the direction from which he
has come. Hule suggests the third option by way of reiterating his offer
to go with Weddel, bringing his sister as Weddel's wife: "We could go
back to the house now, since paw and Vatch are . . . We could ride down
the mou-tin, two on one horse and two on tother. We could go back to
the valley and get married at Mayesfield" (774, Faulkner's ellipsis). Presumably Weddel understands Hule's ellipsis to mean that the father and
Vatch are in ambush at either the main road or the side path. Weddel is
prepared to guess which. But when Hule keeps reemphasizing his offer,
we suspect that he is steeling himself to an uncommunicated act of des-
peration all his own.

It is only at the last minute that we, with Weddel, learn what the meditated treachery was. Hule has led Weddel into the path knowing that the
father and the brother are there. It appears that the path to the left is no
alternative path at all: it "doubled back upon itself and into a matted
shoulder of laurel and rhododendron" (776). Hule has not thought that
his relatives would kill the rider of the sorrel horse: "They think you will
be riding the good horse . . . ; I told them you would be riding . . . " (776,
second ellipsis is Faulkner's). Hule has intended to sacrifice the rider of
the thoroughbred, that is, Jubal. He has all along meditated this private
tradeoff, this compromise in which both his relatives and Weddel would
be partially balked. His final act of despair is his act of complete submis-
sion to Weddel, in accepting completely Weddel's view of the worth and
importance of the Negro. In pushing Jubal off the thoroughbred and tak-

ing the lead himself, Hule intends to save the Negro and sacrifice himself. He reckons without his relatives in thinking the rider of the sorrel will be spared. He has undoubtedly not failed to convince them that Weddel will be on the thoroughbred, but he has failed to comprehend their hatred of both southerner *and* Negro. We have watched the boy's machinations, but there is another will we have not fathomed. In fact, there are two wills. For the father, though he participates in the murder, remains separate from Vatch, though equally unmanageable. We can deduce the father's continued unwillingness to kill Weddel, his continued desire to warn him away; it is surely the father who runs to the supposed body of Weddel "crying monotonously, 'The durned fool! The durned fool! The durned fool!'" (777). As Hule has failed to understand his relatives, in turn they have failed to predict what he would do. All this complex human machination is outside Weddel's power to control or even predict. The climax is not simply a matter of doom, or of making the wrong guess. Weddel is doomed, not by fate but by the unmanageability of people. This, not contrivance, is the irreducible plot.

The Hamlet

Relevance and Plenitude

In the Snopes trilogy, Faulkner will work out a variety of forms, each based on events and moves, and each requiring a unique accommodation between event and contemplation. The Snopes trilogy is a chronicle that spans Faulkner's career and has features in common with, by turns, his most episodic sequences and his tightest examples of cause and effect. These novels particularly emphasize the variety of Faulkner's resources, for the "same" characters participate in the several different kinds of sequence. The Snopes novels create three major solutions to the interaction of characters: a simple collision and recoil, a long and complicated series of strategies, and an anecdote-like reliance on a surprise ending. In each of the novels the presence of interpolated episodes calls attention to Faulkner's intricacies and the demands they make on the reader, and also to the complexity that results from the wide variation in plot relevance of the material assimilated. Repeatedly the text calls for a consideration of the independence and relevance of the treasure chest of things in the novels. The Snopes novels together can be seen as a portfolio of all the things Faulkner makes happen.

In *The Hamlet*, Faulkner calls attention to discontinuities, incidents, irrelevancies. The form of *The Hamlet* requires the reader to focus attention on both the governing incidents and the separate moments with which they coexist. The created world is filled out with episodes, anecdotes, observations, and jokes. But it is also *built* on episodes. The novel shares features with all of the novels Barbara Hardy mentions in her survey of the possibilities of story structures in novels:

> [The novelist] tells a story. . . . It may be the chief principle of organization, as it is in *Wuthering Heights* or *Jane Eyre,* where the

actual physical events provide the primary means of delineating character and change, or it may provide a fitfully recurring tension as it does in Dickens, where the story line does not always coincide with moral criticism or social satire. It may be placed in the context of long spaces of routine or randomly flowing experience, as it is in *Anna Karenina.* . . . But if the novel does not possess the form of the story then it is not a novel. (*Appropriate Form* 1–2)

In *The Hamlet* Faulkner does celebrate "long spaces of routine or randomly flowing experience," but the "fitfully recurring tension" of the story is nonetheless still the "primary means" of delineating the central "change" of the novel. The plot of *The Hamlet* is much like the paradigm Paul Goodman describes for the plots of epic poems:

The action must of course have a beginning, middle, and ending, otherwise it would not be one poem. Yet . . . the hero can finish an exploit and his habitual virtue survive for another, and within limits the other characters may perform independent exploits, for the group may have other representatives. All these considerations point to the following type of plot: an episodic plot in which the episodes are partial actions of the one action. . . . On the one hand, the unity of the over-all action must not be lost. . . . On the other hand, the greatness of the individual exploits must not be lost; they must not be underwritten to hasten to the end, or they will not be epic. The whole must not fall apart into an "episodic plot"; yet each episode must not be pusillanimous. (70–71)

Goodman's general remarks might suggest to readers of *The Hamlet* the independent exploits of Flem, the connected central encounters between Flem and Ratliff, the long interruption between these encounters, the limited independent roles of the Frenchman's Bend community and the Snopes group, and the overall habituality of challenges and stability of characters.

At the same time, it is important to combine a respect for the central plot with an awareness of plenitude or marginal relevance:

Middlemarch is indeed a novel with no irrelevant digressions, no disturbing loose ends, no padding either of humor or circumstantial description or local color. It is not, however, a novel where every episode, every description, every psychological observation, and every metaphor, is of equal importance. Its total design is that of an intricately graduated order. . . . Some of the details could be dropped without much loss to the main figure in the carpet. (Hardy, *Appropriate Form* 12)

For one pregnant scene of the kind I have mentioned, there are many which have slighter general reference, like some of the domestic scenes in *Middlemarch* or the comic scenes in Dickens, where it would be hard to argue the pressure of total relevance. (16)

The question is whether *The Hamlet* is a plotted novel, or what kind of plot relevance Faulkner imposes there. Everyone who has read *The Hamlet* has conceded that Faulkner has strong *local* controls over his narrative; some have wondered if he has anything else.[1] But the novel does gain forward propulsion through plot, and it also leads to a climax in a conventionally plotted manner, without sacrificing its satisfying randomness. Not only do we see Flem Snopes winning a few isolated contests, but we see him accumulating. We know that we will reach an ending when he has gradually "grazed up" the total of the local resources (80).[2] At the same time, we know that he cannot have it all until he has bested the man who has, from the first, both claimed to be the one man able to beat him and called attention to the conflict between Flem and the stability of the whole community. That is, *The Hamlet* is built on conflict issuing in event.

The major antagonists are V. K. Ratliff and Flem Snopes. We meet Ratliff as raconteur-with-an-edge before we ever see Flem. Ratliff tells Jody Varner about the barn-burning episode (15–21). Jody goes from that genially voluble needling to the first major move in the novel, the confrontation where Flem "talks" his way into the store job—with about seventy words, including the ominously direct phrases "What benefit?" and "Guarantee what?" Ratliff and Flem are contrasted, but they are not yet in conflict. Faulkner uses much of chapters 2 and 3 of book 1, however, to establish almost simultaneously both a precedent of rivalry and a medium for contest between the two characters.

The Fool About a Horse sequence is a first attempt to dramatize the medium of barter or cash interchange, the primary medium for the meeting of characters throughout the novel. As everyone has recognized that *The Hamlet* is a novel about money, the desire for it and the abuse of its power, it is important to see that Faulkner has made his form directly enact this reference. Balzac, in *Cousin Bette,* vaguely uses fiscal collapse to measure the power of ungoverned lust. In *Dombey and Son* Dickens measures the force of capital largely by its effects on a family's private lives. James, wishing to talk about money but cut off from the "downtown" world, uses economic language to express the mentality of business working in the drawing room. It is rare that the cash interchange is made the immediate grounds of encounter of characters. But *The Hamlet* enacts business. It is a world "where breath inhaled and suspired and men established the foundations of their existences on the currency of coin" (228). Thus it is with special appropriateness and seriousness that economic metaphors appear in the novel. Ratliff can express with total seriousness the loss of Eula in economic terms because trading is the mode of communication with others in all the phases of his life: "What he felt was outrage at the waste, the useless squandering; at a situation intrinsically and inherently wrong by any economy, like building a log dead-fall and baiting it with a freshened heifer to catch a rat" (182). Similarly, information passed back and forth takes its place in the total context of buying and selling. News is said to be "retailed," with the implicit metaphor of an understood markup between cost and selling price (62).

Clearly, too, the basic form of the interchange cannot be called into question, for without it the characters would have no common language. Ratliff believes moral action too can be converted into this language, as he refers ironically to "social overhead" (95) and attempts to beat Flem on this common ground. In a sense, by making the form of the novel dependent on the "theme," Faulkner has refused to consider the possibility of a radical moral repudiation of money. The importance of Ratliff's trip to New York in *The Mansion* is its vertiginous glimpse of a world where money as Ratliff knows it has no importance (in this case, simply because there is so much of it). Madame Allanovna's gesture of repudiation of money is based not simply on her own financial independence but on a show of patriotic emotion for a fellow Russian (just as other renunciations of the cash nexus might be motivated by love or art or politics or honor). But Faulkner shares Ratliff's incredulity at the sight of money about to he burned: "Because it's money. . . . Somebody somewhere at some time went to—went through—I mean, money stands for too much hurt and grief somewhere to somebody that jest the money wasn't never worth—" (*M* 176–77). When at given instants Ratliff himself repudiates money, his is a greater sacrifice, for he gives up specific dollars that mean something to him. And he always gives them up for the *use* of others. Faulkner thus condemns only abuses *within* a necessary structure. He is not slow to remind us, in his authorial narrative voice, of "a people's heedless greed" (196); nor does he shrink from characterizing Ratliff's self-betrayal, in extravagant terms reminiscent of Dickens and Frank Norris, as due to the power of gold, cosmically present in the probing golden rays of the sun (410). Greed is the confusing of the means with the ends, forgetting "the pleasure of the shrewd dealing which far transcended mere gross profit" (77).

Ratliff responds to the Snopes phenomenon with a significant self-appraisal:

> "I think the same as you do," Ratliff said quietly. "That there aint but two men I know can risk fooling with them folks. And just one of them is named Varner and his front name aint Jody."
> "And who's the other one?" Varner said.
> "That aint been proved yet neither," Ratliff said pleasantly. (31)

This one sentence, reinforced by repetition at a key point, in itself defines and makes explicit the structure of the most significant plot conflict of the novel. The sentence has what Harold Toliver calls "saliency." By having an importance disproportionate to its actual duration, it contributes to the "stress system" of the work.[3] It crops up; it forces the reader to give it a place in the synchronic shape he is forming of the plot.[4]

Faulkner establishes the precedent for rivalry not merely with Ratliff's boast but by establishing parallel displays of skill in the trading medium by both Ratliff and Flem. Ratliff establishes his own ability with his excursion in Tennessee (63–64). But his one deal is offset by Flem's seemingly inexorable rise in fortune—his move into town (65–66), his passing Jody at the cotton gin (67–69), his herd of scrub cattle transmogrified into a herd of Herefords on Varner property (70), the appearance of Eck and I.O. in the blacksmith shop (71–75), and the complex manipulations with two blacksmith shops (76)—reaching at last the "point [where] even Ratliff had lost count of what profit Snopes might have made" (76). Perhaps most appropriately, as Ratliff deduces and verifies (82–83), and as Mink is not slow to notice, Flem now owns not only land and cattle but a hay barn, "something that will burn," the traditional target of have-not Snopeses. The observers are setting up the next impossible state ("Anyhow, he aint moved into Varner's house yet") while the narrator himself reveals enough of the future to make it clear that nothing is impossible (" . . . later, after he had become president of his Jefferson bank . . . ") (65, 66). All that is in doubt is the accommodation Ratliff will make to this inevitability. It is appropriate that after his initial draw with Ratliff, Flem's next contest in the "usurpation of an heirship" (101) is pre-cisely what the coffee-shop commentators have used as a comic hyper-bole, an impossible next stage—he moves into Varner's house (102).

Joseph Urgo (*Faulkner's Apocrypha* 177) suggests that Flem is able to rise because Ratliff in a sense vouches for him. Richard Godden pursues this line of argument and finds that Ratliff misunderstands Ab's souring and thus is an enabler of Flem ("Earthing *The Hamlet*" 110). But there is no evidence that the Varners estimate Flem based on Ratliff's story or that Flem needs any help from anyone. Flem trades on Ab's reputation and apparently does so without anyone else knowing what he is up to; as Jody realizes, "he was standing just exactly where couldn't nobody see him from the house" (*H* 27). The emphasis is on the way Jody's desire to ex-ploit Flem makes him vulnerable to Flem, and how little effort in words it takes Flem to complete a blitzkrieg of moves. Ratliff's somewhat nos-talgic and benign tale of Ab in the past does fail to estimate correctly the present-day Ab; but as everyone is about to find out, Ab is not the problem.

The communal grounds of encounter and the established independent drives of Flem and Ratliff prepare for and lead to the goat-trading se-quence, Ratliff's first attempt to "think of something" to do about Flem (81). Ratliff provokes the contest. He knows that he presents not just a random chance for money-making but a particularized target as well: "I had to trade not only on what I think he knows about me, but on what he must figure I know about him" (94). It is here that Ratliff whimsically raises the question of "social overhead," incorporating the moral champi-oning of the community into his personal contest of skill. But the conflict does not solve the issue. Though Ratliff salvages a nominal profit in the episode, there is no satisfaction. Ratliff's excuses for himself are surely an admission of the feeling of failure: "It was because I have been sick, was slowed up, that I didn't—" (97–98). His "sardonic, humorous" message for Varner casts back to the original boast and forward to the encounter that *will* prove which is the better trader: "Just tell him Ratliff says it aint been proved yet neither" (101). Some repetition of the conflict is here pledged; the continuing antagonism provides the plot conflict of the novel.

We may say, then, that a chain of cause and effect is set up in the novel. It is not the sort of cause and effect that is expressed in a radical change of circumstance; Ratliff is not forced to challenge Flem again by physical or financial necessity. The financial relation between the two is not greatly changed, as it will be after the final encounter, but the need for a symbolic victory is stronger for having been frustrated. The characters have not developed radically new relations to each other. Ratliff's *attitude* toward Flem does not change, but his desire or willingness to put his attitude into practice does, even if he must wait some time for the opportunity. The connection between the encounters is the inveteracy of his character; his clear motive is simply his constant desire to beat Flem. What is perhaps a matter of some ambiguity is the motive behind the motive, the question of the purity of the desire: to what degree does Ratliff challenge Flem out of pride (or even greed), and to what degree from a sense of social overhead? It is not difficult for us to strike a plausible balance; we have here nothing like the bewildering and contradictory multiple motivations of Quentin Compson. The most important thing is that the immediate desire to challenge (for whatever reason) has been built into the very fabric of the social order. The habituality of trading means that challenges are probable whether the challenger is pledged to good, evil, or merely skill. Because it is not proven, the first event requires a rematch; situation, then, combines with character to *cause* the second event.

The episodic events represent the collision and recoil of implacably defined wills. Faulkner's characterizations entail no book-long strategies (though within each episode the calculations are, perhaps disconcertingly, of another order of complexity entirely). No overall balance sheet is kept by Ratliff between the goat trading and the salted gold mine, and Ratliff does not appear to have a plan of attack between the episodes. The characters simply find, at intervals, new opportunities to assert their fixed attitudes. Mink Snopes is another figure whose character is destiny, no matter how great the lapses in time between outbreaks. Ratliff thinks, "So that wasn't the last time this one is going to make his cousin trouble" (104). Faulkner's characters are evidently built on the conviction that each man is a stable entity, each man a troublemaker in his own way.

In an odd way, however, the structuring collisions have been to a great degree localized. The major conflict between Flem and Ratliff is far more important in book 1 than in books 2 and 3, and this leisureliness does have large implications for the novel's narrative structure. The plot is generated in the first ninety pages, and as far as the central conflict is concerned, is not resumed until the last chapters of the book. Unlike Dickens, who seems to sense late in *Martin Chuzzlewit* the need for a murder plot, Faulkner here starts his plot early and lets it lie nearly dormant. Actually, novels are rare in which any two characters are consciously, unremittingly at war with each other. In *What Maisie Knew,* James gives us some relief from the enmity between Beale and Ida by their elimination from the presented action for large segments of time; and even the more continual interaction between Sir Claude and Mrs. Beale is made challenging to the reader's curiosity by many variations in the degree of friction. It is true, however, that *The Hamlet* is particularly casual about its conflicts, allowing antagonists to go on seemingly unaware of their role until the time is ripe for the renewal of their interchange. Flem characteristically pays no attention to Ratliff at all. There is no indication, even when he condescends to salt the Old Frenchman's place himself, that it is Ratliff he is looking to catch. As Ratliff says, "He didn't care. He just come out here every night and dug for a while. He knowed he couldn't possibly dig over two weeks before somebody saw him" (414). From the reader's point of view, the gulling of Ratliff is formally necessary; from Flem's, it is just another day's work, only the last in a long series of encounters that constitute the grazing up of Frenchman's Bend.

The delay, then, is completely in character for Flem. And Faulkner spends much of books 2 and 3 explaining what is holding up Ratliff. Though Ratliff and Flem do not act out their roles as antagonists, their stances between encounters importantly prepare for the outcome of the foreordained renewal of combat. Flem's self-sufficiency and Ratliff's dependent and subordinate role prefigure the moment when Flem will officially defeat his major antagonist. Throughout the dormant stage, Ratliff is not an equal antagonist. In book 2 he is reduced in stature, becoming only an observer and fantasist. Meanwhile, Faulkner connects the Labove episode to Flem through Labove's prediction: "He could almost see the husband which she would someday have. He would be a dwarf, a gnome, without glands or desire, who would be no more a physical factor in her life than the owner's name on the fly-leaf of a book. There it was again, out of the books again, the dead defacement of type which had already betrayed him: the crippled Vulcan to that Venus, who would not possess her but merely own her by the single strength which power gave, the dead power of money" (135). The entire Eula section is made merely another stage in Flem's rise, as Eula (along with three hundred dollars, the Old Frenchman's place, a wedding license, and two tickets to Texas) becomes an acquisition of "the froglike creature" (169).

Yet it is in the third section, "The Long Summer," that Faulkner deliberately forfeits his chances of making *The Hamlet* a tightly plotted novel. In that section, representing almost a third of the novel, the story opens out into new material, forcing the reader's attention to Mink, forcing Ratliff into a side skirmish with minor Snopeses, and virtually forcing the novel to become a chronicle and go into extra volumes.

The third section not only begins with Ratliff but emphasizes again his spiritual heirship to Will Varner, the king of Yoknapatawpha traders: "[Ratliff] was a good deal nearer his son in spirit and intellect and physical appearance too than any of his own get" (180). Yet if the legitimate heir has long since been displaced, we find Ratliff himself mired in fantasy that has ceased being indulgence or symbolic prophecy and become something like hysteria: "Snopes can come and Snopes can go, but Will Varner looks like he is fixing to snopes forever. Or Varner will Snopes forever—take your pick. What is it the fellow says? off with the old and on with the new; the old job at the old stand, maybe a new fellow doing the jobbing but it's the same old stern getting reamed out?" (185). His last fantasy (Flem in Hell) has been a magnificent comic tour de force. Now, talking without pause, he seems to revel in the sordid vision of Flem and a "black brute from the field with the field sweat still drying on her that she dont know it's sweat she smells because she aint never smelled nothing else" (187). His argument that Flem will manage Eula if he can dress her in black tights and paint up a screen to look like the inside of his store is an absurdity that reveals the speaker, not the subject of the fantasy.[5] It is significant that Ratliff here for the first time is speaking without heed of his audience, and in such a way as to worry Bookwright. As Ratliff steps off the gallery, still spinning his noisy joke, with new horrific things to see, the novel steps off into the unexpected private world of Ike H-mope.

Yet despite that long excursion (188–224) from the main narrative line, the Ike Snopes episode is finally linked to Ratliff much as the Eula section is finally connected to Flem. First, after Houston takes the cow to Mrs. Littlejohn (224), Ratliff is implicated through the reappearance of the money he has given to Mrs. Littlejohn for Ike on page 100. The change of hands of this particular money starts up a short subnarrative somewhat analogous to the account of Georgie's finances in "That Will Be Fine"; the subnarrative might be called "The Story of Sixteen Dollars and Eighty Cents." When Mrs. Littlejohn gives the money itself in trade for the cow, the cow becomes Ike's. When Ratliff separates Ike and the cow and makes the Snopes relatives pay for the separation, he insists that the amount of reimbursement be $16.80, so that Ike will come out even. Ratliff generates the series and completes it, and he is explicitly mentioned in the Houston–Mrs. Littlejohn interchange as well.

Ratliff's new involvement with Ike follows the lyric interlude of Ike and the cow. With no transition the narrative abruptly shifts from Houston's words "Goddamn it, keep them both away from my place. Do you hear?" back to the original September afternoon, with Ratliff walking to the Ike Snopes "engagement" (224). As if Ratliff had listened to the intervening narrative, "He knew not only what he was going to see but that, like Bookwright, he did not want to see it, yet, unlike Bookwright, he was going to look." The narrator links him with the previous narrative, saying that he curses "as Houston had: not in rage and not even in outraged righteousness" (225). Ratliff thus takes on the role of intervening in a process of which he has not originally been a part, much as Flem intervenes in the Eula saga. But his role as terminator of the engagement gives hardly anyone satisfaction. Significantly, at this point the townspeople are seen accusing him of greed and questioning his motivation. Told that the $16.80 is Ike's, Houston says, "I reckon it is, if Ratliff gave it up" (224). When Ratliff closes the performance, a bitter voice says, "I notice you come to have your look too" (225). Mrs. Littlejohn says, "It aint that it is, that itches you. It's that somebody named Snopes, or that particular Snopes, is making something out of it and you dont know what it is. Or is it because folks come and watch? It's all right for it to be, but folks mustn't know it, see it" (226–27). Ratliff's confessions of guilt—"I aint cussing you folks. I'm cussing all of us" (225); "I aint never disputed I'm a pharisee. . . . Maybe all I want is just to have been righteouser" (227)— show an awareness of the precariousness of his actions. His action over the cow is intended as a protection of Ike from use as an object by his relatives and the community. Cleanth Brooks denounces the moral relativism that sentimentally sees Ratliff's actions as cruel: "What would [T.Y.] Greet have Ratliff do? See to it that Ike is allowed to continue to practice his 'act of love' as a kind of sympathetic magic? Take Ike and his beloved cow on tour throughout the county?" (*Yoknapatawpha Country* 409). But Faulkner has encouraged this relativism by allowing us to see Ike's possession of the cow lyrically, as an "act of love." Furthermore, there is something unsettling about the means of disposal of the cow: Ike is not only forced to eat the cow, but "the fellow has got to know that's what he is eating" (231). Ratliff seems willing to abandon Ike to the cruelty of his relatives (and his preacher) in a new form. Nor does he make an attempt (aside from one cryptic jibe) to protect Eck Snopes from gulling.

> "How do I need fifteen dollars worth of moral value when all you need is a dollar and eighty cents?"
>
> "The Snopes name. Cant you understand that? That aint never been aspersed yet by no living man. That's got to be kept pure as a marble monument for your children to grow up under."
>
> "But I still dont see why I got to pay fifteen dollars, when all you got to pay is—"
>
> "Because you got four children. And you make five. And five times three is fifteen."
>
> "I aint got but three yet," Eck said.
>
> "Aint that just what I said? five times three? If that other one was already here, it would make four, and five times four is twenty dollars, and then I wouldn't have to pay anything."
>
> "Except that somebody would owe Eck three dollars and twenty cents change," Ratliff said.
>
> "What?" I.O. said. But he immediately turned back to his cousin or nephew. "And you got the meat and the hide," he said. "Cant you even try to keep from forgetting that?" (234)

But perhaps the major impact of Ratliff's intervention is not its moral efficacy or inefficacy but the fact that it is inescapably a *minor* episode.

For Ratliff is confronting not Flem but Lump, whom he calls "that Snopes encore," or, as he corrects himself: "I said encore. . . . What I was trying to say was echo. Only what I meant was forgery" (226). Lump is, as has been frequently noticed, a Flem surrogate while the master is off-stage. His most important function is making grotesquely verbal the un-stated premises of Flem, whose own characterization as the almost per-fectly discreet man is thus protected. It is Lump who tells Mink "there aint nothing personal in this because it is a pure and simple business matter" (281); Lump who objects not to the murder but to Mink's failure to take Houston's money, thus making it perfectly clear which is to him the greater charge when he calls Mink a "durn little tight-fisted mur-derer" (278). But Lump is not even remotely equal to Flem. His harass-ment of Mink and his (presumed) use of Ike and the cow for profit are played for only tiny stakes, and are completely without subtlety. Yet Ratliff does not in fact even challenge Lump head-to-head. It is perhaps a sign of his shrewdness that he characteristically attacks the weakest link, as he has made use of Mink in trying to outdo Flem. But it seems a deflation of his own prowess to bypass Lump for I.O., and when I.O. passes the buck to Eck, Ratliff's victory seems even more to have been accomplished with the minimum expenditure of skill. Eck is a Snopes to be pitied, not outwitted. Ratliff himself, at least temporarily, has con-descended to fight minor skirmishes in default of his announced aim of taking on Flem. The devaluation of Ratliff does not undercut the long-promised resumption of trading in book 4; but it helps to give that trad-ing a sense of inevitability, of logic, when it turns out as unfortunately for Ratliff as it does.

In the Mink episode (250–96) it is appropriate that Ratliff be to-tally absent, for here Mink establishes himself as a serious though late-blooming antagonist in his own right. Ratliff has suggested early (104) that Mink's hostility to Houston, which we have seen developing as a minor consequence of the Snopes invasion (103–4, 180–84), will find a way to become related to the hostility to Flem, which we have also seen (83–87). But even at the end of the Mink section this has not yet come about. Mink, in fact, is waiting patiently for Flem's succor, in the belief that "after all, blood is blood" (301). When reading the novel for the first time we must be aware that we are now very close to the end, and must wonder whether there is time for the promised conflict to take final form. There is not. Mink is in jail, and Flem need do absolutely nothing. In characteristic fashion he has (like Pat Stamper) used the impetuous motion of a potential antagonist to place that person beyond harm. Only Flem's avoidance of conflict actually raises Mink's anger to the full:

> Toward the end of the first day the faith went out of his face, leaving only the hope, and at the beginning of the second day the hope was gone too and there was only the urgency, the grim and intractable sombreness, while still he watched the door. . . . He was speaking himself even before the Judge had ceased, continuing to speak even while the Judge hammered the desk with his gavel and the two officers and three bailiffs converged upon the prisoner as he struggled, flinging them back and for a short time actually successful, staring out into the room. "Flem Snopes!" he said. "Flem Snopes! Is Flem Snopes in this room? Tell that son of a bitch—" (381–82)

Nevertheless we can hardly believe that Mink's hostility can be so easily dispatched, contained by a prison; the ironic non-conflict is as frustrating to the reader as to Mink. Though by the end of the novel Mink has appeared only four times, over a sixth of the novel has dealt with him, and he has been the subject of much speculation from the talkers. The Mink narrative takes up so much of the end of the novel that the reader is left with the sense of what has not taken place, the feeling of a violence that will not be averted by inertia and ended with irony. A narrative line has been developed that opens up the end of the novel—in addition to the more obvious open ending of "on to Jefferson in triumph." Mink does not yet seem like a canceled note (366). In this sense, Faulkner has committed himself to the resumption of a specific conflict, requiring the novel to expand into the additional volumes of the trilogy.

Mink's part in *The Hamlet* is the education of an antagonist; for this, Flem is more useful in absentia, and Ratliff is irrelevant. Ratliff's return from fantasy to combat I.O. over Ike's cow has had only mixed results, but Ratliff is more credible there than in his rather forced appearance in the Mink episode. It turns out that Mrs. Mink Snopes and her children are Ratliff's guests, that he buys them new overcoats, and that he takes an attitude of great relativism about her alleged promiscuity: "But that was her affair. Ratliff knew nothing about that and cared less and, to his credit, believed even still less than that" (299). Faulkner is restoring Ratliff's original serenity and sense of proportion, and leaving no doubt about the "credit" of his good intentions. Yet this wealth of charity verges on the sentimental, makes Ratliff into too blatant a do-gooder, allows him too easy a control of the situation. It is perhaps Faulkner's least successful way of allowing the tension to ebb and flow, of allowing characters for long periods of time to function as observers rather than antagonists. The ebb and flow allows a return to stability, while keeping the potential of further lapses. This particular appearance, however, makes Ratliff too much an exemplar of *caritas*. In the subsequent volumes, Faulkner finds ways of rendering subtler hints of more self-effacing forms of Ratliff's goodness. The disclosure that Ratliff has gained information from Eula and that Eula knows his given names suggests a wholly private existence for Ratliff's humanity (*T* 322; *M* 141).

Even within *The Hamlet,* Ratliff's more open succoring of Mrs. Armstid in book 4 is a compelling case of balked sympathy, compassion not so easily issuing in charity. The charity is inextricably connected with Ratliff's own hesitation about dealing with Flem, his own anxiety about his role as antagonist. Ratliff needles Flem Snopes, preparing him for Mrs. Armstid's request for the five dollars; but this form of conflict is not trading and gets no rise from Flem. When Bookwright in turn taunts Ratliff for his excessive meddling piety, Ratliff reveals that he has done nothing for Mrs. Armstid, and that he still is not able to tell himself what he has done for Ike Snopes and why. At this point, just before his own gulling, Ratliff seems in fact eager to escape completely his role as antagonist. He is still claiming his abilities as at the first, but he is also trying to disclaim his inclination for the combat:

> "Oh," Bookwright said. "Hah," he said, with no mirth. "I reckon you gave Henry Armstid back his five dollars too." . . .
> "I could have," [Ratliff] said. "But I didn't. I might have if I could just been sho he would buy something this time that would sho enough kill him, like Mrs Littlejohn said. Besides, I wasn't protecting a Snopes from Snopeses; I wasn't even protecting a people from a Snopes. I was protecting something that wasn't even a people, . . . just like I wouldn't stand by and see you steal a meat-bone from a dog. I never made them Snopeses and I never made the folks that cant wait to bare their backsides to them. I could do more, but I wont. I wont, I tell you!"

"All right," Bookwright said. "Hook your drag up; it aint nothing but a hill. I said it's all right." (367)

Ratliff's compelling mixed attitude toward his social responsibility joins with his own desire to escape from conflict with Flem altogether. It is not a promising attitude this late in the day for the character whose longtime status as the One Good Trader (non-Snopes variety) has inevitably come to incorporate a near-Miltonic aspect of the One Good Man.

Book 4, "The Peasants" (309–421), over a quarter of the text, marks the return of Flem and the return to prominence of Ratliff and the main plot. The climax is a double one. First is Flem's cataclysmic gulling of the entire community at once, in the Spotted Horses sequence. Then Ratliff himself, the last vestige of original Frenchman's Bend cunning, is done in by Flem's buried treasure routine at the Old Frenchman's place, the value of which Ratliff has conspicuously pondered before (at the very beginning of the third section, pages 179–80, not to mention his listening to Will Varner's hints on page 7). It is interesting to assay the relation and positioning of these important episodes.

Flem's last successes in *The Hamlet* hold the very key to his method. Flem is surely the most self-effacing villain ever. Almost unsurpassably laconic, he draws to him the indiscretions of all other men. In a sense Flem never needs to be greedy; he makes use of the pride and greed of others. At crucial moments, he always profits by making his antagonists forget that it is he they are challenging. Flem lets them bare their backsides to him. At first (in the Spotted Horses sequence), their speculation as to the ownership of the horses diverts them from the fact that gradually they are talking themselves into buying the horses. Ratliff reminds them: "[W]hen a man's done got trimmed, I dont reckon he cares who's got the money" (315). But the question of Flem's ownership, were they to confront it seriously, *is* the question. If Flem owns the horses, the chances are that someone is going to be gulled, and few would tackle Flem directly. The idle speculation that Flem may own the horses thus turns out to be also a way of forgetting Flem, of making a real danger into an academic question. Instead, Flem's antagonists allow themselves to think of the possible bargain in absolute terms of economy: "When a man dont have to invest so much into a horse or a team, he dont need to expect so much from it" (316). Behind the abstract economy lies the rivalry between the members of the gallery community itself. Not only do they all participate in talking each other into buying the horses, but each man is forced to participate by the fear that his neighbors will make a killing without him. After the sale, so great is their eagerness that they allow Henry Armstid to prod them all into abandoning Freeman's original scheme to cooperate and capture the horses one at a time (343). Here again is the communal stampeding, the desire not to be outdone by one another, that allowed them to spend good money for the horses in the first place.

Godden sees the Spotted Horses episode as a sign of Flem as "residual Populist and ur-iconoclast," the "enemy of all relations": "Between 1887 and 1890, Flem is Ab's son, at a loss for political agency but loathing a system which gives rise both to Mink and to Varner" ("Earthing *The Hamlet*" 113). Godden considers and rejects the idea that the horses might be a "carnival" used to control "the free time of a coerced labor force." But Flem's silence, the ambiguity or deception that conceals whether he is involved at all, makes it a large inference to find anger behind Flem's disruptions. The text instead foregrounds the self-deception of the victims, the flaws that make Flem possible.

We are not sure at first where Ratliff has come out. His lack of confidence as antagonist is mingled with a new composure as observer. But his status as observer separates him further from his community. His very common sense in not joining in the horse fiasco leads to a certain bitterness that Lump Snopes voices for the gallery watchers: "We done all admitted you are too smart for anybody to get ahead of. . . . So maybe it aint none of your business and maybe you better just leave it at that" (355). On the other hand, that Ratliff has recovered some of his composure is implied when we are told that the justice of the peace is in the position Ratliff was once in: "an expression not only of amazement and bewilderment but, as in Ratliff's eyes while he stood on the store gallery four weeks ago, something very like terror" (370).

The terror has not returned. If anything, we see Ratliff full of a new excess of confidence, summarizing his long observations of the Frenchman's place and concluding with what must be a conscious reference to his first encounter with Flem: " . . . and then he sold out to Will by taking that old house and them ten acres that wouldn't hardly raise goats" (384). As a character Ratliff remains free, not subjected to any obvious sequence of moods. In the final encounter, his lapses from self-control are temporary, but they reflect the fact that Flem is working his old trick on

Ratliff too, making him think about money when he ought to be out-thinking Flem.

> Ratliff plunged down beside him and began to scrabble among the weeds for the other shovel. It was the pick he found first. He flung it away and plunged down again; he and Bookwright found the shovel at the same time. Then they were standing, struggling for the shovel, snatching and jerking at it, their breathing harsh and repressed, hearing even above their own breathing the rapid sound of Armstid's shovel up the slope. "Leave go!" Ratliff whispered. "Leave go!" The old man, unaided now, was struggling to get up.
>
> "Wait," he said. "Wait." Then Ratliff seemed to realize what he was doing. He released the shovel; he almost hurled it at Bookwright.
>
> "Take it," he said. He drew a long shuddering breath. "God," he whispered. "Just look at what even the money a man aint got yet will do to him." (393)

Greed thus creates competition even among the three treasure hunters; and at the sound of Eustace Grimm's horse, greed creates fear of competition from the rest of the community. Instead of thinking about Flem, instead of outwitting his real antagonist by stopping to think what it is he knows about Eustace Grimm, Ratliff allows himself to be stampeded into immediate purchase of the property. Specifically, he thinks it is Lump Snopes and "his agent, Grimm" that he is bidding against for the right to buy the property from Flem (403). In the goat sequence, he "never went far enough" (101). Now he seems to remember the lesson he learned there, that "even a Snopes was not safe from another Snopes" (403). But once again he does not go far enough to see that Eustace Grimm is a Snopes too, and that a Snopes can use two other Snopeses to make a fool of a Ratliff. He has forgotten his true antagonist, or at least he has assumed he has already beaten him; he feels confident enough to remind Flem that this is the long-promised rematch, telling him he wants the Frenchman's place "to start a goat-ranch" (406). Faulkner's narrator makes it explicit that this lapse, too, is ultimately caused by greed: "dreaming of gold," the sleeping treasure hunters turn their heads from the "golden sun," "as though, still sleeping, they fled the weightless shadow of that for which, awake, they had betrayed themselves" (410–11). Ratliff has failed in precisely the ways the rest of the community has failed in the paired climax.

But why does this episode, first written as "Lizards in Jamshyd's Courtyard," follow the cataclysm that bilks the whole community at once? If the "Father Abraham" fragment is the earliest bit of Snopes writing, and if it represents the first chapter of a novel instead of a short story, then Faulkner originally intended to use the Spotted Horses episode at the beginning of his narrative.[6] But "Lizards in Jamshyd's Courtyard" was also an early piece of Snopes writing, and it included both of the two major episodes of the Ratliff-Flem plot, in essence the frame of the novel as it now exists. Both of these early pieces very likely figured in the original conception that Faulkner described as usually coming to him "like a bolt of lightning" (Gwynn and Blotner 90). Clearly, Spotted Horses proves to be too universal a gulling to be an opening episode; it must be placed at the climax, for in many ways it cannot be gone beyond. But as Faulkner demonstrates, it can be topped once. The final blow is not provided by the general victory but by the victory over the one good man. Structural tension comes from the conflict between individuals. Faulkner allows this intention to be made very explicit when someone says as the last word from the community: "Couldn't no other man have done it. Anybody might have fooled Henry Armstid. But couldn't nobody but Flem Snopes have fooled Ratliff" (420).[7]

The ending has the feel of a certain finality, as if Frenchman's Bend is finished as a factor in Flem's life. Flem moves on to Jefferson, ready to provide new adventures for the next volume of the chronicle. Ratliff is gone, eliminated, not even there to watch the exodus. Flem's antagonists are usually reduced to taking consolation in small gestures, like the wavering look in Flem's eyes that Ratliff saw when he showed him the two notes from Mink: "an instant, a second of a new and completer stillness and immobility" (96); "And then he knew that the jaw had stopped chewing" (97). There is a similar self-revelation even in Flem's moment of triumph. Flem's success is based on his ability to efface himself, to let others make the false moves, to give the impression that he does not even care. There is, then, a comic revelation of his own pleasure in viciousness in the fact that he has to drive "three extra miles" to have a look at Henry Armstid's digging (417). His last gesture—spitting over the wagon wheel—should be seen as a posturing, the awareness of which will not restore anyone his money but might restore equilibrium to the quality of the reader's last laugh. Flem has finished off Frenchman's Bend, but we can perhaps give him a comic unmasking with a provisional finality of its own. We remember that when last seen Ratliff was making a comic wager with Bookwright over the age of his salted coins. Though eliminated as major trader and as restaurant owner, there is a basis for the hindsight with which, in *The Town*, Ratliff will be able to claim he would just as soon have lost as not: "Oh sho, he beat me out of my half of that little cafe me and Grover Winbush owned, but who can say jest who lost then? If he hadn't a got it, Grover might a turned it into a French postcard peepshow too, and then I'd be out there where Grover is now: night watchman at that brick yard" (*T* 296–97). For both Ratliff and Flem, then, there is at the end of *The Hamlet* an ending and a basic continuity.

I have said that the basic form of the trading interchange cannot be called into question in *The Hamlet*. Yet perhaps Ratliff's suggestion that the waste of Eula is "wrong by any economy" does call into question the economy he lives in, does suggest the possibility of what John Matthews has called "various economies of lack and substitution" (163). Many readers have explored the idea that Eula is degraded by being made into a commodity sold in a patriarchal economy, that she is reduced to a (reduced) transaction value.[8] Eula can be described as sold to Flem with the Frenchman's Place as a dowry; by that logic, what Flem gives in trade is presumably a cover story to legitimize Eula's baby. This line of analysis certainly applies to *The Town*, where Flem does trade on Eula's adultery and where Eula is reduced to a "twenty dollar gold piece" (*T* 29). In *The Hamlet* there is perhaps a greater sense of the illogical, the implication that in some inevitable way Eula too has been grazed up as part of Flem's progress. It is the senselessness that most dismays Ratliff. The event is in fact less about Flem than about the failure of any other man to be worthy of Eula or even to put in a claim to have been sexually capable of encountering her. The waste is the fact that Eula's value is squandered, thrown away on a froglike victor whose only sexuality (as mis-imagined in a disturbed fantasy) is with the crudest of field hands. Eula represents "a word, a single will to believe . . . ; the word, the dream and wish of all male under sun capable of harm" (169). But no passion was worthy of that word. What has happened to Eula violates any possible conception of an appropriate "exchange value" under any economy.[9]

In the prophetic vision of Labove, where the schoolteacher foresees in demented fury Eula owned by the "dead power of money," and the husband "without glands or desire" who will own her, Faulkner also allows the postulation of "that quality in her which absolutely abrogated the exchange value of any single life's promise or capacity for devotion, the puny asking-price of any one man's reserve of so-called love" (134). The metaphor of exchange points not only to the possibility of, but also to the inevitable failure of, any economy of emotion—not only because of the limitation of any one man to have adequate reserves of love, but also because of the destructive grandeur in her that prevents Eula from accepting any mere mortal's capacity for devotion. Thus the universal language of interchange is used not simply to point to commoditization but also to assert the tragedy of men and women unable to connect under any economy whatsoever.

In addition to the waste of Eula, many readers have focused on the pervasive and apparently intrinsic presence of waste and loss in Frenchman's Bend—in Mink Snopes, in a nameless tenant farmer, in Henry Armstid and his wife. In place of the timeless sanity of the folk community once extolled by Cleanth Brooks, many readers have tended to postulate something like that presumed community's dark inverse—a patriarchal world characterized by oppression, exploitation, and cruelty.[10] Frequently these readings find that the economic basis of interchange is itself the cause of the damage.[11] Joseph Urgo describes a "homosocial" or "homosensual" world:

> Homosensuality is a cold thing in the marketplace as men buy, sell, and trade without concern for the sensual well-being of one another. If anything, homosensual *cruelty*, not caretaking, typifies the marketplace. (*Faulkner's Apocrypha* 178)

> A human community founded not upon the life and welfare of the human body but upon "the currency of coin" is no human thing at all but some form of perverse incarceration of the flesh. (180)

> Out of the hatred of the community which is produced by the consciousness of dispossession emerge two kinds of people in Faulkner's trilogy: criminals and entrepreneurs. (204)

One major consequence of this reading is the inclination to view Flem Snopes as the victim of and perhaps the rebel against a hypocritical community that demonizes the outsider even though his values are its values. Urgo describes the "Snopeslore" in *The Town* as a sign of "bigotry," of "incipient fascism" (*Faulkner's Apocrypha* 187–88). Richard Moreland associates the response of Frenchman's Bend with fascist anti-Semitism, arguing that the men of the hamlet demonize Flem instead of the oppressive system. Flem thus becomes a "'structural' Jew" (145). Urgo sees Flem's own response as a "revenge" that is "legal and is actually encouraged by the American rags-to-riches mythology": "the only way in which a man can express antagonism or hostility toward the system . . . is by turning the tables and exploiting other men" (*Faulkner's Apocrypha* 180).[12]

These readings, with their frontal assault on the trading system and its economic metaphors, offer subversive motivations both for Flem and for Flem's victims. These motivations would create a countercurrent to the apparently authoritative views of the narrator and Ratliff about "them folks" (31). These explanations, essentially unsubstantiable, can be true enough to coexist with the rhetoric of the narrator, in the way that dissonant interpretations can both be true at the same time. As Donald Kartiganer has written, it is valuable to acknowledge the "text's . . . capacity for unmaking as well as making, its desire to violate its hard-won coherences" ("Faulkner Criticism," 94). Such readings complicate, but need not replace, the dominant notes. They create tension against the novel's form. Certainly they call our attention to the fact that the plot, like the economy itself, is prepared to accept losses. The plot contemplates, tolerates, requires winners and losers, even while the text provides voices to mourn the losses.

In the case of Flem, provocative critical readings that attribute to him a sense of violation highlight the degree to which the text refuses to give us these things directly. The text does not offer trenchant ethical or sociological analysis of Flem or of a phenomenon called Snopesism. What it does in formal terms is create Flem as a differentiated source of energy or force, and for this it does give us a word—power, the dead power of money. The plot defines Flem as an antagonist, explains him situationally in terms of the expression of his antagonism within the trading medium. For that matter, the plot does its own form of Snopes-watching, makes its own implied definition of Snopesism. In formal terms Snopesism is

Flem Snopes. His lesser adjuncts or echoes or uncivic ditches (*T* 257) are part of the phenomenon of Flem. They are part of his tribe; he is the one truly patriarchal structure in *The Hamlet*. As the title of Faulkner's early fragment might suggest to us, Flem (not Ab) is a Father Abraham. Formally, the tribe is part of the force that is expressed by Flem Snopes; individual Snopeses are moves that Flem makes or refuses to make, persons he uses, or, finally, even antagonists he allows to come into existence.

~

The perception of the large form, the narrative architectonics, of *The Hamlet* requires the recognition that *The Hamlet* is still an episodic novel, that the major conflict is not always at center stage. The valid desire to follow causal sequences, to emphasize important events in the novel, encourages us to follow the sometimes-antagonist Ratliff even in periods of dormancy. Perhaps we pay too much attention, in structuring the story, to the intermittent glimpses of him in the long summer of discontent that Faulkner makes him undergo. Hysteria and terror will be seen by some readers as impossible for the "bland, shrewd, intelligent" sewing-machine salesman; some will feel Ratliff could never so lose control as to start a fight with Bookwright over a shovel. But even if these are violations of character they are minor ones that merely accentuate real sequences in the action: first Ratliff's loss of status as antagonist, and then his loss of poise. And, too, the hysteria is easy to overemphasize if seen out of context. For Ratliff is only one of the things in the novel, his story only first among many. His hysteria, whether we believe it or not, need not necessarily alter our sense of the tone of the novel. For a proper sense of plot must take account of non-plot. That the Ratliff-Flem episodes can be told (even in rudimentary fashion) in one short story ("Lizards in Jamshyd's Courtyard") only reminds us once again of the looseness of the anecdotal framework in the novel, and of the transparency of improvisation with which Faulkner has filled in the gaps of the frame.

Among the episodes in which, as James might say, incident is made of mere gesture, there are in *The Hamlet* scenes in which words are made into something like events, scenes existing for the verbal wit within them. The five-page scene (78–82) between Ratliff, Bookwright, and Tull in Ratliff's Jefferson coffee shop seems generated out of verbal wit, one-liners. It enacts, even before Ratliff's visit to Frenchman's Bend, what Ratliff looks forward to in that visit: "the sheer happiness of being out of bed and moving once more at free will . . . in the sun and air which men drank and moved in and talked and dealt with one another" (77).

As always in these scenes, some new information passes hands, some is hinted at, and some old information is "retailed" back and forth. Ratliff misses the reference to the teacher (Labove) and to the fourth Snopes (Ike). He is catching up on the news about I.O., taking a moment to improvise a little on the previous version of the shoeing of Houston's mare: "That other one. I.O. That Jack Houston throwed into the water tub that day in the blacksmith shop" (79). We are being prepared for the future by mention of the goats and the teacher, and particularly by Ratliff's desire that someone "do" something. Faulkner also uses the scene to control our expectations about the long-range possibilities for change in the situation. Ratliff makes predictions that are not wrong, only incomplete, about the major stages of Flem's progress:

> Flem has grazed up the store and he has grazed up the blacksmith shop and now he is starting in on the school. That just leaves Will's house. Of course, after that he will have to fall back on you folks. . . . (79)

> So he's working the top and the bottom both at the same time. At that rate it will be a while yet before he has to fall back on you ordinary white folks in the middle. (80–81)

Clearly also the commentators are looking to the past, using jokes as a means of accommodation to the rise of Flem Snopes. Their verbal gestures make the Snopes phenomenon usable, hence perhaps more tolerable. The scene is thus part of the consequences of past events. It is not isolated from the past or the future. It is, then, marginally functional, and some effort is being made to establish its relevance.

But the real substance of the scene is not the accommodations or resolves it contains, or even the new information it communicates. We are not much concerned with what Ratliff misses (on first reading, we do not ourselves know that the teacher has any significance) or with what he learns (simply that I.O. is going to teach the school). The focus of the scene is the one-liners, some of which, like most good remarks, we will have to hear again.

"What was it that Memphis fellow cut outen you anyway?"

"My pocket book," Ratliff said. "I reckon that's why he put me to sleep first." (78)

"I'll have steak," Tull said.

"I wont," Bookwright said. "I been watching the dripping sterns of steaks for two days now." (78)

"What kind of pie, Mr. Bookwright?" the counterman said.

"Eating pie," Bookwright said. (80)

"This here cup seems to me to have a draft in it," [Ratliff] said to the counterman. "Maybe you better warm it up a little. It might freeze and bust, and I would have to pay for the cup too." (81)

In the first of these remarks the questioner willingly acts as straight man, not really expecting a serious answer. In the others, the joke takes advantage of the opportunity that arises in ordinary conversation. But in none does witticism reflect individual personality. Wit is a communal activity in which each must participate. Even Ratliff's crack at the counterman about the cold coffee is not so much personally directed as it is unavoidable, built into the ground rules of such a conversation. Every opportunity must be taken advantage of.

In this tissue of verbal wit, Snopes stories and comments take a natural part. Part of the act of making up wisecracks is the attribution of characteristic language to absent or imaginary characters. Bookwright tells his anecdote not really to retell an event but for one remark, the speaker's ignorant self-revelation and his simultaneous unveiling of one of Flem's usuries: "'Go to Mr Snopes at the store,' the other nigger says. 'He will lend it to you. He lent me five dollars over two years ago and all I does, every Saturday night I goes to the store and pays him a dime. He aint even mentioned that five dollars'" (80). Ratliff's attempt to get serious—"Aint none of you folks out there done nothing about it?"—is parried back into the joke medium: "Yes. . . . And wind up with one of them bow ties in place of your buckboard and team. You'd have room to wear it" (81). (Bookwright here caps his own joke by suggesting that Ratliff would lose not only his buckboard and team but his clothes to boot.) The scene appropriately comes to a climax on the best of the Snopes jokes, one which we cannot but suspect has been the genesis of the entire scene: "If I was you I would go out there nekkid in the first place. Then you wont notice the cold coming back" (82). Faulkner thus establishes the pleasure of talking, not even of telling stories but merely of making jokes about the general situation. In its marginal relevance and its reliance on verbal wit, the coffee-shop scene functions as a sort of Puddnhead Wilson's calendar of Snopeslore, interpolated into the actual sequence of events.

Verbal glossing of events provides intermittently in *The Hamlet* the afterthought that typically caps the anecdotal short story. The glossing is invariably a gathering of facts from separate sources, a summation of what "the countryside knew" (166). After the departure of Eula and Flem, for example, the postmortem (166–67) involves discussions of the size of Varner's check, the mass exit to Texas, and the wedding license. Even this scene of less than a page is constructed by the participants as a continually growing joke, with each remark topped by a better one, and the final straw kept for the last.

> Tull said [Varner's check] was for three hundred dollars. Book-wright said that meant a hundred and fifty then, since Varner would discount even his own paper to himself fifty percent.
>
> "The bride and groom left for Texas right after the ceremony," [Tull] said.
> "That makes five," a man named Armstid said. "But they say Texas is a big place."
> "It's beginning to need to be," Bookwright said. "You mean six."
> Tull coughed. He was still blinking rapidly. "Mr Varner paid for it too," he said.
> "Paid for what too?" Armstid said.
> "The wedding license," Tull said.

Another pair of scenes synthesized for the retailing of information takes place with the coming of spring in the restaurant (301–2) and in French-man's Bend (303–5). These scenes collect new incidents and keep us up to date on old characters whose episodes are essentially complete. We are told quickly of Eula's return and of her girl baby; of I.O.'s second wife; of the name of Wallstreet Snopes; of Mink's continuing wait for Flem; and of Ike Snopes's toy cow. The scene is a summation of old business, preparatory to the coming climaxes. Such scenes suggest that in *The Hamlet* events do not exist without postmortems, that actions must be processed through wit. And each wisecrack must itself sooner or later be "amended" (68).

Events exist in their own right, but also to be extravagantly improvised upon. It has perhaps not been adequately noticed how often in the minds of Faulkner's characters meditation or anticipation or speculation turns into fantasy. Fantasy is in a sense the expanded form of the verbal commentary improvised in the coffee-shop scene. In *Intruder in the Dust*, Faulkner shows Chick Mallison's fatigue becoming something very like hallucination, in Chick's fantasies of "How Miss Habersham got home," of "How the Gowries would pass judgment on their traitor," and of "How you could have crossed the square by riding Highboy across the backs of the cars" (*Intruder* 186–89, 219–20, 238). In *The Hamlet*, Ratliff and Labove are particularly prone to these "bizarre phantasmagoriae" (*Intruder* 197). We have noted how Labove is given the gift of prophecy to see Flem as Vulcan to Eula's Venus, thus usefully swinging the entire episode into line with the major narrative sequence. Labove's other fantasy, though explained and rendered simply as memory, acts almost as a parable to explain his own present situation. Labove remembers the shooting of a black man, the man's peaceful resignation to death, and the comic undercutting of his willingness to die when the bullet rolls out of his many layers of underclothing (142–43). Labove thinks the lesson is to not wear an overcoat when he goes to be killed by Jody. Instead, the parable is a prophecy of the way his anguish, too, will be undercut, will fail to get its expected catastrophe. More generally, the story is a parable of the way the terrible turns out, after all, to be only another failure, only sad—or comic, depending on your point of view.

With the inscrutable Flem, particularly, it is inevitable that most of our thinking should be speculation. Ratliff's fantasies begin as conjecture about Flem: "But I reckon I can guess the rest of it, he told himself. . . . He could almost see it . . . " (76). But they are never merely conjecture. They attribute to characters words the characters undoubtedly think but could not possibly say—"How many more is there? How much longer is this going on? Just what is it going to cost me to protect one goddamn barn full of hay?" (76)—or they go even further and revel in the horrific and grotesque—". . . laying there and looking up at them every time his head would get out of the way long enough, and says, 'Mr Snopes, whut you ax fer dem sardines?'" (188). The fantasies' common feature is their insularity and their quality of the improvised (by character and by author), even when couched as memory or as a sudden, privileged look at the future, such as Ratliff's future sightings of the transmogrifying buggy of one of Eula's suitors.

Unquestionably the virtuoso fantasy is Ratliff's version of Flem in Hell (171–75). It is a comic, hyperbolic extrapolation of a real series of events, Flem's actual conquest of Frenchman's Bend. The initial trade, the Faustian bargain, has long since taken place; the scene in hell is the legal controversy growing out of that bargain. It is also in a sense a renovation of the original bargain, the parties attempting to strengthen their bargaining positions with legal abstractions and a verbal parrying like that of Dostoyevsky's episode of the Grand Inquisitor. The presupposition of the scene is its first and best joke, that Flem's soul has shriveled up and therefore the devil cannot redeem Flem and soul into hell, and cannot himself in abstract terms Fulfill The Bargain. Flem, then, is not only off the hook; the devil is now on. Faulkner pauses to allow some pleasant and yet fairly obvious peripheral improvisations, such as that there are plenty of superfluous souls "*raising all kinds of hell to get in here, even bringing letters from Congressmen, that we never even heard of*" (172), and the possible claim that Flem's soul might have been lost when "*we had a flood, even a freeze*" (172). But the central question is whether the Prince, the ultimate legalist, can find a flaw in Flem's legal position. Instead of attacking the question directly, the Prince offers to absolve Flem, and then assumes that any second-rate legalist with a "*mouth full of law*" will naturally accept a bribe. But Flem is the man without fleshly desires: "*He says that for a man that only chews, any spittoon will do*" (173). Flem's stolidity achieves immediately its usual results. He has his adversaries quarreling among themselves, comparing each other as tempters to the Prince's father, and therefore comparing Flem, albeit not favorably, to the "*greater man*" who successfully resisted the temptations of that great sophist.

The Prince does return at last to the legal question, and the hairsplitting gets very complicated. Flem, the Prince is told, does not want Paradise: "*He wants hell*" (174). Does this mean that his goals are limited, or that he knows not to ask more than the Prince has to offer? It would seem that Flem's part of the legal bargain has been the formal avowal of the Prince as master, including an acceptance of the Prince as his creator and the real owner of Paradise. It might be an inconsistency on Flem's part not to ask for everything, but the Prince does not take it up. Instead he seems to try to catch Flem in the same inconsistency. But as it turns out, it is the Prince himself who next forgets he is supposed to be Flem's maker.

> He turned his head and spit, the spit frying off the floor quick in a little blue ball of smoke. 'I come about that soul,' he says.
> 'So they tell me,' the Prince says. 'But you have no soul.'
> 'Is that my fault?' he says.
> 'Is it mine?' the Prince says. 'Do you think I created you?'
> 'Then who did?' he says. And he had the Prince there and the Prince knowed it. (174)

But when Flem answers the next display of "*the temptations, the gratifications, the satieties*" only by spitting "*another scorch of tobacco onto the floor,*" the Prince thinks to lull him into the same mistake by a hyperbolic "offer."

> 'Then what do you want?' the Prince says. 'What do you want? Paradise?'
> 'I hadn't figured on it,' he says. 'Is it yours to offer?'
> 'Then whose is it?' the Prince says. And the Prince knowed he had him there. In fact, the Prince knowed he had him all the time, ever since they had told him how he had walked in the door with his mouth already full of law.... 'You have admitted and even argued that I created you. Therefore your soul was mine all the time. And therefore when you offered it as security for this note, you offered that which you did not possess and so laid yourself liable to—'
> 'I have never disputed that,' he says.
> '—criminal action. So take your bag and—' the Prince says. 'Eh?' the Prince says. 'What did you say?'
> 'I have never disputed that,' he says. (175)

The confidence of the Prince "all the time" betrays his lack of general confidence in legalism; but he immediately falls back on some circular legal reasoning of his own, intended to undermine Flem's legal position. By selling his soul to the devil Flem has agreed to say that the devil is the creator; but when he says that, according to the Prince, he is invalidating the very basis of the sale. Flem's rebuttal, made without recanting his promised allegiance, implies that the devil was under no obligation to buy what was already his own, and that "criminal action" is precisely what he has been offering to undergo. He himself has never made any pretense that the soul was his own, or guaranteed that it would last. Bested on every count, the Prince is allowed to make the comically hyperbolic response more appropriate to grotesque farce than to the preceding sophistries, "*choking and gasping and his eyes a-popping up at him setting there with that straw suitcase on the Throne among the bright, crown-shaped flames. 'Take Paradise!' the Prince screams. 'Take it! Take it!'*" (175). If seen as a comic cataclysm meaning "Take Everything," the Prince's words are simple enough. In the context of legalist debate they are more ambiguous, and the reader may be uncertain how to respond. Is this a last desperate, unavailing, repetitious offer of something the Prince does not in fact have to offer? Or is the Prince the real owner of Paradise (in Ratliff's view) after all? If so, is he offering Paradise as a means of keeping hell to himself? Or is he giving up everything not only rhetorically but literally, conceding as inevitably lost both hell and Paradise to this appalling casuist who has seen through the very premise of the age-old Faustian bargain? The reader must give up certainty about the specific state of negotiations at this point, which seems unfair, having come so far. Nonetheless, there is no questioning the thoroughness with which Flem has put us through our paces, or the appropriateness of the Prince's incredulous cry, "*Who are you?*" (175). The density of this four-page scene illustrates Faulkner's enthusiasm for even his smallest episodes and shows his unmatched ability to make a virtue of the episodic.[13]

We have been willing to see *The Hamlet* as a narrative multiverse that includes episodes and even paragraphs largely independent of the central narrative line.[14] Yet the unqualified praise of irrelevance would disarm the judgment necessary not only to the reader but, more importantly, to the writer himself, who must ultimately decide what goes in and what goes out. If we are to accommodate the plot to all the other details of the novel, however, we ought to be certain why we value some extraneous material and not all.

The Russian Formalist Victor Shklovsky, emphasizing as he does the tactics and deceptions of the storyteller, points out that irrelevance and loose ends are one of the storyteller's best methods of withholding the relevant, making the relevant seem important. Central occurrences too easily won are affectively unsatisfying, and so the writer makes use of some of the available material, notably anecdotes, simply as "delaying action" (49). Seen in these terms, all of book 3 of *The Hamlet* acts as delaying action for the promised rematch between Ratliff and Flem. But from the point of view of discrimination, for this function any padding will do. A similar problem arises with Martin Price's questioning of the very possibility of an irrelevant detail. Price has argued for the relevance of "implication" of Emma Bovary's blue merino dress, a relevance "only retrospectively clear." As Price sees it, the detail may shift from figure to ground and back without warning, and its multiple function is never easy to follow. The irrelevant detail "is not, of course, irrelevant, but it has so attenuated and complex a relevance as to confirm rather than directly to assert a meaning. Its meaningfulness, in fact, may become fully apparent only as the total structure emerges. It serves meanwhile a sufficient function in sustaining the virtual world in which the structure is embodied" (87). While sympathetic to Roland Barthes's attempt to see realist writers showing their mimetic intentions through the use of patently irrelevant details, Price is forced to conclude that all of those details do in fact have functional importance. But Price, like Shklovsky, leaves no grounds on which the writer may judge how best to confront alternatives of inclusion and exclusion. There must surely be degrees of functionality, just as some delaying actions are more appropriate than others. Liberality may undermine judgment, and the writer must know that without judgment the work will never be shaped.

Other critics who have dealt with the irrelevant detail or anecdote have been more willing to suggest grounds of discrimination between cases. John Bayley works on the supposition that the act of creation must be at least partially involuntary and instinctive:

> As creator he has brought into being something which he did not and could not have expected. It is real because it is of a different order of being from the blueprint, the necessary artifice of projection. . . . The potentially great modern writer probably has lost all instinctive and unselfconscious confidence in his power to create, and to convince an audience of the truth of his creation. . . . It may be that our last hope lies in inadvertency. . . . An author may stumble upon a world while in the process of decreating a fiction. ("Flexner Sonata" 216–17)

Even having subjected the inadvertent discovery to the disciplines of craft, the writer must preserve the *appearance* of the spontaneous: "All right; the figure of the Leechgatherer *was* pondered, altered, and so was the poem, but its appearance, its dramatic inadvertency, its air of creation ambushed and surprised, is surely as I have described?" ("Flexner Sonata" 216). Eudora Welty, writing of *Intruder in the Dust,* similarly praises this quality: "It could be that to seem impromptu is an illusion great art can always give as long as profundities of theme, organization and passionate content can come at a calling, but the art of what other has these cadenzas? Even the witty turns and the perfect neatness of plot look like the marks of a flash inspiration" ("In Yoknapatawpha" 597). Her observation as it applies to the plot may seem undercut by Cleanth Brooks's very critical analysis of the plot of *Intruder in the Dust.* As Brooks sees it, the mystery plot is so laxly conceived that its intricacies are perhaps literally impromptu, and not felicitously so (*Yoknapatawpha Country* 103–4).[15] But though Welty specifically mentions the involuntary quality of "even" the central plot, by implication she is praising that quality in all parts of the work of art. John Bayley's observations, too, apply to the peripheries. Even the Leechgatherer, Bayley implies, manifestly takes his place at the center of Wordsworth's poem in spite of his inappropriateness to the poet's own original central solipsism, so "finely fondled and meticulously explored"; and even the didactic conclusion, which might have been the means of glibly processing and co-opting the intrusion, is only an "imperfect and intense reaction to an equally intense, incomplete, and disturbing encounter" ("Flexner Sonata" 216). This notion of the appearance of inadvertency, then, offers one ground, however subjective, for discrimination among those peripheral episodes, some of which we would like to praise for their freedom, their contribution to the plenitude of great novels.

Without going so far as to attempt to compare the spontaneity of different episodes, it is still possible to find grounds to make some discrimination among episodes. Surely what we have been valuing in the episodes of *The Hamlet* is simply the ability to *exploit* the immediate situation. Faulkner exploits his episodes by developing them and by limiting his demands of relevance. He lingers over his episodes; he *intends* his irrelevance. The extraneous episodes that fail to convince are those which are excessively cautious, or merely derivative, or which self-consciously attempt to justify themselves as actually of central importance to the plot or to an abstract "theme."

Faulkner's career is not without such failures. His third novel, *Sartoris* (1929), is conspicuously a work continually laboring against waste, continually beset with unexploited plenitude. Undoubtedly the difficulty is related to the extreme conventionality of the central character, Bayard Sartoris. Bayard embodies the wasteland sensibility expressed also by the subadar of "Ad Astra," who asks, "What will any of us do? All this generation which fought in the war are dead tonight. But we do not yet know it" (*CS* 421). Usually the wasteland hero was possessed of the extreme sensitivity of the romantic artist, his powers of expression smothered by his inward awareness. Faulkner may be seen attempting to vary this convention, making Bayard's dead brother the artist manqué: "Were they poets? . . . I know the other one, the dead one, was" (*S* 186). Faulkner also attempts to connect Bayard's World War I deracination with the death wish, seen in periodic catastrophes, of a "funny family" that is "always going to wars, and always getting killed" (*S* 167). But Bayard is nonetheless defined by "the lonely heights of his despair" (*S* 288); he is "dying from the inside out" (*S* 354). He enters, strikes a pose, and eventually does die. It is a brilliant act of planning to have Bayard's desire for death impinge on his grandfather's life and become responsible for his death; it is no less brilliant for that death to unmask the essential cowardice behind Bayard's posture. So rigidly confined by his conventionality, however, Bayard is for long periods fictionally inert.

Given so difficult and inert a central figure, Faulkner frantically used up all of his anecdotal material simply to provide the solidity of a background. In his inference of a folk community, Brooks says, "The folk society that lies around [the characters] goes on in its immemorial ways. It is neither sick nor tired. It has all the vitality of an old and very tough tree" (*Yoknapatawpha Country* 115). Yet much of this folk material is simply wasted, for instance the two pages of rudimentary Snopeslore (*S* 172–73). Nothing is fully developed in the material. *Sartoris* may be a "source-book" (Millgate, *Achievement* 85), but it is still only a sketchbook.

But more importantly, the inertness of Bayard causes Faulkner to attempt to use his background material as the actual forward motion of the novel. In many ways the background becomes the foreground; and many of the episodes are attenuated in the telling, calling attention to their shallowness. The novel is, more than any other, a pastiche of episodes, none of which have any real narrative complexity: the exploits of Colonel

John Sartoris, the passions and financial difficulties of Simon Strother, the rebellion of Caspey, and the letters of Byron Snopes, to name only a few. These episodes are not more developed than the cryptic Snopeslore, only more insistent. The episodes involving Old Bayard's facial blemish, in particular, seem embarrassingly strained. The irrelevance has been asked to provide the form itself. Consequently, the incident is spread over no less than 160 pages (*S* 81–241), appearing in no less than seven scenes (*S* 81, 83, 88, 89, 93–105, 220–228, 229, 234, and 238–41).[16] Long before the visit to the Memphis doctor we can see the obvious punch line to this one feeble joke: the wen will come off just as predicted by the folk doctor, Old Man Falls. We must be embarrassed that so little has been prolonged for so long.

In *The Hamlet,* as in *Sartoris,* there are episodes that do not adequately exploit their status as improvisations within the formal structure. Faulkner is never guilty in *The Hamlet* of underdevelopment: the very size of some of the episodes makes them formidable. Yet somewhere in book 3 his inclusiveness has gone awry; we must say that he is not easy about his episodes of love. He seems to wish to justify irrelevance by repetition, to claim relevance to theme by exhaustive thoroughness in depicting the varieties of love. The loves of Ike, Houston, and Mink are accumulated with encyclopedic regularity, as if in alphabetic sequence: Love (Idiot Style); Love (Passive Magnetism); Love (Sexual Voracity). It is clearly right to say that these episodes justify each other as relevant to the "theme" of love. The question is whether such a systematic justification does not undercut the incidents' functions as independent demonstrations of plenitude. Juxtaposition and theme are so blatant that the incidents cease to be free events. No amount of variation-in-repetition is likely to conceal their organizing principle. This is formalism at its most constricting.

Insofar as any of these episodes achieves something, it does so not by its contribution to overall structure but by its appropriateness to the situation at hand. For instance, the struggles of Houston against his love, and then the torment, rigidity, and despair caused by his wife's death, act as a prelude to demonstrate in Houston the effect of the complete cataclysm, his own death. The "rigid, indomitable," Houston (248), who screams at his murderer with his last breath, is suddenly seen to undergo the ultimate relaxation, bringing an involuntary physical reaction that is almost like the human sorrow he has fought for so long: "'God damn it, couldn't you even borrow two shells, you fumbling ragged—' and put the world away. His eyes, still open to the lost sun, glazed over with a sudden well and run of moisture which flowed down the alien and unremembering cheeks too, already drying, with a newness as of actual tears" (249–50). The humanity of this, its total absorption in itself, is worth more than all the contrived linkages to other episodes. And the immediate transition to Mink is even more compelling in its continuity. Mink in fact becomes a part of Houston, "wedded and twinned forever now by the explosion of that ten-gauge shell—the dead who would carry the living into the ground with him; the living who must bear about the repudiating earth with him forever, the deathless slain" (249). The two are one, the continuity and identity are real. Yet as we move in easy transition from Houston to Mink, Faulkner also exploits the wrench from death back into life, from rest into furious motion, from silence into ceaseless sound: "That shot was too loud. It was not only too loud for any shot, it was too loud for any sound" (250). These immediate linkages are free of Faulkner's textbook demonstration of the varieties of love. It is possible, then, to value episodes in *The Hamlet* for their self-coherence, their intrinsic value, and their exploitation of their own resources, instead of for some contrived relevance to theme. In a narrative multiverse, we need not be without discrimination.

Yet it would be wrong to say that these episodes do not contribute to overall plot structure in the end, whether as consequence, as antecedent, or simply as pacing. "The irrelevant detail is not, of course, irrelevant." We are really speaking only of degrees of relevance. Faulkner carefully forms the coexistence of plot and non-plot. If the contrived relevance to theme is obvious and embarrassing, the indirect relevance to event ultimately suggests a complete world where events have multiple ramifications and are connected to seemingly independent antecedents.

We have noted already the marginal relevance of the coffee-shop scene. There, Ratliff acts as the balance, the point of coexistence between the plot and the non-plot. The other characters are in some sense adjusting to past events by making jokes; but as a response to rather than a simple confirmation of this new situation, the verbal wit is a tentative gesture at best. Ratliff in effect reminds his fellow talkers that telling stories as a means of coping with the situation does not mean changing the situation:

"Aint none of you folks out there done nothing about it?"
he said.

"What could we do?" Tull said. "It aint right. But it aint none
of our business."

"I believe I would think of something if I lived there," Ratliff
said. (81)

Ratliff does not place too much utilitarian importance on his jokes. He is
able to exploit the moment for its own sake while at the same time preparing for immediate action. His contemplation of the situation is not
offered as event in itself, or even as adjustment of someone else's change
of circumstances, but as the pause that follows one event and precedes
another. The scene is thus momentarily poised between the public assertions that change relations through circumstances.

The fantasy of Flem in Hell also represents part of the reverberations
of event, a not wholly successful attempt by Ratliff to make manageable
a change of circumstances in which he has not been able to take any part.
He is trying to convince himself that the loss of Eula to Flem is not
serious, not really waste: "Of course there was the waste, not wasted on
Snopes but on all of them, himself included—Except was it waste? he
thought suddenly. . . . He looked at the face again. It had not been tragic,
and now it was not even damned, since from behind it there looked out
only another mortal natural enemy of the masculine race" (171). But when
we see Ratliff again at the beginning of book 3, we see that he has not
convinced himself. He is still feeling "outrage at the waste, the useless
squandering; at a situation intrinsically and inherently wrong by any
economy" (182). The fantasy is the momentary stay of this confusion and
is thus always implicitly concerned with the changes that have provoked
it. It is even an inward intensification of Ratliff's preexisting antagonism
to Flem, the antagonism that has been overt before and will be overt
again. With his storytelling, Ratliff implies for the moment a confidence
that reaches beyond confusion forward and backward to those confident
attacks. Thus this episode too is marginally relevant to more lasting
changes, even though it is made memorable by Faulkner's willingness to
develop an inner coherence to the episode itself, to make the fantasy a
followable and challenging intricacy in its own right.

The episodes of Ike Snopes and the cow are part of the antecedents of
event, the beginning of the chain of cause and effect that culminates in

Ratliff's challenge of Flem's echoes. When the story is being told it is presented as a lyric celebration with its own inner coherence. It is only by following the action that we discover that this phenomenon, seemingly so unrelated to anything but itself, also is absorbed by the main thrust of the plot. Ike and the cow become eventually another opportunity for exploitation—or for chivalry. The independent event originates its own series of events, which inevitably feeds into the progress of Snopesism. We are made to feel, of course, that "all things" must be exploited and abused by Flem's inevitable drive, yet we do not specifically apply the abstract certainty to this specific case until in fact Ike too is "grazed up." Even though the episode is preceded by Lump's announcement that "He's started" (186), there is a chapter division, and we are not guided to make the connection, to see the Ike episode as a flashback and as an explanation of Lump's announcement. In the interim, we experience the lyric encounter almost without expectations. It seems an interlude—a lull and an excursion. Only later do we learn that this created world is not so fragmented as Faulkner's exploitation of instantaneous experiences has led us to believe.

The Houston story, too, is the antecedent of an important conflict, the near-challenge of Flem by Mink, a conflict that is finessed in *The Hamlet* and saved for *The Mansion*. We follow sequentially Houston's courtship, his marriage, his wife's death, his grief, his arrogance, his murder, Mink's travails, Mink's capture, Mink's expectations of Flem, the coming to fruition of Mink's antagonism, and finally the seeming dead end by which Mink's challenge is avoided. But the ultimate reference to Flem is by no means emphasized when we are watching Houston. Though Faulkner has documented the tension between Mink and Houston, while we are following the Houston story nothing could be further from our minds than Mink. That is why Faulkner can so thoroughly shock us with the sudden line, "He was still alive when he left the saddle" (249). Like the other episodes, the Houston story seems at first a pause from Snopesism, specifically from the confrontation between Ratliff, I.O., and Eck. The non-plot provides the pacing of the plot; the abrupt change of pace encourages us to see the episode as not one of the central events. Relevance to plot is not contrived and emphasized even as much as in the coffee-shop scene; it is allowed to become apparent in its own time. The plot and the non-plot of *The Hamlet* thus form a coexistence in which the ultimate authority and omnivorousness of the one does not inhibit the instantaneous independence of the other, and in which the constant interplay of the two makes for moments of contemplation in the middle of the chain of reactions.

The non-plot of *The Hamlet,* then, marks time with contemplation, incidents, and an array of performances, while the simple plot provides a sequence of major conflicts in the trading medium. For *The Town,* Faulkner moves to a greater population of conflicting wills, but he never dispenses with the fabric of wit, anecdote, reverie, and observation.

4

The Town

Dialogue and Complex Action

Plots depend on characters at odds, and in *The Town* Faulkner greatly complicates his conflicts by increasing the number of independent actors. He is clearly attempting a much more complex convergence of his narrative lines toward a narrative climax. The narrative foregrounds varieties of action and inaction, forms of encounter both intended and inadvertent, and new forms of failure. The intermittence of direct challenge in *The Hamlet* is replaced with continuous and simultaneous moves, and there are more people capable of making material moves than in *The Hamlet*. Interestingly, some notable readers have suggested that *The Town* has very little plot. Joseph Urgo says that "nothing seems to happen in the novel" (*Faulkner's Apocrypha* 185). Perhaps this is because the non-plot is dominated by the drama of storytelling. Urgo's view is that the novel is a "meditation" with an "epistemological thrust," an examination of "community knowledge" and its role as an expression of "political" activity (184, 186). It is true that although there is a dramatic expansion of actors, there is at the same time a foregrounding of an alternative to action, in the dialogue of storytellers and watchers. This environment of conversation through complex stories requires the active engagement of the reader. It also implies a Faulkner who continually complicates his own stories through "improvement" over many retellings. But *The Town* demonstrates that there is a place in Faulkner's narrative universe for both fabulation and event.

Even the medium of encounter has changed from *The Hamlet*. Though the rise of Flem Snopes continues, marked most notably by his elevation to vice-president of the bank in chapter 7, Flem is shown winning not a single financial contest. Only the revelation of his private interest in Miz Hait's insurance money (chapter 16) shows the continuity of his victorious methods of financial dealing. His only detailed contest (chapter 1) is a defeat. We do see him indirectly in his attempt to take over Wall Snopes's grocery business (146–49),[1] but even that adroit use of financial power is foiled, however narrowly, by Ratliff. Of the two encounters in which he is motivated by his new concept of civic virtue or respectability, one involves his use of out-and-out skullduggery to frame Montgomery Ward Snopes, the other results in his taking of a large financial loss to expel I.O. Snopes from Jefferson. The new form of conflict even radically changes the demeanor of the Flem whose trading pattern has hitherto been so uniform. For a Flem paying *out* money, taking overt steps to earn respectability, is a greatly more active and more *vocal* Flem than the self-effacing trader of *The Hamlet*. And yet, though neither of these encounters is a financial trade in the classic sense, both derive from such trades. Flem's manipulation of Montgomery Ward entails argument and strategic action against the legal authorities, specifically Gavin Stevens, who want to send Montgomery Ward to prison for the "wrong" offense. The planting of illegal whiskey is thus, like horse trading, a strategy in a contest of wits and wills, even though the end result is not financial gain.

Charles Mallison suggests that the "work" of curiosity is also rewarded with "profit": "Another Snopes industry wouldn't be the right word for this one, because there wasn't any profit in it. No, that's wrong; we worked at it too hard and Uncle Gavin says that anything people work at as hard as all of us did at this has a profit, is for profit whether you can convert that profit into dollars and cents or not or even want to" (129). This implies also that any strategic work toward a definite goal is analogous to or formed by the financial medium, whether the work is in words and the end in property (as in the Flem in Hell fantasy of *The Hamlet*) or whether the work is in criminal action and the end in (presumably) non-negotiable respectability.

In the end Faulkner manages to convert non-financial contests to financial consequences. As readers we may be dulled into non-material language by the controversy between Gavin and Ratliff over whether Flem wants revenge or respectability. We should not forget that the ultimate respectability, the presidency of the bank, is inseparable from the greater financial stature which that office also carries. In using the moral indignation of Will Varner (and the town) against Eula and De Spain, Flem has made morality pay, and has in fact made economics the measure of morality. Flem arouses the town against De Spain for having so long made economics excuse and even necessitate continuing adultery:

" . . . outraging morality itself by allying economics on their side since the very rectitude and solvency of a bank would be involved in their exposure" (307). But as Charles puts it here, Flem fits right in with a town that sees an outrage to "morality itself" only when money is at stake; economics thus stands behind and encompasses the mundane rights and wrongs of "morality."

But if Flem's goals are ultimately financial, his opponents' are not. De Spain does use bribery to solidify his relation with Flem; but Gavin needs a different medium. Gavin tries to connect De Spain to financial mismanagement and only evades his own problem. Gavin's contests are sexual or paternal, his goals as unfinancial as sending a schoolgirl off to Radcliffe. His medium for action varies from poetry and argument to the elaborately sophomoric one-upmanship of suitors' rivalries. The fact that Eula, De Spain, and Gavin are almost completely outside the money medium (even though they do seek "profits" in Faulkner's metaphorical definition) means that the conflicts of *The Town* must be more complicated than those of *The Hamlet*. Furthermore, the greater number of antagonists working at these diverse means necessitates a multiplication of cross-purposes that goes far beyond the simple collision-and-recoil plot between Flem and Ratliff.

Initially, however, there are no antagonists, only "curiosity" (4). The characters of *The Town* establish the field, or the limits, within which they are prepared to operate. Harker in the Centaur in Brass episode is typical. He does not complain to the marshal that Flem is stealing from the power plant; he prefers to watch and tell about it, "talking about him with the kind of amoral amazement with which you would recount having witnessed the collision of a planet" (17). Even when he does get involved in the confederation of Tom Tom and Turl, he denies it:

> "He holp us," Turl said.
> "Be durn if that's so," Mr. Harker said. "Have you and Tom Tom both already forgot what I told you right there in that ditch last night? I never knowed nothing and I dont aim to know nothing, I dont give a durn how hard either one of you try to make me." (28)

Gavin later questions Harker's "pretence of simple spectator enjoyment" (30). But if Gavin is offering any different response it is only the idea of wit as a weapon, clever words as a defense: "But the horse which at last came home to roost sounded better. Not witty, but rather an immediate unified irrevocably scornful front to what the word Snopes was to mean to us" (43). Laughter is the first response of both Gavin and Ratliff, until the day Ratliff sees something else in Gavin's face: "'At first you laughed at them too,' he said. 'Or maybe I'm wrong, and this here is still laughing?'—looking at me, watching me, too damned shrewd, too damned intelligent" (44). A whole community is initially defined by the desire of Harker and Gavin and Ratliff to watch and even to laugh.

Superficially, there is a simplicity about Gavin's moves. The three interviews between Eula and Gavin seem to create three equal stages, particularly since Gavin summarizes them at the third interview: "'Marry her, Gavin,'" she said. I had known her by sight for eighteen years, with time out of course for the war; I had dreamed about her at night for eighteen years including the war. We had talked to one another twice: here in the office one night fourteen years ago, and in her living room one morning two years back. But not once had she ever called me even Mister Stevens. Now she said Gavin. 'Marry her, Gavin'" (332). The Matt Levitt episode, particularly, is emphasized as a comic repetition of Gavin's rivalry with De Spain. Gavin's attempt to form Linda's mind is connected with his earlier poetic association with Melisandre: "It's the same thing again: dont you remember?" (179). But his attempt to "save" Linda is a repetition of his earlier desire to "save" Eula (49): "To save a Snopes from Snopeses is a privilege, an honor, a pride." (182). Matt's racer with the two-toned horn reminds all the characters of "the other one when it was Mr de Spain's cut-out" (186). Charles's father is particularly hard on Gavin, claiming to notice "something we haven't smelled around here in . . . how long was it, Gavin?" (186, Faulkner's ellipsis) and emphasizing the comic differences between the two incidents at Gavin's expense: "'By Cicero, Gavin,' Father said. 'You're losing ground. Last time you at least picked out a Spanish-American War hero with an E. M. F. sportster. Now the best you can do is a Golden Gloves amateur with a homemade racer. Watch yourself, bud, or next time you'll have a boy scout defying you to mortal combat with a bicycle'" (187). Even Matt uses the earlier episode to add insult to injury: "You aint much of a fighter, are you? But that's O.K.; I aint going to hurt you much anyway: just mark you up a little to freshen up your memory" (190). Charles meditates on this lack of originality in events: " . . . as if the sole single symbol of frustrated love or anyway desire or maybe just frustration possible in Jefferson was an auto-mobile cut-out" (195–96). Faulkner thus uses repetition as a source of whimsy and wit; narrative structure is a matter for comic exploitation rather than a puzzle left to be divined by the detective reader.

Yet such obvious correlations do not, after all, constitute a structure made of a series of simple challenges. For Gavin Stevens's contest against "Snopeses" is more theoretical than actual, and he is never a direct an-tagonist of Flem. In the two skirmishes of his first contest (chapters 3–6) he cares nothing at all about Flem. Ratliff says, "I dont even think he especially hunted around for something. I think he just reached his hand and snatched something, the first nearest thing, and it just hap-pened to be that old quick-vanishing power-plant brass" (82). He is com-batting De Spain for the love of Eula. He is also "saving" Eula from what he claims are lies and gossip, saving her from not just De Spain but "You too. . . . You and your husband too. The best people, the pure, the unimpugnable" (49). With her usual percipience, Maggie reveals his mixed motivation: "Just what is it about this that you cant stand? That Mrs Snopes may not be chaste, or that it looks like she picked Manfred de Spain out to be unchaste with?" (49). We know that Flem is using Eula's adultery to move up in the world and that De Spain's role would be impossible without Flem's connivance. Any consequences of the adul-tery may ultimately be traced to Flem, may be called "footprints" that "Mr Snopes left" (77). But it must be remembered that in tackling De Spain, Gavin is not thinking about Flem.

In his second conflict (chapters 12–15), Gavin does come closer to conflict with Flem, but only indirectly. In fact, the implication is that for Gavin it is interpretation, not action, that is most important. We see Gavin agonizing not between two courses of action but between two in-terpretations, two "premises":

> Back there in that time of my own clowning belated adolescence . . .
> I remember how I could never decide which of the two unbear-ables was the least unbearable; which (as the poet has it) of the two chewed bitter thumbs was the least bitter for chewing. That is, whether Manfred de Spain had seduced a chaste wife, or had simply been caught up in passing by a rotating nympholept. This was my anguish. (133)

Because the second premise was much better. If I was not to have
her, then Flem Snopes shall never have. . . . So that girl-child was
not Flem Snopes's at all, but mine; . . . since the McCarron boy
who begot her (oh yes, I can even believe Ratliff when it suits
me) in that lost time, was Gavin Stevens in that lost time. . . . (135)

The decision to support the second premise does not lead to a resolution
for action—"Flem shall never have her"—but an interpretation of the
past: "Flem must never have possessed her sexually." This decision, which
allows Gavin to pretend "it might have been me" or at least to identify
himself with McCarron, also leads him to think of himself as the father-
grandfather of Linda. But this reasoning is only talk, looking "back there
in that time." It confers no program of action. Gavin sees Linda, about
fourteen, walking "like a pointer" (131) when he returns to Jefferson in
chapters 7 and 8. But any action to assume a paternal role toward Linda
is attenuated and gradual to say the least. "Forming her mind" (179) does
not begin until chapter 12. Gavin's second conflict thus is not originally a
deliberate challenge.

Yet Gavin soon does attempt to explain the second conflict as an attempt "to save a Snopes from Snopeses" (182). The problem with that
theory is that the immediate antagonist is Matt Levitt, who misunderstands Gavin's new form of idealism and makes the whole affair a knock-
about rehash of that earlier "clowning belated adolescence." With a real,
separate will of his own, Matt insists on being the antagonist, however
temporarily. After that, Gavin thinks he must treat Linda as an adversary
for her good name's sake. He spends his strategic energies dodging Linda,
in a Prufrockian "thousand indecisions which each fierce succeeding harassment would revise" (206), a ludicrous "adolescence in reverse, turned
upside down" (208). When Gavin proposes an actual scheme, to send
Linda away to school, a more complicated resistance arises. Gavin looks
beyond Linda to combat the source of the resistance, but he thinks the
source is Eula: "the mother who said *Certainly, meet him by all means. Tell
him I am quite competent to plan my daughter's education, and we'll both thank
him to keep his nose out of it*" (218). Ratliff warns him he is wrong, but Gavin
is a little too eager to indulge his bitterness against Eula and will not
listen to Ratliff. Ratliff would have told him that the real antagonist is
Flem Snopes, but Gavin once again is not even thinking of Flem Snopes.

"What?" he said. "You're going to see Eula because Eula wont let her leave Jefferson to go to school? You're wrong." . . .

"But wait, I tell you! Wait!" he said. "Because you're wrong—" But I couldn't wait. Anyway, I didn't. . . .

But she was prepared, self, house and soul too; if her soul was ever in her life unready for anything that just wore pants or maybe if any woman's soul ever needed pre-readying and pre-arming against anything in pants just named Gavin Stevens. . . . (219)

The visit to Eula reveals not only that it is Flem who won't let Linda go off to school but also that when he became vice-president of the bank he bought the house and picked out the furniture himself.

"I dont want coffee," I said, sitting there saying *Flem Snopes Flem Snopes* until I said, cried: "I dont want anything! I'm afraid!" until I finally said "What?" and she repeated:
"Will you have a cigarette?" (223)

Gavin has reached an antagonist he fears to attack, but he does make one last gesture of bravado. Even that last gesture is foiled by his failure to understand the complexity of the situation. Linda has a will of her own too, and a private love for the man she thinks is her father. That life "to her . . . isn't nothing" (226). When Gavin threatens to tell Linda she is not Flem's daughter, Eula must explain that Linda simply would not believe him. The problem can never be reduced to a simple coalition of opposition to Flem Snopes. After his brief last try, Gavin gives up: "So there's nothing I can do" (226). Eula disagrees, urging Gavin to marry Linda. But Gavin's revolt against Flem is short-lived, and he is stymied by the complexity of the contest. At the end of chapter 16 he is still trying to sort out the separate wills of the three agents he has faced in his second conflict:

"All right," I said. "All right. Just tell me this. When you went home first and changed before you met me in the drugstore that afternoon. It was your idea to go home first and change to the other dress. But it was your mother who insisted on the lipstick

and the perfume and the silk stockings and the high heels. Isn't
that right?" And she still wrenching and jerking faintly at the arm
I held, whispering:

  "Please. Please." (230)

Gavin is no longer involved in the conflict, or even in the telling of it. It
is only at the end of chapter 16 that Ratliff mentions almost inadvertently
that someone "finally persuaded Flem to let her quit at the Academy and
go to the University after Christmas," that in fact Linda has already left
town (260).

When we see Gavin again he is no longer even deliberating on how to
act; he is retreating for extended evaluation. He is confusing the reader
by insisting on elaborately expanding his sentimental theory of Flem's
intentions, which Ratliff has already refused to give credence to as far
back as chapter 8 (142). Gavin hides behind talk of Flem and "the humility of not knowing," the "arch-fiend among sinners" (De Spain!), and
"the altar of mankind" (266, 270, 276). He actually allows himself to suggest that Flem has misappropriated the brass "not for the petty profit it
brought him but rather to see what depth De Spain's base and timorous
fear would actually descend to" (273). When he finally does come back to
the immediate problem that has been his crusade, he brings only conjecture and not personal knowledge: "Why? It's obvious. Why did he ever
do any of the things he did? Because he got something in return more
valuable to him than what he gave. So you don't really need to imagine
this" (290). Nor is Gavin now contemplating a third conflict, with Flem
or anybody else. We are in the climactic third conflict, but it is not initially Gavin's conflict at all. Eventually his history as Linda's protector will
give him a role in the climax, but only a secondary role in the second shift.
The third conflict is Flem's big move.

Though the climactic series of events leads to the third of Gavin's
meetings with Eula, and thus appears to be a third in Gavin's series of
contests, actually the third conflict belongs to Flem. Up to the final chapters Flem has not really appeared in Gavin's series of conflicts at all. He
has been seen directly only in the hermetic episodes (chapters 1, 10, and
16) interspersed between Gavin's two previous projects (chapters 4–5 and
12–15), together with a few scattered clusters of interpretation and prediction (most notably in chapter 8, pages 136–43). But despite Flem's lack of
visibility, the final conflict comes as no surprise. Beginning in chapter 1, a

series of speculations on "How It Will End" has been established as a major subnarrative running throughout the novel. Flem has not caught Eula and Manfred, Ratliff says, because "he dont need to *yet*" (15, emphasis added). In chapter 8 this subnarrative of speculation on the end is associated with another subnarrative, the conjecture over Flem's intentions in moving his money out of his own bank (150, also 142, and 262–64). Ratliff here first suggests some connection between the bank presidency and Eula, the "one Snopes object that he's got left . . . that-ere twenty-dollar gold piece" (151). During this whole preliminary period, despite Flem's relative inactivity in the plot, Faulkner creates an environment of conflict and of movement, through rhetoric. First there is the series of references to footprints, beginning with the water tank at the end of chapter 1: "Except that it was not a monument: it was a footprint. A monument only says *At least I got this far* while a footprint says *This is where I was when I moved again*" (29). When Flem appears in a rented dress suit, the town comes "to realize that it wasn't any more just a footprint than that water tank was a monument: it was a red flag. No: it was that sign at the railroad crossing that says Look Out for the Locomotive" (73). After the "Mrs Rouncewell panic," Flem has "left more footprints" (77).

Even more pervasive is the language of combat and of strategy. Flem is described as winning (24), as "farming Snopeses" (31), as "moving his echelons up fast now" (39). The Snopes watchers are looking for his next move, trying to see where he will "break out": "Confound it, the trouble is we dont never know beforehand, to anticipate him. . . . You got to move fast when he does break out, and he's got the advantage of you because he's already moving because he knows where he's going, and you aint moving yet because you dont" (143).

But eventually there begins to take place a series of moves that Flem does initiate. Ratliff hints as early as chapter 8 that something besides rapacity and money now motivates Flem. In chapter 10 he names "this-here new discovery" as "civic virtue" (175). In his short chapters 9 and 11 he hints that there is an interpretation Gavin is not making: "Because he missed it. He missed it completely" (153). It is only in chapter 16 that he gives it the name "respectability" and predicts that "there aint nothing he will stop at, aint nobody or nothing within his scope and reach that may not anguish and grieve and suffer" (259). This interpretation gives a shape to the moves that begin with the eliminations of Montgomery

Ward and of I.O. Snopes in chapters 10 and 16: there are "two down and jest one more to go," only one Snopes left for Flem to eliminate, "one more uncivic ditch to jump" (257). Ratliff is stretching a point, for Eula is not really a Snopes and has nothing in common with the other Snopeses Flem eliminates: Flem wants not to be rid of her as an embarrassment but rather to use her to achieve his goal of the bank presidency. But a conflict between Flem and Eula is definitely seen as the coming end of the series.

Charles has very early given away what will happen to Eula: "a while more still and she was dead and Mr de Spain had left town wearing public mourning for her" (74). But even after Uncle Billy Varner comes to town, and even after Charles repeats less explicitly that "this one was going to have death in it too though of course we didn't know that then" (301), Faulkner still maintains the suspense, the feel of the town's watching and waiting in suspended animation to see how it will work out. Townspeople like Mr. Garraway take sides in the interim on how it ought to come out. It is not until the end of chapter 20 that Gavin, now knowing the means of Flem's machinations, thinks he can say conclusively that the climax has really taken place: "*He has unpinned it now* I thought" (335).

The end, then, is prepared, and our appetites for the climax are still being encouraged even while it is already taking place. The climax of *The Town* is what Gavin has called a "long series of interlocked circumstances" (140). It is a difficult achievement, one that requires of us a concentration on narrative intricacy and detail. Gavin in particular has long made the actual functioning of the climax the subject of his predictions. His thought in chapter 8 is that to complete the final blackmail of De Spain, Flem would need Eula's cooperation, which he is not likely to get: "'Because, to use what you call that twenty-dollar gold piece, he's got to use his wife too. Do you mean to tell me you believe for one moment that his wife will side with him against Manfred de Spain?' But still he just looked at me. 'Dont you agree?' I said. 'How can he hope for that?'" (151). Gavin has gone on record asserting the impossibility of Faulkner's conclusion, but he has missed the ominous likelihood that Flem will "use" Eula in the sense of "expend." Later, Linda is seen as a potential figure in the equation. The possibility of her marrying forces Flem to act fast "because he knows that Eula will leave him too then" (228), which would mean "he'll lose the weight of Uncle Billy's voting stock" (261). Gavin supposes that in return for his permitting Linda to go away from Jefferson to school, Flem would make *Eula* sign a paper guaranteeing him half of her inheritance (291). The paper would be necessary to gain the assistance of Uncle Billy. As Gavin sees it, Flem's paper would shake Uncle Billy: "It wasn't her it was to alarm, spook out of the realm of cool judgment" (291). Flem would trade the paper to Varner in return simply for his help in getting his revenge on De Spain: "All you got to do is help me take that bank away from Manfred de Spain—transfer your stock to my name, take my post-dated check if you want, the stock to be yourn again as soon as Manfred de Spain is out, or you to vote the stock yourself if you had druther—and you can have this paper. I'll even hold the match while you burn it" (294–95). The virtuous Flem of Gavin's conceiving does not even want to be president of the bank, or "a prominent man in Jefferson" at all (292). He cares nothing about any inheritance from Varner. And he never considers exposing Eula to her father or anyone else.

Ratliff scoffs at the notion that Uncle Billy could be scared by a "joked-up piece of paper" (299). For Ratliff, only the facts about people could prompt Uncle Billy to an unforeseen action. The people who could matter much are not Flem and De Spain but Linda and Eula, and Ratliff has no doubt that the crucial fact at Flem's command is "that she's been sleeping around again for eighteen years now with a feller she aint married to" (300). Because Ratliff's unfailing common sense has been right in every dispute so far, there is little reason to doubt him. We are not certain how Flem will bring about his goals, but we are certain how he will not bring them about. It is, therefore, something like a betrayal of Ratliff's character and our own expectations that Ratliff is not corroborated about the piece of paper and Will Varner's anger. It is also a cause of some confusion in our unsorting of the actions of the climactic conflict.

In fact, when the climactic series of events does begin, it is Linda who takes the initiative that gives Flem his gambit, and the result *is* a piece of paper, a contingency will. Flem's manipulation of Linda is masterly. His acceptance of his inability to force her to stay home completely deflates her rebellion. Apparently frightened by the loss of the security of home, she comes immediately to heel: "She said: 'I will go! I will! You cant stop me! Damn your money; if Mama wont give it to me, Grandpa will— Mr. Stevens' (oh yes, she said that too) 'will—' While he just sat there— we were sitting then, still at the table; only Linda was standing up—just sat there saying, 'That's right. I cant stop you.' Then she said, 'Please.' Oh yes, she knew she was beaten as well as he did. 'No,' he said. 'I want you to stay at home and go to the Academy'" (321–22). Flem's generosity in every other matter proves to Linda that he loves her, and leaves her struggling: "You know: the one that said 'Please' accepting the clothes, while the one that defied him to stop her refused the picnic" (324). Linda believes that "if he wouldn't let her go off to school it was because he loved her" (326). His sudden capitulation then proves he loves her enough to be indulgent about even "the one thing in her life he had ever forbidden her" (326). It is natural that she should wish to respond with a comparable generosity, and she would not have to know much about Flem to make the particular gesture she does. So Ratliff seems to have been wrong about the "joked-up piece of paper."

It is apparently the paper that angers Will Varner as well, Ratliff notwithstanding. Linda is Will's "one remaining weapon," and apparently the thought of losing her allegiance simply makes him angry. He knows the paper itself is worth nothing, but Eula dismisses that from consideration: "As if that mattered, legal or illegal, contingency or incontingency—" (328). It would seem that the question of Eula's fidelity is not necessary to begin the series of events. What is not clear is how Flem introduces his exposure of Eula into the equation, to channel Will's anger against Eula and De Spain. It seems awkward to suppose that Linda's contingency bequest and Eula's adultery are simply mentioned as totally independent facts. It would be easy to concoct a connection—for instance, by claiming that Eula's unfaithfulness actually caused Linda to demonstrate her loyalty to Flem—but Faulkner strangely does not bother. Another problem is that Uncle Billy has not before seemed the sort of character who would even care about the immorality problem. The difficulty is that without the revelation of adultery, there is no one for an outraged Will Varner to "act" *against*—except Flem himself. However, Eula's version of the events does not really paint her father as an outraged moralist, but as a man shocked by finding out about something that has gone on without his knowledge for eighteen years (329). Eula also depicts Varner as a man eager to do whatever is necessary for the restoration of his peace, even if it means his daughter is run out of town: Eula says Varner sees that Flem gets the bank "since that was what all the *trouble and uproar* was about" (330, emphasis added).

When Uncle Billy gets to Jefferson, both Flem and Manfred are seen as his antagonists: "He wanted both of them out of the bank" (329). And yet his anger seems to shift away from Flem, for even when he supposedly wants Flem out of the bank he is overseeing the sale of De Spain's bank stock to Flem and arranging for the projected elopement of Eula and De Spain. Later suggestions that Flem may yet be run out of town thus do not represent real possibilities: " . . . unless your father really does get shut of the whole damned boiling of you, runs Flem out of Jefferson too . . . " (333); " . . . *provided of course old Will Varner leaves him time* . . . " (334); "Whether old Mr Will Varner ran Mr Flem Snopes out of Jefferson too after this, Mr de Spain himself wouldn't stay" (338). Though these continued references gradually reduce the idea to merely an *unlikely* possibility, they do have the effect of keeping that possibility in our minds. We are forced to ask why, if Will Varner really had the power, he did not take care of his old enemy while he was in the process of running his own daughter out of town (and out of life). The question cannot be satisfactorily answered, and it represents a flaw in the way Flem is represented as bringing off his move for the top. The revised version in *The Mansion* is that Varner would trade the paper for the bank presidency (*M* 145). But the swap is hardly more satisfactory, for Ratliff still concedes that the paper is worthless. If the paper is only a token of Flem's successful annexation of Linda's affections, there can be no reason to place value on the paper itself.

The initial intricacy, whatever its possible flaws, does not exhaust the chain of cause and effect in the climax. Gavin Stevens enters the climax after it enters its second shift: "Yes, Uncle Gavin too; Mr de Spain was finished now as far as Jefferson was concerned and now we—Jefferson—could put all our mind on who was next in sight, what else the flash of that pistol had showed up like when you set off a flashlight powder in a cave; and one of them was Uncle Gavin" (341). After the individual wills of Linda and Flem have set Will Varner in motion, and after De Spain's pride insists on an elopement or a fight (336), Eula comes to Gavin looking for someone to take care of Linda after she is gone. Gavin figures in Eula's own private equation, in her decision of how to react to the central catastrophe; he is one of the human resources available to Eula in her response to Flem, De Spain, and her father. The implication seems to be that Gavin actually is the determining factor in Eula's decision, presumably in failing to convince her that if she elopes with Manfred he will take care of Linda by marrying her.[2] But Gavin is not merely a factor in Eula's decision. The last act of the chain of circumstances is Gavin's own decision about how to react to Eula's suicide. His decision is to reassert normality, to attempt to reassure Linda that her family is not a monstrosity, that her mother may have been an adulteress and a suicide but was not a whore. Gavin's decision ends the collision of wills.[3]

The climax is followed by two anticlimaxes, one sinister, one comic. The addition in chapter 23 of the outrageous Snopes Indians episode is a suggestion that the saga is never over, that there will always be "one more thing" (359). It prefigures further attempts to defeat outrageous minor Snopeses, particularly the isolated episodes of chapters 13 and 14 of *The Mansion*, comic situations that lead to serious formulations of "how to trust in God without depending on Him" (*M* 321). There is always another Snopes, but as Ratliff will say, it is "jest another Snopes" (*M* 349). While the Snopes Indians show the recurrence of Snopesian "behavior," they are also interpreted by Ratliff as an ending of that behavior in its purest "unvarnished" form, a throwback to pre-respectable days for the tribe (370). And at the same time these Snopeses benefit from Ratliff's pity for them as inarticulate and abused children, even while Ratliff continues shielding his pity behind humor:

> "Watch out, now," Ratliff said. "Maybe we better set it on the ground and shove it up with a stick or something." But he didn't mean that. Anyway, he didn't do it. He just said to me, "Come on; you aint quite growed so they may not snap at you," and moved near and held out one of the oranges . . . ; until the girl, the tallest one, said something, something quick and brittle that sounded quite strange in the treble of a child; whereupon the first hand came out and took the orange, then the next and the next. (370–71)

The episode manages quite contradictory effects, suggesting "the last thing" as well as maintaining the continuity of never-ceasing episodes; suggesting pure danger, and the uses of pity and kindness toward the dangerous.

The other anticlimax, which precedes it, also suggests a continuity. Flem is shown not to be satisfied by a merely utilitarian achievement of certain goals, but to be capable of an overreaching and gratuitous exercise of power. He forces Linda to stay for the dedication of Eula's monument:

"So you would think he would a been satisfied now. But he wasn't. He had to make a young girl (woman now) that wasn't even his child, say 'I humbly thank you, Papa, for being so good to me'" (347–48). Ratliff's notion is that the situation represents for Flem a "contest," a "game of solitaire" against Jefferson: "The only remaining threat now was what might happen if that-ere young gal that believed all right so far that he was her paw, might stumble onto something that would tell her different. That she might find out by accident that the man that was leastways mixed up somehow in her mother's suicide, whether he actively caused it or not, wasn't even her father" (348).

This makes clear the precise way that Gavin's reassuring pity for Linda in chapter 22 (346) has perfectly served Flem's ends. Yet in chapter 22 the threat was not that Linda would hate Flem and expose him in some way but that she would hate her mother: "When I thought he wasn't my father, I hated her and Manfred both. . . . But now that I know he is my father, it's all right. I'm glad. I want her to have loved, to have been happy" (346). It is not clear just what might happen if Gavin or anyone else did tell Linda, what scandal she might cause that could shake a respectability already solidified by a wife's suicide. It is also unclear why Flem would be so eager to give Linda a last, debasing reminder of his power and authority. His action is another of the rare self-revelations in which he shows emotion or an uncharacteristically unprofitable and impractical ruthlessness more appropriate to lesser Snopeses. Because such moments are not unique, they are not seen as violations of Flem's character but as glimpses of another dimension to the character, a really frightening dimension of motiveless malignity. Flem's journey out of his way to get a look at his handiwork at the end of *The Hamlet* is similarly revealing to the reader; here his meanness can only be considered revealing to Linda as well, can only be accounted the creation of a new antagonist.

> . . . and him setting there chewing, faint and steady, and her still
> and straight as a post by him, not looking at nothing and them
> two white balls of her fists on her lap. Then he moved. He leant
> a little and spit out the window and then set back in the seat.
>   "Now you can go," he says. (355)

His act is a dismissal. Faulkner does not allow us to know until the end of *The Mansion* what Linda's attitude toward Flem has become; the new conflict is not confirmed by being made explicit. But the "two white balls of her fists" give a hint, a first portent, to suggest that beyond the end-plotted conflict and the game of solitaire, a new contest of wills is in preparation. The dialectic of wills seems to escape any final formulation.

The moves, then, are:

1. Gavin moves against Manfred to "save" Eula. (chapters 3–6)
2. Flem eliminates Montgomery Ward. (chapter 10)
3. Gavin is in conflict with Matt Levitt to "save" Linda. (chapter 12)
4. Gavin moves to send Linda to school and finds his antagonist is Flem. (chapter 15)
5. Flem eliminates I.O. He has one last "uncivic ditch to jump." (chapter 16)
6. Flem "unpins it." (chapters 17–21)
   a. Linda moves to give Flem a joked-up piece of paper
   b. Will Varner moves against De Spain
   c. Flem secures the bank presidency
7. Eula moves to use Gavin to take care of Linda—a failed move. (chapter 20)
8. Eula moves to zero herself out. (chapter 21)
9. Gavin moves to reassure Linda about her mother. (chapter 22)
10. Flem makes a contemptuous move and creates an antagonist. (chapter 23)

The Town is, then, a plotted novel, a chain of interlocked circumstances, despite the possible flaw in the orchestration of wills—Will Varner's inexplicable forbearance—and the misleading rhetorical pointers —Ratliff's unexpected unreliability.

Faulkner puts a great deal of stress on his intricacies both local and central. When he directs our attention to a profit-and-loss sequence, for instance, he does so in ways that Balzac does not, even though Balzac is continually mentioning numbers. Balzac's numbers express a general trend toward bankruptcy through unfathomable squanderings.[4] Faulkner asks us to believe that the numbers work out to a sum. Some readers may find themselves taking it all on faith; such a response puts us in the position of the readers of the most annoying "omniscient" narrators, who constantly reassure their readers that the characters are responding perfectly and that events are transpiring rapidly—offstage. The danger is that we may feel that the intricacies are obscurantist and may even doubt whether they work at all. It is comforting to know that Cleanth Brooks can concoct a workable explanation of the goat trading in *The Hamlet* (*Yoknapatawpha Country* 279–82). But the very usefulness of double-entry bookkeeping suggests that Faulkner's communication with the reader during the reading of the novel has been less than complete. We must wonder about the intended accessibility of the episodes. Are the actual details meant for rereaders only?

Suspicions of plot failure may be a mark of a rhetorical lapse, a failure to involve the reader. Some readers have suggested that occasionally such suspicions are well founded. Cleanth Brooks indicts the readers of *Intruder in the Dust* with an uncritical acceptance of a hopelessly farfetched plot. Yet paradoxically this very possibility is not an invitation to dismiss Faulkner's plots but rather the greatest challenge to our attention as readers. Even as first readers we cannot risk being cheated. Our own self-respect requires us to place as high a value as Faulkner does on *curiosity*. It is not a wasted curiosity. Faulkner's intricacies reveal not abstract patterns but human actions; they require not erudition but the following of cause and effect. In a sense Faulkner dares his literary readers to become as money-wise as he, not to concede their stake in a world of complications. Even catching Faulkner out is a mark of the high respect we have for him, a demonstration of our willingness to follow him all the way into his world. The goat trading does remain somewhat elusive, but it is an extreme case. The working of *The Town* (notwithstanding the flaw) is a followable chain of cause and effect generated by the willful independence of human actors. Faulkner's plot is not obscurantism, but a challenge.

～

The non-plot of *The Town* suggests that human interaction requires communication as well as independence. Faulkner emphasizes this combination in the intricate dialogue between the novel's narrators. He chooses to enact through the storytelling in the novel the interplay of separateness and dialogue that is at the heart of the plot. The same individual willfulness that takes form among the central actors as plot, the contest and collision of wills, works among the narrators to create and preserve narrative freedom. The narrators are engaged in the same interest in human interaction that draws the readers into the working of the plot.

Faulkner explicitly calls our attention to the function of storytelling as a communal dialogue through the ongoing colloquy between characters and narrators. In the first paragraph of *The Town* we are reminded of the complicated manner of transmission of all our information:

> I wasn't born yet so it was Cousin Gowan who was there and big enough to see and remember and tell me afterward when I was big enough for it to make sense. That is, it was Cousin Gowan plus Uncle Gavin or maybe Uncle Gavin rather plus Cousin Gowan. . . . They sent Gowan down to stay with us and go to school in Jefferson until they got back. "Us" was Grandfather and Mother and Father and Uncle Gavin then. So this is what Gowan knew about it until I got born and big enough to know about it too. So when I say "we" and "we thought" what I mean is Jefferson and what Jefferson thought. (3)

We might account for this confusion over sources by arguing that in this chapter, which tells of events before the birth of Charles Mallison, verisimilitude requires Cousin Gowan and the tradition of verbal repetition. But Charles also implies that even Gowan himself did not and could not tell all of what happened. The inclusion of Gowan is appropriate, then, in suggesting the *necessity* of communal and continual telling. Similarly, Charles's discussions of the meaning of "us" and "we" are more than explanations of conventional abbreviations. By positing an "us" (a family) and a "we" (a town) existing even before his birth, Charles insists on the basic continuity of groups. It is within such groups, extending beyond any one lifetime, that telling (or "thinking") goes on, as an activity requiring more than one person and more than one occasion.

In the actual telling of the stories, Faulkner insists on a confusion about sources that verges on obscurantism. The original "Centaur in Brass" story alternates scenes told omnisciently by a depersonalized observer from "our town" (*CS* 149) with scenes using Harker as a quoted source, also apparently omniscient. In the novel Faulkner avoids the feeling of oscillation between two kinds of narration not by reducing the tale to a uniform narration but by multiplying the number of contributors and denying omniscience to any of them. He uses not only Harker and Turl but also Tom Tom, Gowan, and even Gavin Stevens. The scenes once told by the disembodied narrator are now attributed to several different characters, including even Harker.

Clearly, Faulkner delineates his sources with ever greater complexity not only to simulate greater accuracy in determining the facts and our means of knowledge of the facts but also to emphasize the communal endeavor necessary in getting any story told. Very little of this complexity is necessary from strict verisimilitude alone. Since Harker has already been the source for one private interview between Tom Tom and Flem, there is no logical necessity that Gavin, and not Harker, should have found out from Tom Tom the substance of the second interview with Flem. It is perfectly credible that "all Mr Harker knew at this time was that the junked metal would accumulate slowly in the corner behind the boilers, then suddenly disappear overnight" (21), but it is not credible that for some reason Gavin should know more, and in fact Charles never claims that he does. There is no real reason for Gavin's privileged position as a source. Nor is there any reason that Turl could not have been asked what really happened before Tom Tom got on his back, since he willingly offers information on what happened afterward. Faulkner simply appears to wish to maintain Harker's freedom to speculate: "Jest exactly time enough for him to creep across the room to the bed and likely fling the quilt back and lay his hand on meat and say, 'Honeybunch, lay calm. Papa's done arrived'" (26). Faulkner tells the Centaur episode not from a niggling desire for overprecise verisimilitude, but out of an abstract sense of the necessity of a variety of characters and of the desirability of a complex interaction.[5]

The precise recognition of individual contributions is maintained not just in the opening chapter but throughout the novel, and not just to distinguish the sources of bits of information but to note the sources of the characteristic verbal commentary as well. Charles Mallison is particularly willing as a narrator to include opinions as he has presumably heard them in the voices of his elders, and he always credits the voices:

That was the first summer, the first Summer of the Snopeses, Uncle Gavin called it. (4)

... Texas (that bourne, Uncle Gavin said, in our time for the implicated, the insolvent or the merely hopeful) ... (6)

Because Uncle Gavin said this was still that fabulous and legendary time when there was still no paradox between an automobile

and mirth, before the time when every American had to have one
and they were killing more people than wars did. (13)

. . . what Uncle Gavin called the divinity of simply unadulterated
uninhibited immortal lust which they represented . . . (15)

The frequency of these attributions suggests the degree to which the
young Charles relies on the good lines of others, particularly his Uncle
Gavin. But this does not simply reflect Charles's youth. If anything, it is
Gavin himself who takes the method to its eclectic extreme: "I could feel
my shirt front getting wet. Which was what Ratliff would have called tit
for tat, since what Victorians would have called the claret from my nose
had already stained the shoulder of her dress" (192).

Even in the telling of the early incidents, however, the scrupulous
Charles does not give credit to Gavin for all the fancy language; he takes
a few flights that would seem to be his own:

. . . just moving, walking in that aura of decorum and modesty
and solitariness ten times more immodest and a hundred times
more disturbing than one of the bathing suits young women
would begin to wear about 1920 or so, as if in the second just
before you looked, her garments had managed in one last frantic
pell-mell scurry to overtake and cover her. Though only for a moment because in the next one, if only you followed long enough,
they would wilt and fail from that mere plain and simple striding
which would shred them away like the wheel of a constellation
through a wisp and cling of trivial scud. (9–10)

Yet the prose sounds very much like Gavin's language. Perhaps Faulkner
identifies his sources not simply to distinguish the various speaking styles
he commands through them but also to emphasize that stories in this
novel are made up of a multiplicity of contributions. Here he does not
hesitate to achieve the same purpose by the very different technique of
attributing manifestly *inappropriate* language to a character. Faulkner's
mixture of styles—such as Ratliff's "The sybaritic indolence and the
sneers was gone" (*H* 174), or the fancy word assigned to Old Het in the
phrase "She said it was like a tableau" (239)—at times seems incongruous

and intentionally mannered, a highly anti-mimetic and artificial enterprise of fusing the author's high style and the character's folk grammar. But in *The Town*, Ratliff explains his growing interchange of language with Gavin as the effect of that very complicity which Faulkner is at such pains to recognize:

> "I'm sorry," I said. "I didn't mean it that way. It's because I like the way you say it. When you say it, 'taken' sounds a heap more took than just 'took,' just like 'drug' sounds a heap more dragged than just 'dragged.'"
> "And not jest you neither," Ratliff said. "Your uncle too: me saying 'dragged' and him saying 'drug' and me saying 'dragged' and him saying 'drug' again, until at last he would say, 'In a free country like this, why aint I got as much right to use your *drug* for my *dragged* as you got to use my *dragged* for your *drug*?'"
> (260–61)

The mixture of styles thus becomes the fruit of freedom and of confederation. The good lines of Gavin and Ratliff are living and independent proofs of their autonomous activity and their continuing dialogue, but so are the voluntary modifications of language which on the surface might tend to call in question the stability and individuality of their characters. In *The Town* these characters are stable enough and maverick enough to effect interchanges in their very speech, our primary means of knowing them as literary characters.

Thus each narrator incorporates into his narrative the voices and stories of others. Yet the precision of attribution was dismissed by Stephen Marcus in one of the influential early critiques that put *The Town* into a lingering critical disrepute: "Often we reach Ratliff only through Mallison, who has gotten to him through Stevens. This extreme refinement in point of view is inherently undramatic and indicates how exiguous Faulkner's direct grasp on experience can become" (387). The direct grasp on experience does not seem to be what Faulkner has in mind. For this very reason he has employed a method that is precisely dramatic, if by dramatic we mean formed by the interacting voices of two or more characters.

The dialogue between characters is most immediate in the complicated interaction Faulkner has devised for the narration of the novel as a whole. The form of the novel is made to enact the compilation of narrative material through dialogue, through talk and storytelling. Series of chapters such as 4–6 and 12–14 exhibit continuities in which each speaker contributes what information he has. Ratliff and Charles Mallison, respectively, must leave gaps in their narratives that only Gavin Stevens can fill in: in chapter 7, the first night interview with Eula; in chapter 13, the short scene in which Linda says that she does not want to marry Gavin *because* she loves him. Another example of privileged information is Ratliff's knowledge of who *really* put up the money to save the business of Wall Snopes (149). But once again the aim is not mere verisimilitude. Faulkner is suggesting that voluntary communal telling is *desirable,* not simply necessary because of the privacy of some experience. He implies that everyone in his community of talkers has a chance to make his approach to the true assessment of the facts, that the facts are not the property only of those who have the most intimate knowledge of them. The narrators, then, like the sources, are chosen arbitrarily, but intentionally so. In the dramatic situation of *The Town,* the speakers willfully fasten on stories to tell each other.

Several pairs of chapters are linked as if by a continuous dialogue between two speakers in a dramatic scene, one storyteller commenting on his predecessor's last words before beginning the episode he wishes to tell.

[Charles Mallison] Gowan said you would even have thought she was proud of it. (end of chapter 3, 77)
[V. K. Ratliff] She was. (beginning of chapter 4, 78)

[Charles Mallison] "I know what you mean," Uncle Gavin said. "I know exactly what you mean." (end of chapter 7, 131)
[Gavin Stevens] I knew exactly what he meant. (beginning of chapter 8, 132)

[V. K. Ratliff] He leant a little and spit out the window and then set back in the seat.
"Now you can go," he says. (end of chapter 23, 355)
[Charles Mallison] So the car went on. (beginning of chapter 24, 356)

These perfect continuities seem to require an actual conversation between storytellers, seem to imply a conventional dramatic situation, until we notice that some tellers seem to have no cognizance of the tales told ahead of them. After we have just heard Gavin's testimony in chapter 5, Ratliff goes on as if it had never happened: "So something happened somewhere. . . . Some day Lawyer his-self might tell it" (99). We might account for Ratliff's failure to hear Gavin as due to an aside between Gavin and the audience. In fact, Gavin twice implies such an audience when he addresses directly a "you" which he treats as if it had not heard the story before: "But I dismissed that as immediately as you will too if we are to get on with this" (211); "So you will have to imagine this too" (291).[6]

There are discontinuities in the storytelling situation that are greater than mere asides—the discontinuities caused by variations in the *time* different tellings are supposed to take place. Frequently expressions like "yesterday afternoon" (214) or "an hour ago" (227), which seem to imply that the time of telling is not far removed from the events being told about, are actually used only relatively, to mean "the previous afternoon" or "an hour before." The most confusing time complication is caused by the repetition of Ratliff's remark: "Except that that one dont really ever lose Helen, because for the rest of her life she dont never actively get rid of him. Likely it's because she dont want to" (102). The remark closes Ratliff's telling of chapter 6. When Charles Mallison begins chapter 7 by referring to the remark, we might suppose it is being implied that Ratliff's narration has taken place at a previous point in time, which Charles remembers: "I remember how Ratliff once said that the world's Helens never really lose forever the men who once loved and lost them; probably because they—the Helens—dont want to" (103). But on the very next page Charles says that Ratliff made the remark when Gavin took Montgomery Ward Snopes with him to France for Eula's sake (104). And shortly thereafter Charles quotes Ratliff as having made a variant of the remark to him by way of mentioning that he has already made it to Gowan: "Which reminds me of something I may have said to your other cousin Gowan once when likely you wasn't present: about how some of the folks that lost Helen of Troy might some day wish they hadn't found her to begin with" (114).

The repetitions and variations seem intentionally introduced to undercut any assurances we might have in placing the telling of the previous chapter, chapter 6, at a particular time. The narrators seem to insist that the narration, like the individual remark, *did* take place several times and that any individual narration is only one of an unfinished sequence of tellings. As Ratliff says to Charles, "You're going to have to hear a heap of it before you get old enough or big enough to resist" (112). Confusing and mannered though the device may be, it does suggest abstractly the independence from time of the storytelling dialogue. The innovative convention does indeed create an oscillation between past and present, suggest the evolution of stories. In its own confusing way it suggests the jarring necessary on the way to whatever communal consensus can be achieved.

The jarring between narrators can be productive, can lead to the truth of such matters as Flem's motive. Ratliff's two magnificently terse chapters (9 and 11) explicitly contradict Gavin and raise the contested question Gavin summarizes as "*whether I was right and your husband just wants your lover's scalp, or Ratliff is right and your husband doesn't care a damn about you or his honor either and just wants De Spain's bank*" (318). But the conflicts among narrators are more often simply assertions of their own individualities. This storytelling is a communal dialogue, but it is a dialogue that depends on individual freedom. Each narrator tells his story partly as a cryptic and tantalizing performance, keeping his listener guessing, not letting the act of listening be too easy. Ratliff resumes a story after a year's lapse with the pretense that he expects Gavin to know what he is talking about:

> "A salted goldmine," Uncle Gavin said, "One of the oldest tricks in the world, yet you fell for it. . . . "
> "Yes," Ratliff said. "Almost as old as that handkerchief Eula Varner dropped. Almost as old as Uncle Billy Varner's shotgun." That was what he said then. Because another year had passed when he stopped Uncle Gavin on the street and said, "With the court's permission, Lawyer, I would like to take a exception. I want to change that-ere to 'still.'"
> "Change what-ere to 'still'?" Uncle Gavin said.
> "Last year I said 'That handkerchief Miz Flem Snopes dropped.' I want to change that 'dropped' to 'still dropping.' They's one feller I know still following it." (8)

The jostling between narrators is not only an assertion of freedom from each other and from us but an affirmation of novelty in narrative, of narrative freedom from fact. In retelling any episode, each narrator feels free to tell it with a difference, so that no bit of Snopeslore appears in the same form it had in *The Hamlet*. Each character tells scenes in his own way, so that we have within two pages (44, 46) two different versions, from Gavin and from Gowan, of the scene in which Gavin tells Ratliff to get out of his office. They may represent two different occasions, but so much of the dialogue is the same that we feel justified in supposing that they are the same occasion told with liberties. Ratliff's remarks on Helen and the continuing meditations on "What constitutes a Snopes" and "What is the difference between women and men" are other materials that belong to all jointly and which are not required ever to take final form. Any narrator can appropriate these materials at will, and turn a new twist if he can. The result, as Warren Beck says, is "somewhat coincident but still dissident" (*Man in Motion* 132). As far as the facts of the story go there are always details that "even now we dont know," which "we will never know exactly" (30). Omniscient storytelling seems not even desirable. In his revisions of "Centaur in Brass," Faulkner incorporates a new liberating reliance on conjecture, an engagement with what "likely" happened or what "must a" happened (26). Ratliff is not the only narrator who realizes the value of being "secured as he was from checkable facts" (134). Where facts would inhibit or would require that the case be closed, they are the last thing desired.

In fact, curiosity is something to be sustained for its own sake. In a distinction that seems uncharacteristically critical, young Charles seems to say that Gavin and Ratliff are interested in curiosity *rather than* in people: "He and Uncle Gavin were both interested in people—or so Uncle Gavin said. Because what I always thought they were mainly interested in was curiosity" (4). There is a good deal of talk in the novel about women's interest in facts, or their interest in what will fit together like facts whether they are facts or not. But finally the characters most liberated from fact, most interested in finding something interesting that will fit, are the narrators themselves. For Ratliff, the absence of an authoritative version of any kind is proof of the way he wants to tell it: "Because them five boys (I knowed two of them) never told it, which you might say is proof. . . . Between what did happen and what ought to happened, I dont never have trouble picking ought" (100). We cannot be sure that even yet we have the final, verifiable account of *The Town*. But perhaps neither do all the narrators. Even in chapter 21 Charles does not know about the last meeting between Gavin and Eula: "I know now what Uncle Gavin believed then (not knew: believed: because he couldn't have known because the only one that could have told him would have been Mrs Snopes herself and if she had told him in that note she gave me that afternoon before she was going to commit suicide, he would have stopped her or tried to because Mother anyway would have known it if he had tried to stop her and failed)" (340).

The characters thus assert, even while engaging in dialogue, their independence of the facts and each other. It is this jarring, this incorrigible willfulness, that preserves in *The Town* the randomness and plenitude so prominent in *The Hamlet*.[7] In moving from Frenchman's Bend to Jefferson and from Jefferson to the world, the characters seem to have if anything a greater range of subjects for random wit, whether Texas or automobiles or Greenwich Village or respectability. There are also the ongoing efforts at individual definitions and explanations of those phenomena which are by common agreement undefinable and inexplicable—women and Snopeses. What is relevant to an immediate narrative can always be an excuse for narrative excursions that evade any strict criteria of economy. In explaining why the bank needed a new president (and vice-president), Charles Mallison recounts the circumstances of the death of Colonel Sartoris, which entails telling about Bayard Sartoris, his war experiences, and his sports car (116–17). An explanation of why school happened to be closed the day of Eula's death leads to a short treatise on "the very best time of all not to have to go to school," followed by a return to the narrative with the rambling unconcern of an oral storyteller glad to make his story as long as possible: "Anyhow we had the holiday" (301–2). Faulkner's transitions to and from the irrelevant are never disguised. Charles's descriptions of Gowan at thirteen naturally lead him to tell some of his own experiences, simply some of the things boys do: "Because even now I can remember some of the things Aleck Sander and I did for instance and never think twice about it, and I wonder how any boys ever live long enough to grow up" (53). There follows the lengthy anecdote about how Aleck Sander shot John Wesley Roebuck in the back and ruined Charles's hunting jacket (53–55). Both anecdotes and folk wisdom are kept alive by the incorrigible undiscipline of the narrators. They preserve the reality that comes in at the corners of the narrative; they appeal to our sense of the right word for our common experience in the world.

> "What did Grover Cleveland like for fun back then?"
> "For fun?" Ratliff said. Then he said: "Oh. He liked excitement."
> "What excitement?" Uncle Gavin said.
> "The excitement of talking about it," Ratliff said.
> "Of talking about what?" Uncle Gavin said.
> "Of talking about excitement," Ratliff said. (126)

The Town is a dialogue, an exercise in communication, precisely because of the freedom and extraordinary willfulness of the communicating figures. Gavin, Charles, and Ratliff *enact* an interchange of stories that shows a group consciousness in continually vital re-formation and evolution. In this sense they capture the sense of the community better than the gallery loungers of *The Hamlet*, who are always present in great numbers but do not make nearly so definable a set of individual contributions. Tull and Bookwright are often little better than names; their contributions are by and large limited to one-liners not expressive of their individual characters. *The Hamlet* is Ratliff's book. In *The Town*, however, everyone participates. *The Town* forces us to remember that community begins with individuals, that we cannot really have dialogue unless we know and believe in the individuals who enact the communication.

In fact, *The Town* seems to bear out the assertions of John Bayley, who says that successful stories require communication between teller and listener or reader: "The only really boring stories are those which we can always tell ourselves, and the only essential paradigm of fiction . . . is that it is made up by someone else" ("New Formalism" 68). In a noteworthy interchange Bayley's strictures are disputed by Gabriel Josipovici, who argues abstractly that a story need not by definition take place between teller and listener because "it is hypothetically possible for each of us to tell ourselves all the stories that could ever be imagined." At any rate, he says, perfect communication is impossible: "No writer can really say what he wants to say because no writer ever possesses language as his own" (301). Josipovici thus praises modern art for giving up the illusion of communication and "calling attention to itself" (288). But the conditions that

Josipovici thinks should paralyze a storyteller are taken by Faulkner's characters as the most necessary requirements for the telling of stories. The narrators of *The Town* are not worried about perfect communication. They cannot always tell their stories the same way twice, and they do not try. Nor do they ever consider telling their stories to themselves. Not only does an imperfect command of facts and language not deter them or turn them to solipsism, it positively protects them, ensures them against the need ever to stop talking. The novel thus exploits the instability that Josipovici sees as inherent in language. And we must feel that Faulkner's narrators are just independent enough to communicate, that any greater freedom could only inhibit their ability to tell and retell stories. Entertainment of a listener encourages the teller's own eccentricities, even requires that at each telling there be some novelty. The listener makes possible both the freedom from the listener and the freedom from fact. Individual freedom can only be expressed to others. This is communication in the only practical sense, the shared desire to hear a story made up or at least embellished by someone else. As Gavin believes, talk in itself is not art, but dialogue is; Gavin wishes "to concentrate on talk in order to raise it to conversation, art, like he believed was everybody's duty" (51). In many ways Jefferson is impotent and derelict, but in Gavin's terms the very form of the book forbids us to condemn the town. Despite its failure to rise to Flem's challenge, in a more long-lasting way, through its storytellers, the town continues to do its "duty," to turn mere talk into conversation—which is art.

But telling is not acting, and it cannot be confused with acting. Theresa Towner correctly asserts that *The Town* documents the failure of talk to combat Flem. "Sharing information about Snopeses clearly has no effect on their progress in *The Town*" (105). Talking is an aesthetic reaction, not an action. In that sense the formation of community can be seen as avoidance. But it does not necessarily follow that this implies "the tragic consequences of failed narration" (Towner 76). The friction of telling, commentary, and speculation does not undercut the action but rather exists simultaneously and separately. All the Snopes novels create space both for traditional agency and for the detachment of essentially aesthetic reactions, for both event and conversation about event. Faulkner shows that plot and the fabulation which is a reaction to plot can both coexist easily in the same novel. If this improvisation around the events, this fabulation, is postmodern play, then postmodern play must be as old as gossip. If, on the other hand, this is "incipient fascism," as Joseph Urgo humorlessly asserts (*Faulkner's Apocrypha* 188), then so is all gossip.

The dialectic of communication is present implicitly even in the complicated form of the individual episodes, which carry within them an entire tradition of telling and retelling. *The Town* includes several of those hermetic episodes that have led so many of Faulkner's critics either to dismiss the Snopes saga as a tissue of short stories or apologetically to offer thematic continuities as true sources of "unity." Those critics have no doubt been prompted to their views by the knowledge that many of the episodes were in fact printed previously as independent short stories.[8] And yet there is in some of the episodes something more important than the history of their composition. From the reader's perspective, the point about these episodes is not that they have been or could be published elsewhere but that they *appear* to have been *told* elsewhere. The later forms of the stories show complexities that look to have been added to earlier forms. The joints are apparent. As in the scenes of *The Hamlet* that are built like jokes, the added sections of the episodes function to go always one step further into a more outrageous narrative complexity. They perpetuate an implicit dialogue carried on from one telling to another.

In the Centaur in Brass episode (the first chapter of *The Town*) the evolution is verbal, a developing of the Last Word that closes the chapter: "It was not a monument: it was a footprint" (29). In the original short story "Centaur in Brass," the notion of Flem Snopes's "monument" (the water tank) is not really a last word so much as a reiterated idea whose meaning is at least partially obvious from the beginning. Since Faulkner does not economize on his references to the monument, it is no surprise that the monument appears in a little portentous meditation at the end:

> In our town Flem Snopes now has a monument to himself, a monument of brass, none the less enduring for the fact that, though it is constantly in sight of the whole town and visible from three or four points miles out in the country, only four people, two white men and two Negroes, know that it is his monument, or that it is a monument at all. (first sentence of story; *CS* 149)

He built his monument slowly. (first sentence of part 2; *CS* 153)

. . . he had set the capital on his monument and had started to tear the scaffolding down. (from first paragraph of part 3; *CS* 158)

So they wondered what Snopes was looking at. They didn't know that he was contemplating his monument: that shaft taller than anything in sight and filled with transient and symbolical liquid that was not even fit to drink, but which, for the very reason of its impermanence, was more enduring through its fluidity and blind renewal than the brass which poisoned it, than columns of basalt or of lead. (final paragraph of story; *CS* 168)

In *The Town*, the monument idea is not only more subtle but more complex. Because it appears only twice, and in a more complicated form, we are not allowed so easily to guess its meaning. "At first we thought that the water tank was only Flem Snopes's monument. We didn't know any better then. It wasn't until afterward that we realized that that object low on the sky above Jefferson, Mississippi, wasn't a monument at all. It was a footprint" (third paragraph of novel; 3). It is not until the final page of the episode that Faulkner allows himself to amplify on this brief preview of his Last Word. The brief introduction of terms (monument, footprint) must wait for the full exercise in definition: " . . . looking at his own monument, some might have thought. Except that it was not a monument: it was a footprint. A monument only says *At least I got this far* while a footprint says *This is where I was when I moved again*" (29).

The revision is functionally necessary in explaining the role of this episode in a novel that continues the previously inexorable rise of Flem Snopes. There is something unsettling about beginning with a failure, and the core story is definitely one of failure. As readers of *The Hamlet* we find it hard to believe that the old methods expressed in "I can find somebody else" (*T* 23) could have failed even once. But the rhetorical last word (in the novel) establishes the unusualness of such a federation as well as the certainty that Flem will not be finished by one little miscalculation. The somber last page of "Centaur in Brass," in which Flem is seen first sitting alone in the dark and then in the "hopeless" little house (*CS* 168), is deleted, and we are assured that the water tank is not a funerary monument to foiled ambition but, like Flem's incongruous nose, a frantic and desperate warning.[9] Faulkner thus affirms in a way not completely supported by the tale itself that this is still the old Flem. And he couples the last word with a first word, a look forward that suggests Flem has absorbed a minor setback willingly, his major assets far from depleted.

> "Not even now?" Uncle Gavin said to Ratliff.
> "Not even now," Ratliff said. "Not catching his wife with Manfred de Spain yet is like that twenty-dollar gold piece pinned to your undershirt on your first maiden trip to what you hope is going to be a Memphis whorehouse. He dont need to unpin it yet." (29)

But the Last Word does more than persuade us of the plausibility of the episode. It calls attention to the need for those who have "thought" about the episode—or *told* about it—to become more complicated in their last words. Faulkner's reiterated "at first we thought" and "some might have thought" calls attention to the rejected interpretation or quip, calls attention to Ratliff's old problem of going *far enough*. In the revised version, both the pundit (Charles) and the subject for whom he is finding words (Flem) must keep going farther: not "only" the satisfaction of "I got this far" but, in addition, "I moved again." We can of course verify from the original "Centaur in Brass" our suspicion that Faulkner is revealing for us his own history of engagement with his material. In evolving the best last words, the storyteller who conceals his identity behind the general "we thought" has also found it desirable to say "More! More!" to the monument quip.

We can see, then, that Faulkner's characteristic "not . . . but" construction represents not merely a stylistic mannerism but the record of the writer's dialogue with himself. Without stopping to reject past tellings, Faulkner fossilizes them, makes them steps in an evolving complexity. His willingness to let us see him going himself one better through retelling is an important cause of our sense of the implied storyteller behind these continually developing episodes.

In other well-known episodes, more than the Last Word is being evolved. We cannot but be aware in some of the trading stories of how negotiations have been reworked, reheated to a fine pitch of confusion. It is as if subsequent tellings must establish their autonomy by capping the joke. In the original published story "Fool About a Horse," Pap starts off with the Beasley Kemp horse and the mule and the $3.65 for Mammy's separator. He trades with Pat Stamper for the "matched team" of mules and buys the separator. When he trades the matched team back to Stamper he gets his mule and a new horse (the Beasley Kemp horse in disguise), but he must throw in the separator (reconverted to cash). Mammy then trades the horse and mule for the separator. Before the last trade, Stamper's profit was the separator money; now it is the horse and mule. Pap is now out everything he started trading with, but Mammy is even. The joke is that instead of a resignation before mistreatment, irate womanhood insists on her hard-earned luxury at the expense not only of the man's luxury (the horse) but even of the indispensable farming machinery (the mule).

In *The Hamlet* the story goes one step farther, forcing Miz Snopes to give up something of her own before Pat Stamper will "dicker" with her. She must trade the horse, the mule, *and* the *cow* for the separator. Before, she had only the one gallon of milk to run through the separator again and again. Now, she hasn't any prospect of getting another gallon ever without charity. As the equation becomes more complex, the story takes Miz Snopes into the realm of comic monomania: she has traded the source of milk for the separator. Faulkner emphasizes this comic capping. Before the last trade, the lot looked "like all Texas" (*H* 51); now it looks "like it would have held all Texas and Kansas too" (*H* 53). It is perhaps cheating on Faulkner's part never to have mentioned the cow before it suddenly figures in the equation at the end. There is no way we could have guessed the story could be capped in this way. If we stop to think that even further things could be pitched into the sequence (goats? chickens?) we will lose the obviously intended sense of total gulling, of comic disaster at the end of the story. In these inflationary retellings, we are meant to look back on the new end as conclusive, the original story as nothing by comparison: "That was easy but this is the ultimate."

Unlike the novel versions of Fool About a Horse and Spotted Horses, the retold story of Mule in the Yard does not turn the original conclusion into another false ending. Its additions are made within the basic narrative structure that leads up to Miz Hait's revelation of her "justice" (256). In *The Town*, I.O.'s argument with Miz Hait takes a minor role alongside the more substantial negotiations in which I.O. is ousted from town by his cousin Flem. The story of Miz Hait's trading with I.O., then, is told *concurrently* with the new story of Flem's involvement. As in the original tale, Miz Hait offers to buy the offending mule and is told by I.O. that the price is $150. She sends I.O. $10 by Old Het, later making her lucid explanation of her own calculations:

> "Hait said you paid him fifty dollars a trip, each time he got mules in front of the train in time, and the railroad had paid you sixty dollars a head for the mules. That last time, you never paid him because you never would pay him until afterward and this time there wasn't no afterward. So I taken a mule instead and sent you the ten dollars difference with Het here for the witness." . . . [Uncle Gavin] said they were so still that Mr Flem himself spoke twice before they even noticed him. (251)

In the original tale, Snopes simply refuses to accept the deal and insists on getting his mule back. When he insists on returning the $10, Miz Hait tells him where the mule is, without telling him the mule is dead. The fact that I.O. buys back a dead mule with Miz Hait's $10 is the core event in both the story and the novel. But in *The Town* this final step comes as a cap, a last insult after I.O. has already been eliminated by Flem.

Flem's role is what is new in the episode. The story of Hait's demise as previously told is revised, and it is revealed that Flem actually got half of Miz Hait's $8,500 insurance money, while I.O. got $100 to keep quiet. But Flem's silent role in past events, though it represents an important surfacing of the nose for money that was more overtly seen in his earlier days, is in contrast to his role within the episode. Not only does he redeem Miz Hait's mortgage, presumably in the name of Snopes public relations, but he buys I.O.'s entire stock of six mules at the exorbitant rate of $150 a head on the condition "that you move back to Frenchman's Bend and never own a business in Jefferson again as long as you live" (253). Flem has also cleaned out the Snopes nest: he reveals that he has just sold the Snopes Hotel. Financially, I.O.'s dealings with Flem are very profitable. It is the particular way that Miz Hait's trickery joins with Flem's prodigality that leaves I.O. in no doubt that he has been bested by Flem as well, or at least that Flem can outwit him whenever and to whatever degree he chooses. For I.O. makes too quick an assumption that his negotiations with Miz Hait are independent of Flem's; he taunts Flem: "At least I got one ten dollars out of the mule business you aint going to touch" (251). At this point he is through trying to get any more than $10 out of Miz Hait. It is only when Flem begins paying $150 per mule that I.O. starts trying to get his mule back and insists on returning Miz Hait's $10. Flem's refusal to give up one last $150 without a seventh mule lures I.O. into ignoring the rather pointed way Miz Hait asks, "You giving this back to me . . . before these witnesses?" (252). His greed to get money out of Flem has in fact made his dealings with Miz Hait an even greater disaster, depriving him of his last $10. Even though he has grossed $900 on his mules, when he comes back begging for the $10 "he did look cold, small, forlorn somehow since he was so calm, so quiet" (255). It is the last stage of "utter hopelessness" (248). He has lost the symbolic $10 which was the last solace of his hatred of Flem, and Flem is at least indirectly the cause. Faulkner has thus connected the basic story to a whole new range of negotiations, so that the resulting total episode is just as much a narrative of expanding complexity as if its expansion were temporal. Like the "not . . . but" construction, episodes like this imply with each telling their long periods of growth, their preexistence both as oral tales and as elements in a creative dialogue between tellings.

We can find these complexities in many of the previously published stories: the trial added to "Spotted Horses"; the interference of Lump, the intended help of Miz Snopes, and the repeated struggles with the dog and the body added to "The Hound." But a story need not have been printed to have had a long previous existence or to have been accreting complexities over a period of time. The important quality of these stories is that we sense their evolved structures through reading them, not through private knowledge of their history. We can sense in the story of Flem's elimination of Montgomery Ward Snopes a complexity evolved through retelling. The episode has the basic form of a simple Snopes-elimination story like Ratliff's disposal of Clarence in *The Mansion*. Despite Montgomery Ward's complex protests against the method of arrest, he is simply arrested for making money from obscene postcards.[10] A greater complexity is introduced in relating Flem to the elimination, but since both Gavin and Flem want Montgomery Ward disposed of, the next logical step in the evolution of the tale would require no action from Flem at all: since Montgomery Ward, like Mink, is in jail anyway, Flem would simply have to wait for conviction. The twist invented for the episode in *The Town* turns on Flem's "new discovery," his new "civic virtue" (175), which is later called respectability. Gavin thinks that Flem is going to use the good of Jefferson—"not for me, my kinsman . . . For Jefferson"

(170)—as a dodge to free Montgomery Ward after all. Ratliff jumps to no such conclusions: "So he wants Montgomery Ward to go to the penitentiary. Only he dont want him to go under the conditions he's on his way there now" (170). The twist, then, is that Flem himself salts Atelier Monty with whiskey to have Montgomery Ward sent to prison on the more common and respectable charge.[11] Faulkner lends credibility to the new complexity in Flem's motive with an ironic echo from Hub Hampton that shows just how well Flem has made use of the pieties of Jefferson's "normal" citizens:

> "Damn it," he said, "it's Jefferson. We live here. Jefferson's got to come first, even before the pleasure of crucifying that damned—"
> "Yes," Uncle Gavin said. "I've heard that sentiment." (174)

Then, as a last straw, Flem returns to Gavin the key to Montgomery Ward's studio, which he has stolen right from the sheriff's office. New outrageous actions are engendered by the application of Flem's new motive to a situation that has much in common with simpler Snopes-ridding operations. The obvious simple ending is passed up as new narrative material is added to the basic anecdote: first Flem, then the respectable Flem (with all the possible variations growing out of that novelty). As readers we can sense the story adding, under the pressure of retelling, new touches that are not necessary but welcome.

Each episode's inbuilt history thus preserves the writer's dialogue with himself between present and past tellings, thereby reinforcing the implicit temporal dimension of the communal tradition of storytelling. We do sense the active presence of the storyteller. And we are made to feel that the dialectic of storytellings, like that of the wills in plotted conflict, resists any final resting place.

5
The Mansion
Conflict and Contemplation

In *The Mansion* Faulkner offers the paradox of a plotted novel largely given over to reminiscence, reverie, and review. The novel embodies a hidden multiplicity of actors, but the course of the novel essentially is a meditation on those actors before they perform any material moves. In the process, Faulkner implies a conviction of the independence, vitality, and growth of characters. In large part the novel is about and written from the point of view of old men, but while looking retrospectively over the careers of those old men Faulkner affirms the possibilities of agency, the ambiguities of action, and the importance of agents in his fiction. There is a referential dimension to these reveries, as Faulkner repeatedly emphasizes the multiplicity of things real people do, even suggesting rhetorically that in spite of appearances "people just do the best they can" (429).[1]

The plot of *The Mansion* is simpler than that of either *The Hamlet* or *The Town*. *The Mansion* provides the ending of the trilogy; as a novel in its own right, it seems all ending. The major part of the novel is contemplation, the reconsideration of old characters enacting what occasionally seem to be old episodes. The conclusion of the novel, though strongly foreshadowed, turns out to conceal new complications until the end. But the very success of the final revelations depends on an almost total restraint beforehand. *The Mansion,* like the story "Mountain Victory," holds off before one major event; the event is shocking because it interrupts the essential stability of what preceded it. There is a certain structural similarity between *The Mansion* and *The Hamlet* in that Linda, like Mink in *The Hamlet,* becomes an antagonist late in the novel. But Mink's antagonism is seen slowly developing throughout *The Hamlet.* Significantly, in *The Mansion* Linda is revealed as Flem's antagonist only *after* she is already successful (though adequate hints are given beforehand). Prior to the climax, in short, there is a real scarcity of events.

The "Mink" section recapitulates the development of Mink's antagonism to Flem. The murder of Houston, though it is presented in great detail and with new effects that importantly change our attitude toward Mink's character, is not really an event of this novel but a given fact. The novel's first paragraph presents us with the fact of the life sentence and Mink's anxiety about Flem; the rest of the chapter, then, has the effect of explaining the given. From this point Mink's relation to Flem is completely determined, though it is not made overt until the end of chapter 2: "*Yes sir* he thought. *It looks like I done had to come all the way to Parchman jest to turn right around and go back home and kill Flem*" (51). No other relation in Mink's life is ever allowed to have any importance except as it furthers the stated goal of killing Flem. The trick played on him by Montgomery Ward merely intensifies an already irrevocable commitment. The episode is a good example of Faulkner's willingness to expand his stories and offer new justifications for old antagonisms, to include something new about the Mink-Flem conflict. It also is an important example of Flem's tactics. But it is not exactly an event, for Mink takes no notice of Montgomery Ward's role and simply maintains his deferred conflict with Flem. The release from prison permits everything to change. But in the interim between the release and the murder of Flem, nothing is allowed to divert Mink from his challenge. His picaresque adventures are largely discontinuous because they do not affect him in any way. The record of his finances does provide a continuation between episodes,[2] but his financial situation is a source of continued tension to him only because he may not have the money to buy a gun and make it back to Jefferson. His attention is fixed on the ultimate goal, not on the immediate dilemma. All potentially extended interactions are finessed, as Mink makes of himself a predetermined quantity. Mink exists to kill Flem; he kills Flem, and he is not.

Linda's actions before the climax also show little change or reorientation in her relationship to other characters. Since chapter 6 is almost exclusively concerned with the story of Eula, we know little of what Linda's character has been, except for Ratliff's deduction that she wanted "to be needed" (143). The first events that concern her are those which precede her return home: she confederates but refuses to marry; she marries; after her husband is killed she returns home bereaved and deaf (chapter 7). The experiences seem significant, but we cannot be sure that they have actually affected her character or that they have actually caused her to return to Jefferson. The only reason given for her return is Gavin's "Why the hell shouldn't she?" (178). Furthermore, because of the sequence of presentation, the actions of chapter 7 are definitely shown to be past actions with respect to the time of the novel. They are background, events preceding the return of Linda, which Charles and Gavin are first seen awaiting at the beginning of chapter 6. They are as much past as the events of Eula's life, even though they are new to readers of the trilogy. Chapter 8 completes the scene in which Linda arrives in Jefferson, but most of the chapter concerns Gavin's troubles with young women. In chapter 9, Linda seems intent on precipitating some action that will radically disturb the situation in Jefferson: she consorts with the Communists and befriends the Negroes. Still, she never goes beyond the brink of an event: nothing she does is allowed to have real consequences. In chapters 10 and 11 Linda undertakes her handiwork of marrying off Gavin. It is constantly emphasized, however, that Gavin's marriage does not affect his real relationship with Linda in any way. Not until Linda actually gets Mink paroled, then, does an event occur that changes her orientation to any other characters. Until chapter 16, Linda is not definitely involved in anything but static relationships.

Flem participates even less than in *The Town*. Significantly, the new "Flem Snopes monument in that series mounting on and up from that water tank" (164) is his wood footrest, "not a defiance, not a simple reminder of where he had come from but rather as the feller says a reaffirmation of his-self and maybe a warning to his-self too" (156). Unlike the other monuments, the footrest marks the consolidation of no new gain, is the sign of no adjustment of relations. Flem's moving into the mansion has been a foregone conclusion after the events marked by the Eula monument. The footrest if anything reveals the surprising tentativeness of Flem's new achievement, the gingerliness with which he occupies the last goal of respectability; the last monument seems really a sign of lack of assertion.

The Mansion is a novel of waiting. Flem is defined as the man for whom two people wait, but who does not come. He is the man who does not answer (65), the man about whom "ever body was wrong" (63). In a remarkable tableau, Flem and Linda are both immobilized in what seems a kind of permanent stasis. Flem sits and chews on air. Linda is a stillunravished bride of quietude, apparently outside human time (230, 236). Flem is the man who does not talk, Linda the woman who cannot hear. They are twinned in a silent inaction. Flem's acts, such as they are, are mysterious. If one question is what he will do, another is whether there is one thing he would not do (333). We are thrown back on the drama of "ever body" watching, interpreting, and waiting. The watchers are engaged in astonishment but also "good hard fast thinking" (62): "half of Jefferson was doing the anticipating for him and half the waiting too, not to mention the watching" (61).

In this void of waiting the speculation is of portents and outstanding IOUs, but also there is again the pervasive language of competitive games, particularly of chess and poker: "I've been raised" (69); "what he was thinking was *All I got to do now is keep folks thinking this is a cross and not a gambit*" (229); "that match" (116); "that engagement" (116); "this last desperate gambit" (122). So Faulkner continues to embody an environment of conflict and contest.

In fact, Flem participates in only two real actions in the novel. In chapter 3 he passes up the opportunity to take over Montgomery Ward's "French-postcard industry" (53) and spends "twenty-five or thirty dollars to send Montgomery Ward to Parchman when the government would a sent him to Georgia free" (64). This reveals a new motive besides respectability for the events previously told in *The Town*—namely, Flem's desire to keep Mink in prison. In chapter 4, the negotiations between Flem and Montgomery Ward show Flem's trading prowess and make tangible for the readers of this novel the methods that have gotten Flem this far. Montgomery Ward rejects Flem's first offer of payment of "about five hundred, mostly in trade, on the installment plan" and demands first ten thousand, then five (67). Montgomery Ward thinks he has "got to" Flem, but he soon realizes that he is "a pretty slow learner . . . sometimes, now and then, mostly now in fact" (68). For Flem suddenly shows himself willing to see that Montgomery Ward is sent to Atlanta after all, and on the greater charge of sending obscene matter through the mail: he has obtained the postcard that Montgomery Ward sold Grover Cleveland Winbush and has blackmailed Grover Cleveland to run the envelope containing the postcard through the canceling machine at the post office. Flem has "raised" Montgomery Ward, and now he offers only a hundred dollars, a railroad ticket, and a two-day trip to Memphis (69). Another negotiation takes place in chapter 14, when to all appearances Flem buys the Compson golf course under the delusion that the government will want it for an airfield. In fact, Flem wants the land for a profitable housing development, Eula Acres. These two episodes are the only clear examples of Flem's methods, and neither constitutes a readjustment with a major character.

The only other hint of his strategies concerns his attitude toward Linda. Gavin believes Flem has stolen Linda's Communist Party card to hold the threat of turning it in to the FBI; he then decides that Flem will actually turn it in. Gavin even argues that "*It was he himself probably who scrawled Jew Communist Kohl on his sidewalk at midnight to bank a reserve of Jefferson sympathy against the day when he would be compelled to commit his only child to the insane asylum*" (240). Gavin has in fact already been visited by an FBI agent who knows Linda holds a party card. The FBI agent is described as being as "terrifying as the footprint on Crusoe's beach" (234). The metaphor cannot help but remind readers of the trilogy of the series of footprints left by Flem in *The Town;* we cannot be sure that Flem's agency is implied, but the coincidence of metaphors is ominous. At any rate, whether already initiated or merely intended, Flem's planning against Linda would constitute an important reorientation of characters, for it would mean an aggressive challenge on Flem's part, a "gambit," in Gavin's words (229). Flem's alleged plans against Linda actually would promise a major event. We cannot be sure that this aggression is really even intended, but the possibility of it is important in convincing us that Flem is still an active character. It forces us to take him seriously, though as it will turn out he becomes a participant in the one major event through his passivity, not by going on the offensive.

The restraint of the preliminary action in the novel is reinforced by Faulkner's narrative cross-cutting. The "Mink" and "Linda" sections are developed in parallel. The "Linda" section works up in time almost to the point at which the "Mink" section ends in chapter 5. Chapter 5 ends with Mink's parole in 1946; chapter 11 ends in 1942, with Gavin married and Linda working in the industries in Pascagoula. The emphasis is on convergence of the stories; when the stories reach the same point of time and still no direct interaction has occurred, we must believe we have been seeing prologues. The "Flem" section then begins (chapter 12) by advancing Mink in time from the end of chapter 5. But the forward motion once again proves to be temporary, as chapters 13 and 14 go back in time to events of the previous year, the elimination of Clarence Snopes in the summer of 1945 and of Res Snopes in the spring of 1946. Chapter 15 recounts Linda's return home after the war and therefore forms a sequence with the previous two chapters. Chapter 16 finally catches up to and passes the time when Mink was last seen, showing Gavin's anxiety during Mink's days of freedom and ending with the revelation of the murder. This means that the next Mink chapter, instead of being a flash forward, is now a flash back. Chapter 17 shows Mink up to the murder. Only chapter 18, which follows the murder, finally accomplishes the long-expected convergence of Mink and all the other characters, and it could follow either the last Jefferson chapter (16) or the last Mink chapter (17). Though Linda and Mink are once again apart, they are contained within the same chapter; and Gavin Stevens is actually able momentarily to act as a bridge between them. Two sequences, though their actions have been separate both spatially and temporally, have directed themselves forcefully to the single point in space and time where really dynamic action could take place. The expository action in *The Mansion,* then, not only holds back from events but points toward one event, directs expectation toward the significant action that is yet to come. The preliminary events point rather than lead.

The few minor events are not all that point to the climax. From the earliest pages of the novel, we are encouraged rhetorically to think about the inevitability of the end, and the form the end will take—specifically Flem's murder. Mink Snopes, looking back to the time "long before the moment came when he had had to aim the gun and fire the shot" (3), remembers his patience before the necessity for his first murder became absolute: "Maybe in fact They were even testing him, to see if he was a man or not, man enough to take a little harassment and worry and so deserve his own licks back when his turn came" (6). There has been no doubt in his mind that his turn *would* come. This reverie refers to the murder of Houston, but it occurs after Flem fails to appear at the trial; it would be easy to apply Mink's retrospective thinking toward the avowal of yet another inevitable "turn." The subsequent detailed telling of Houston's murder enforces our belief in the inevitability of Mink's actions, once decided on. Well before the actual murder, Mink thinks, *"Maybe I ought to waited till he got back . . .* , turning at last back to the now empty and vacant platform, noticing only then that he had thought, not *should* wait for Flem, but should *have* waited, it already being too late" (35). After he is sent to Parchman, Mink immediately transfers this sense of necessity to a new object: "*If a feller jest wants to do something, he might make it and he might not. But if he's GOT to do something, cant nothing stop him*" (49). These hints prepare us in such a way that when Flem's name is finally made explicit, it affects us as the actual completion of an action: "*Yes sir* he thought. *It looks like I done had to come all the way to Parchman jest to turn right around and go back home and kill Flem*" (51). Much later he wishes he could avoid it:

> in 1948 he and Flem both would be old men and he even said aloud: "What a shame we cant both of us jest come out two old men setting peaceful in the sun or the shade, waiting to die to-gether, not even thinking no more of hurt or harm or getting even, not even remembering no more about hurt or harm or anguish or revenge," . . . as if whatever necessary amount of the money which Flem no longer needed and soon now would not need at all ever again, could be used to blot, efface, obliterate those forty years which he, Mink, no longer needed now and soon also, himself too, would not even miss. *But I reckon not* he thought. . . . *Cant neither one of us take nothing back.* (94)

The effect is that we end the "Mink" section believing not simply that Mink thinks Flem is going to die but that Mink's will has become self-sufficient and independent of himself. Mink's willful choice has become so habituated as to be beyond reconsideration, invulnerable to sentiment. Like the girl and Jubal of "Mountain Victory," he has converted himself into a fixed quantity. It is not a will greater than Mink's own that requires Flem's death; it is Mink's own will become fixed. Faulkner clearly does not wish us to see this certainty as the presence of God, fate, or Faulkner. It is an example of his use of a rhetoric of determinism to condition a dramatic inevitability, to convince the reader rhetorically of the proba-bility of an action. And yet the feeling of necessity is not conveyed over the head of the character but through him.

Faulkner clearly does not intend a determined world. The impend-ing catastrophe is the inevitable result of human choices. Mink's wistful "what a shame" urges us to accept the inevitability but also reminds us of the history of other possibilities not chosen. The effect is much like Joe Christmas's moment of self-objectification, when the possibility of other choices remains real even though it is immediately rejected:

Then it seemed to him, sitting on the cot in the dark room, that
he was hearing a myriad sounds of no greater volume—voices,
murmurs, whispers: of trees, darkness, earth; people: his own
voice; other voices evocative of names and times and places—
which he had been conscious of all his life without knowing it,
which were his life, thinking *God perhaps and me not knowing that
too* He could see it like a printed sentence, fullborn and already
dead *God loves me too* like the faded and weathered letters on a
last year's billboard *God loves me too* (*LIA* 97–98)

Faulkner actually emphasizes fluidity and choice; *The Mansion* is partly
an intermittent meditation on choice and *change*. Mink's initial action in
preparing for his revenge represents a change of character: "He was now
having to change overnight and forever for twenty or twenty-five years
his whole nature and character and being: *To do whatever they tell me to
do. Not to talk back to nobody. Not to get into no fights. That's all I got to do
for jest twenty-five or maybe even jest twenty years. But mainly not to try to
escape*" (49). Mink does find that "Parchman just changed the way a man
looked at what he saw after he got in Parchman. It didn't change what he
brought with him. It just made remembering easier because Parchman
taught him how to wait" (92). Obviously this creature of fixed will is only
pliable in ways that ultimately abet the assertion of his will. But Mink
continues to be able to adapt. He tells himself that to get to Jefferson "he
would have to change his thinking, as you change the color of the bulb
inside the lantern even though you cant change the lantern itself" (397).

The compromise of change and stability is an important one, and the
ability to adapt seems to present a point of comparison between one
character and another. It is clear that Mink has changed "only" his behavior, not his will (though that new behavior has made him a new Mink,
pacific in everything but the original decision to kill Flem). By comparison with Linda and Flem, Mink actually comes off well in showing an
ability to change. "Change" in itself, however superficial, is notably incompatible with Linda, whom Charles sees as "no mere moment's child
but the inviolate bride of silence, inviolable in maidenhead, fixed, forever
safe from change and alteration" (203). Ironically, this changelessness
makes Linda out of place in the postwar Jefferson where even the Communists are rich in spite of themselves (351). Linda is explicitly contrasted
with Charles, who believes or "at least" hopes that something has hap-

pened to him that "met the standards of suffering and enduring enough to enrich his spiritual and moral development" (351).

Flem presents several superficial signs of change, but Ratliff observes that Flem's respectability does not come from a change of character but rather from a deliberate consistency: "But it was jest the house that was altered and transmogrified and symbolized: not him. . . . It wasn't that he rebelled at changing Flem Snopes: he done it by deliberate calculation, since the feller you trust aint necessarily the one you never knowed to do nothing untrustable: it's the one you have seen from experience that he knows exactly when being untrustable will pay a net profit and when it will pay a loss" (154–55). Ironically, the change Flem does undergo is a repudiation of change, a metaphysical development toward the unchangeable, an assumption of the consistency of a rock: "the capitalist . . . who had begun life as a nihilist and then softened into a mere anarchist and now was not only a conservative but a tory too: a pillar, rock-fixed, of things as they are" (222). When Mink sees him again, he notices that he looks "a little changed of course. . . . But no different, really" (412–13).

Faulkner thus keeps the possibility of change before us even in a community whose relations are apparently settled. He reminds us of the mistake made by the antagonists of Clarence Snopes, who thought they understood him until he *changed:* "And, Charles's Uncle Gavin said, since previous to his elevation to grace, everybody had believed Clarence incapable of change, now the same people believed immediately that the new condition was for perpetuity, for the rest of his life" (300). Faulkner emphasizes that his is a world in which, even with Clarence Snopes, change upon change is possible.

Faulkner also makes clear what sort of inevitability he is building toward by his unmasking of the rhetoric of Gavin Stevens in chapter 16. Gavin pretends to believe in the fatedness of Flem's death, pretends even to believe that he wants to be an accessory to the murder. He warns the deaf Linda about what Mink will do, but he does it aloud, and when she says she does not understand he simply writes "*I love you*" on her writing pad. He justifies this restraint by thinking, "*If I say No she will find somebody else*" (ironically ascribing to Linda the time-tried methods of Flem Snopes) (368–69). But when he tells Ratliff about it, he pompously claims actually to have wanted to participate in an inevitability, the murder of Flem: "It was because I not only believe in and am an advocate of fate and destiny, I admire them; I want to be one of the instruments too, no matter how modest" (368). The pretended belief in inevitability would mean that it makes no difference what Gavin does, so that he might as well be an instrument as not. Ratliff plays along with Gavin's rhetoric but hints that it is inadequate:

> "Destiny and fate. They was what you told me about being proud to be a handmaid of, wasn't they?"
> "So what?" Stevens said. "Sign it."
> "Dont you reckon you ought to maybe included a little luck into them too?" (370)

Ratliff realizes that behind Gavin's rhetoric is actually a desire to save Flem: "If you'd a said No, she would jest got another lawyer that wouldn't a said No nor even invented that two-hundred-and-fifty-dollar gamble neither. And then Flem Snopes wouldn't a had no chance a-tall" (370). But he will not let Gavin forget the words he has used. Ratliff sees the situation in all its pathos, which may include fate but also includes a lot more: "us and Linda and Flem and that durn little half-starved wildcat down there in Parchman, all mixed up in the same luck and destiny and fate and hope until cant none of us tell where it stops and we begin" (374). Gavin does not really believe in fate either, and in fact he does try to "fix it," prevent Mink from getting out of prison without a promise to leave the state: "*So I am a coward, after all. When it happens two years from now, at least none of it will spatter on me*" (376); "*So I really am a coward after all the talk about destiny and fate that didn't even sell Ratliff*" (377). Gavin is thus made explicitly to repudiate his high talk; and when he hears that Mink has outwitted him he immediately goes to Flem to affirm his human responsibility: "I'm responsible for this, even if I probably couldn't have stopped it" (381).

Gavin still talks tough, and particularly refuses to abridge his antagonism for Flem, thinking that if it were to occur, the murder would be a "just fate" (382). Even Ratliff suggests it is possible that God might be working against Gavin:

> "By God, God Himself is not so busy that a homicidal maniac with only ten dollars in the world can hitchhike a hundred miles and buy a gun for ten dollars then hitchhike another hundred and shoot another man with it."

"Dont that maybe depend on who God wants shot this time?" Ratliff said. (389)

But the important thing is that Gavin has repudiated his talk of fate, and that both Gavin and Ratliff are doing everything to prevent the crime from taking place. Gavin's former talk about being an agent of fate has shrunk to the ironically small consolation he takes in not reporting immediately to Flem: "'I'm not really an evil man,' Stevens said. 'I wouldn't have loaned Mink a gun to shoot Flem with; I might not even have just turned my head while Mink used his own. But neither am I going to lift my hand to interfere with Flem spending another day or two expecting any moment that Mink will'" (393).

The cluster of discussions of fate and responsibility, occurring just before the event so long foreshadowed, is a powerful caution from Faulkner against the misreading of his rhetoric as an excuse for inaction. When, at the end of chapter 16, Gavin realizes how he has been deluding himself in thinking that Mink is dead, his sense of inevitability returns with a conviction far more profound than his earlier empty talk of fate and destiny: " . . . thinking quietly *We wont stop him. We cant stop him—not all of us together, Memphis police and all. Maybe even a rattlesnake with destiny on his side dont even need luck, let alone friends*" (394). Faced with a specific force that has nothing to do with determinist abstractions, Gavin uses the outmoded rhetoric as a mockery of his own affectations and as an admission that he actually has no words to describe the sort of will he has tried to impede. Clearly we too are meant to accept this sense of inevitability— but only affectively, not literally.

The climax thus is no imposed fate. But it is no surprise, is even a certainty, that Mink will kill Flem. After the complexity of individual episodes throughout the trilogy, the end approaches with a striking simplicity. Faulkner reveals the accomplished fact at the end of chapter 16: "The pistol was here last night. It functioned" (395). In a sense, then, Cleanth Brooks is right in saying that Faulkner is "not playing for gross suspense" (*Yoknapatawpha Country* 238). Of course, we do not yet know what has been Mink's fate, or even for certain that it was Flem the pistol functioned against. The early revelation is thus not unlike Charles Mallison's "this one was going to have death in it" in chapter 19 of *The Town* (*T* 301). But more importantly, the final chapters have yet to reveal the hidden allocation of wills in the apparently simple and inevitable collision

between Flem and Mink. The active role of Linda does come as a shocking surprise, completely undercutting the expected climax. The acquies-
cence of Flem is a third element that shows the ending of *The Mansion*
to have the aggregative structure of other ever-evolving Faulknerian
complexities. Faulkner has not lost his desire for "interesting technical
complications" (134).

Predictions subtle and plainspoken about the danger of Linda have not
been lacking, but they are never clear as to the precise nature of the danger. The earliest warning suggests that the danger is to Linda's lover
(Barton Kohl) and protector (Gavin) and that the greater danger is not
physical: " . . . that it wasn't her that was doomed, she would likely do
fine; it was the one that was recipient of the fidelity and the monogamy
and the love, and the one that was the proprietor of the responsibility that
never even wanted, let alone expected, a bone back, that was the doomed
one; and how even between them two the lucky one might be the one
that had the roof fall on him while he was climbing into or out of the
bed" (163). But there seems no particular reason to blame Barton Kohl's
death on Linda, and so we may even be tempted to ignore Ratliff's dire
prophecies, regularly spaced at the end of almost every chapter in the
"Linda" section:

> "She'll come back here," I says.
> "Here?" he says. "Back here?" then he says, "Why the hell
> shouldn't she? It's home."
> "That's right," I says. "It's doom."
> "What?" he says. "What did you say?"
> "Nothing," I says. "I jest said I think so too." (178, end of
> chapter 7)

> " . . . She's going to marry him," I said.
> "Why not?" he said. "I reckon he can stand it. Besides, if some-
> body jest marries him, maybe the rest of us will be safe."
> "The rest of them, you mean?" I said.
> "I mean jest what I said," Ratliff answered. "I mean the rest of
> all of us." (204, end of chapter 8)

> "You were wrong. They aren't going to."
> "What?" he said. "What's that?"
> "She's not going to marry Gavin."

"That's right," he said. "It will be worse than that."

Now it was me that said, "What? What did you say?" But he was already himself again, bland, serene, inscrutable.

"But I reckon Lawyer can stand that too," he said. (232, end of chapter 9)

"He cant marry her now," I said. "He's already got a wife."

And you never thought of *soberly* in connection with Ratliff either. Anyway, not before now, not until this time. "That's right," he said. "She aint going to marry him. It's going to be worse than that." (256, end of chapter 11 and of the "Linda" section)

This obvious series of warnings regards Gavin alternatingly as either the victim or the danger. In chapter 7 Ratliff does not want Gavin to hear, so presumably he is speaking about Linda herself as the danger. But in chapter 8 he seems content at thinking that Gavin may marry Linda, and he implies that not just "them" (women) but everyone is endangered by Gavin's bachelor idealism. Everyone will become safe not because Gavin marries Linda but because someone (anyone) marries Gavin. The expression "he can stand it" does not sound serious until recalled in the "Lawyer can stand that too" of the next chapter. This is clearly a warning about Linda. But it is a cryptic warning, and at the end of chapter 15 Charles is understandably still wondering "What in hell could Ratliff have meant? Or anyway thought he meant? Or at least was afraid he might have meant or mean?" (360).

Ratliff's next warning is much more explicit:

"I aint worried about her," Ratliff said. "She's all right. She's jest dangerous. I'm thinking about your uncle."

"What about him?" Charles said.

"When she finally thinks of something and tells him, he will likely do it," Ratliff says. (361)

When, in the very next chapter, Linda asks Gavin to free Mink, it is impossible for us not to see the connection. We already believe that the release of Mink is a dangerous, even a deadly, act. But even so we have no reason to think Ratliff is foreseeing intentional complicity in murder. Ratliff even suggests that Linda is well intentioned and harmless in herself. He undercuts her as a threat by saying she is "jest" dangerous and "all right." He says that she will act out of the need to "invent" some "injustice," which perhaps attributes to her a pity for the tricked and harshly · treated Mink that we ourselves have been encouraged to feel (360). There is nothing to imply a malicious intention, and Ratliff seems actually to be worried only about Gavin. Gavin too is aware of the danger of Linda's action. He attempts to protect her presumed naïveté and idealism by arranging for Mink to be released only on the condition that he not return to Jefferson. In fact, the only suggestion that Linda might be hostile to Flem, or that she might have some actual hostile intention toward him, comes earlier, when Charles wonders about the Snopes Christmas dinner in terms initially favorable to Linda as "bride of silence," "invulnerable . . . in that chastity forever pure": "The two of them sitting there face to face through the long excruciating ritual which the day out of all the days compelled; and nobody to know why they did it, suffered it, why she suffered and endured it, what ritual she served or compulsion expiated— or who knows? what portent she postulated to keep him reminded. Maybe that was why. I mean, why she came back to Jefferson. Evidently it wasn't to marry Gavin Stevens. Or at least not yet" (216). Linda's involvement and at least some of its implicit dangers are thus no secret, are in fact ominously pondered.

It is thus not the identities of the participants that constitutes the complexity of the final event. The only thing concealed is Linda's intention, her will to be in conflict with Flem. The revelation of the intention provides a new dimension to a murder that would have happened eventually with or without Linda's will or even her naïveté. This new dimension is revealed to Gavin when he deduces that Linda must have ordered her Jaguar before Flem's death and that she intends Gavin to know it (422–25). But Linda does find an opportunity to become an accessory in more than intention, in a way that Gavin never does know about. After the murder she actually helps Mink escape: "That door is a closet. You'll have to come back this way to get out" (416). Her cool cooperation in the murder is an act of aggression which reveals beyond a doubt that her part in the episode has not been a mere objective or neutral foreknowledge of the killing. In physical action her token gesture alters the central event only slightly; but her participation substantially changes the predicted equation of human wills in the conflict. Apparently it takes Linda to achieve a plot as covert and as mute as those of Flem's better days. Linda proves in the end to be as good a Snopes as Flem.

But there is also a third will acting in the central event of *The Mansion*. Prior to his murder, Flem has permitted quite contradictory impressions —the expectation of a possible aggressive action against Linda and also the perception of a general inaction, a lack of any further stages of success to mark with monuments.[3] The ambiguous ascription of hostile intentions turns out to be a false lead, a sign of life with no plot consequences. The weariness wins out—but in an unexpected way. For Flem's inertia when faced with his killer may be fatigue, but it does seem like a *willed* passivity. Flem makes no attempt to stop Mink when Gavin tells him that Mink is at large. Taking his hint from Flem's calculation of how much money Mink has, Gavin believes that Flem's lack of interest is simply confidence that Mink presents no real threat, or at least that he can easily be tracked down while trying to buy a gun in Memphis. But even during the killing itself, Flem remains impassive: "Now his cousin, his feet now flat on the floor and the chair almost swiveled to face him, appeared to sit immobile and even detached too, watching too" (415). Ratliff later suggests that Flem has been willing to play the game of Give-me-lief (430–31). The implication would be that even when warned by Gavin he has been preparing this forbearance, that his inquiry as to "How much?" has not been a calculation of his chances to survive but merely a habitual interest in all financial activity. And, in retrospect, it looks very much as though he also has sensed Linda's part in the affair. When Gavin asks him if he is going to tell Linda that Mink is free and intends to kill him, Flem simply asks "Why?" (389). He may well mean not (as Gavin supposes) that telling her would serve no purpose, but rather that it would be superfluous to tell her what she must already know. But Ratliff's further supposition is that Flem plays Give-me-lief with Linda: "Now it was her lief" (431). Flem appears, then, to know his antagonists and acquiesce in their actions. He becomes so detached as to be cooperative, hence suicidal. The last surprise in the surprise ending is Flem's action as antagonist against himself. Linda's surprise role is ironically outdone by Flem's own, as Flem remains the master of circumstances, retaining his ability to go everyone one better.

Three cohering wills make the major event of *The Mansion* more complicated than any single event in the series of collisions in *The Hamlet*.

Flem's antagonists in *The Hamlet*—Ratliff, Mink, and all the inhabitants of Frenchman's Bend—are defeated in part because there is no cooperation between them, because their challenges are episodic and uncoordinated. The coordination in *The Mansion* is all the more complex because any cooperation is strictly unintended. Linda, Mink, and Flem form no overt cabal for the elimination of Flem. Mink does not know that he is being used by Linda. Linda, in turn, ironically never realizes that in all her plotting, she works with the indulgence, even the permission, of her victim. The physical action is simple. But the strongly prefigured ending has been coupled with an unexpected complexity of which Ratliff has obscurely warned, a set of surprises that act as contingencies to alter the look of what has always seemed predetermined.

With the combination of surprise and finality in the ending, Faulkner completes the pattern of plotting in the trilogy as a whole. The course of the trilogy may be seen as the search for the one comparable will, the will that can come off even in conflict with Flem Snopes. The previous volumes have detailed the moving failures of Ratliff, Gavin, and Eula. *The Mansion* in a sense resumes and contains all these failures. The entire plot of *The Town*, for instance, is confined within chapter 6 of *The Mansion*.

Gavin and Ratliff are present as living remnants of the past, still attempting conflict with limited objectives. Gavin Stevens is still, as Ratliff described him in *The Town*, "a feller that even his in-growed toenails was on the outside of his shoes" (342). He cannot help showing the world his anxieties and immaturities; his desire to do good is frustrated because he was born in the "wrong envelope," "that fragile and what you might call gossamer-sinewed envelope of boundless and hopeless aspiration Old Moster give him" (128). Ratliff warns Charles that someday he will outgrow Gavin, and eventually Charles does look back on Gavin indulgently but objectively:

> Because he is a good man, wise too except for the occasions when
> he would aberrate, go momentarily haywire and take a wrong
> turn that even I could see was wrong, and then go hell-for-
> leather, with absolutely no deviation from logic and rationality
> from there on, until he wound us up in a mess of trouble or em
> barrassment that even I would have had sense enough to dodge.
> But he is a good man. Maybe I was wrong sometimes to trust
> and follow him but I never was wrong to love him. (230)

As well intentioned as Gavin is, he really is no longer an antagonist of Flem's. His elaborate letter to the "F B & I Depment" turns out to be only a fantasy, an indulgence to solace a lack of will. After outlining the plan of action, an anonymous denunciation of Flem for carrying a "*commonist party Card*" (which of course is not really Flem's but Linda's), Gavin undercuts himself by beginning a new paragraph with the words, "If I only dared" (243).

Gavin's one successful action against the Snopeses comes in foiling the plotting of Orestes Snopes, who has rigged a booby trap hoping that if it works the murder of Old Man Meadowfill will be blamed on the ex-marine McKinley Smith, and that if it fails it will at least cause Meadowfill to provoke Smith to kill him in self-defense (346–47). Apparently Gavin gets help from Flem in subsequently forcing Orestes to give Essie Meadowfill the land he has disputed with her father (348). Gavin's success as detective and fighter of Snopeses undoubtedly encourages him to attempt a major role in preventing Mink from reaching Jefferson, shielding Linda from the knowledge of danger, and actually protecting Flem Snopes.

Gavin has prevented one crime; he hopes to prevent another. But his relegation to a minor role in the catastrophe appears to be due to his willingness to repeat the methods he used so successfully in the Meadowfill episode. Through his scheme to give Mink $250 on the condition that he immediately leave the state, he indirectly comes into a conflict with Mink—and is defeated. Ratliff has raised the possibility that perhaps for Mink "jest money aint enough"; Gavin has posed the problem in terms of a conventional cash interchange, certain that Mink will think he is being offered a real bargain: "He's selling Flem Snopes for these next two years, with a thousand dollars a year bonus thrown in free for the rest of his life" (370). Gavin obviously uses a methodology understood by Flem, for when he tells Flem that Mink has escaped, Flem's first question is "How much was it?" (379). The two share the belief in what Charles cynically refers to as "our native-born Jefferson right to buy or raise or dig or find anything as cheaply as cajolery or trickery or threat or force could do it, and then sell it as dear as the necessity or ignorance or timidity of the buyer would stand" (214). Gavin believes with Ratliff that "the minute a man can really believe that never again in his life will he have any use for two hundred and fifty dollars, he's done already been dead and has jest this minute found it out" (386). But Mink is such a man.

152 / *Chapter 5*

He has been the representative poor man, but in the transaction with Gavin he totally rejects the medium of money for the medium of arms. He breaks the circle, violates the financial medium by which Flem has gained the power Mink takes from him. Ironically, he is not the first in the novel to do so. For Gavin's own successful work of detection has actually been made necessary because Old Meadowfill has made such a rejection of money. Orestes Snopes misreads Meadowfill because he has "the idea, illusion, dream that mere money could move a man who for years now had become so accustomed to not having or wanting one extra dollar, that the notion of a thousand could not even tempt him" (335). In the final conflict Gavin misreads Mink in exactly the same way that Res Snopes has misread Meadowfill, and therefore he fails in his attempt to repeat his success as detective.

The other old antagonist, Ratliff, appears in *The Mansion* preeminently as the exemplar of logic and common sense, deflating Gavin's sentimental excesses:

> "Young people today dont have any [time] left because only fools under twenty-five can believe, let alone hope, that there's any left at all—for any of us, anybody alive today—"
> "It dont take much time to say We both do in front of a preacher and then pay him whatever the three of you figger it's worth." (160)

He speaks for Faulkner's sense of what it is to be *alive:* "Because anybody can see and hear and smell and feel and taste what he expected to hear and see and feel and smell and taste, and wont nothing much notice your presence nor miss your lack. So maybe when you see and feel and smell and hear and taste what you never expected to and hadn't never even imagined until that moment, maybe that's why Old Moster picked you out to be the one of the ones to be alive" (173).

Ratliff's wisdom is not passive. In chapter 13 he steps to the fore to eliminate Clarence Snopes, not only disgracing the senator but trading with Uncle Billy Varner, playing the "low-minded rascal" and "anonymous meddler" (319). In doing so Ratliff gives impetus to Gavin's contest with Orestes; and after that, he encourages Gavin not to lose heart because of the need for unceasing contests:

"You see?" his uncle said. "It's hopeless. Even when you get rid of one Snopes, there's already another one behind you even before you can turn around."

"That's right," Ratliff said serenely. "As soon as you look, you see right away it aint nothing but jest another Snopes." (349)

In the final crisis, it is Ratliff who detects Mink's escape, and Gavin sees Ratliff "alone out of Yoknapatawpha County" as the man to help him: "To be unschooled, untravelled, and to an extent unread, Ratliff had a terrifying capacity for knowledge or local information or acquaintanceship to match the need of any local crisis" (381). But Ratliff is otherwise not an important participant in the climax. His victory over Clarence is inescapably another minor-league contest, which weakens the attempt to present him as the prototype of "how to trust in God without depending on Him" (321). In *The Town* Ratliff has explained his attitude toward Flem as *curiosity*, the desire to learn: "[Y]ou keep on trying. It's because you hope to learn. You know silence is valuable because it must be, there's so little of it. So each time you think *Here's my chance to find out how a expert uses it*. Of course you wont this time and never will the next neither, that's how come he's a expert. But you can always hope you will" (297). In *The Mansion* Ratliff presents himself as only one of many antagonists hoping for small victories over Flem: "a few of us trying to trip him and still dodge outen the way when we could but getting overtromped too when we couldn't" (428). Ratliff has managed to compromise, keeping his status as antagonist by maintaining only limited objectives consistent with his role as sage.

In the process of relegation of former combatants, Gavin and Ratliff become part of the background. But they do not do so inactively. Increasingly their medium is not action but observation, the "actual" listening and watching that Ratliff insistently calls "active": "I was actively watching it, that time back there when Lawyer first got involved into Linda's career" (113).

In the abeyance of action there also comes to the fore the continuing drama of narration, with the narrators of *The Town* now joined by the extradiegetic Faulkner narrator. Here more than ever the narrative is an extreme form of the polyphonic heteroglossia of Bakhtin.[4] All the voices interpenetrate, and verisimilitude is blatantly set aside. There is a sort of postmodern disdain of pure consistency. V.K. Ratliff sounds like the Faulkner narrator with a V.K. accent:

> . . . immolating hit and her both back into virginity. (115)

> The full unchallenged cynosure you might say . . . from sometime in March to the concluding dee-neweyment . . . (117)

> . . . naming him Quick turned out to be what the feller calls jest a humorous allusion. (123)

It might be better to say that here V.K. Ratliff is "doing" the Faulkner narrator. We also have the narrator doing V.K. doing Gavin, and doing Charles doing V.K. The narrator must tell us who is the source and who is talking, because it is no longer obvious: "This is Charles telling it" (308).

Just as if to make sure we know that moves never cease, at the very end of *The Mansion* Faulkner introduces a new struggle and a new actor.[5] The drama of the last pages is the drama of "What the Ground Can Do."

> . . . the ground itself never let a man forget it was there waiting, pulling gently and without no hurry at him between every step, saying, Come on, lay down; I aint going to hurt you. Jest lay down. (434)

> . . . he was free now, he could afford to risk it; to show how much he dared risk it, he could even close his eyes, give it all the chance it wanted; whereupon as if believing he really was asleep, it gradually went to work a little harder, easy of course, not to really disturb him: just harder, increasing. (435)

> But he could risk it, he even felt like giving it a fair active chance just to show him, prove what it could do if it wanted to try. And in fact, as soon as he thought that, it seemed to him he could feel the Mink Snopes that had had to spend so much of his life just having unnecessary bother and trouble, beginning to creep, seep, flow easy as sleeping. (435)

The ground makes the final move.

The Mansion presents at last the final will, the will that *is* comparable to Flem. The irony is that the comparable will is a composite will. The

ending of *The Mansion,* an ironic complication to the apparent predictions of the novel, is also an ironic completion to the seemingly linear
pattern of conflicting wills in the trilogy. The final will is not one will but
the will of a community of people who have nothing in common. *The
Mansion* thus preserves the whole series of conflicting wills and is both a
conclusion and a summation of the pattern of the whole trilogy.

~

The surprise in the ending requires a certain amount of ambiguity in
characterization. But this is appropriate, given the form of the novel's
plot, for the scarcity of events in the novel virtually requires that a large
part of the novel be a contemplation of expository material—that is, of
characters in the static situation that exists prior to the major event.
There are throughout the text moments of prediction, unverifiable and of
different degrees of specificity: I had to kill Flem; it's going to be worse
than that; she's just dangerous. What we call suspense is a form of waiting. Into the temporal gaps created between these predictions, the text
pours a universe of other concerns, preoccupations. One is the reimagining of known characters—Mink, Linda, even Montgomery Ward Snopes.
The effect is to add to the question "What will he/she do?" the additional
question "What will it mean when he/she does it?" Is Mink more than a
cold-blooded killer, and if so, does that change the meaning of any killing
he may turn out to do? More importantly, is Linda's act in getting Mink
released a new form of "tilting" (at windmills), the latest in a series of
futile idealistic challenges of social authority (351)? Does she not know
that what she is doing is potentially the same thing as killing her father?
While we wait we have to think about this, and much of what the text
leaves us to think about in that temporal gap is a series of ambiguous
metaphors: a plume, a collapsed plume, a mechanical duck's quack. These
create not so much suspense as uncertainty. If we are not sure who the
actor really is, we have to have some anxiety about understanding the act
that actor may become engaged in, however much foreshadowing there
may have been. Linda's role in Flem's murder is difficult to predict not
only because we have been uncertain how to react to the cryptic warnings
but also because her character has always been deeply ambiguous. The
myriad rhetorical effects that sway us one way and the other complicate
our sense of Linda's character far more thoroughly than Ratliff's few
warnings of doom.

Descriptive imagery is only one of the more overt of the many ways our attitude toward character is controlled, but what is surprising about the imagery that describes Linda is how often it tends toward the ominous and the sinister. In *The Town*, Linda is first described as walking "exactly like a pointer dog walks just before it freezes onto the birds" (131). The image captures the idea of Linda's slenderness and her headlong, oblivious way of walking straight forward. But the implications of the image may not be pleasant, as Charles implies by breaking off the simile without voicing the consequences to the victims: "She walks like a pointer. . . . I mean, a pointer that's just—" (*T* 131). In *The Mansion* she becomes "something that wouldn't have no end to its appetite" (163). Her voice is the "dry harsh quacking voice that deaf people learn to use" (199). It might seem hard to believe that Faulkner would use the consequence of a physical handicap as an image of insensitivity. But as Charles describes her the voice does seem to make Linda not only inhuman but mechanical: "It was still the duck's voice: dry, lifeless, dead. That was it: dead. There was no passion, no heat in it; and, what was worse, no hope" (217). Even Gavin concedes the lifelessness, and describes the eyes as looking "out of, across, something—abyss, darkness" (238). Gavin is shocked when Linda offers herself to him using a four-letter word, and the unloveliness of the voice seems appropriate to the explicitness of the word:

> "But you can   me," she said. That's right. She used the explicit word, speaking the hard brutal guttural in the quacking duck's voice. That had been our problem as soon as we undertook the voice lessons: the tone, to soften the voice which she herself couldn't hear. (238)

> Then I wrote . . . *what shocks is that all that magic passion excitement be summed up & dismissed in that one bald unlovely sound* (239)

Gavin generously thinks of the voice as simply a physical problem; the reader cannot be sure that it does not mirror some deeper deadness. The deafness permits lofty pity but also strongly pejorative imagery. Charles entertains himself with the ambiguity, within one sentence calling Linda both "absolved of mundanity" and "castrate of sound" (211).

The white streak in Linda's hair is like a knight's plume, and Charles thinks of it as "really splendid" (350). But it is a *collapsed* plume: "a collapsed plume lying flat athwart her skull instead of cresting upward first then back and over." The word partly fits the notion of the obsolescence of knighthood in the postwar world, but it also suggests a more pervasive lack of valor. The narrator appears to be trying to rehabilitate the adjective when he says the plume is "collapsed in gallantry" (351). But the phrase could also be read to mean that Linda's gallantry itself has collapsed.

A similar lingering ominousness must be noted in Charles Mallison's speculations on the sexuality hidden beneath Linda's surface frigidity. Charles does wisecrack that the tall ones can surprise you when you get the clothes off. But such suggestive generalizations give way to his sense of something in Linda he wants nothing to do with:

> . . . not her for him, but rather not him for her: a lot more might still happen to him in his life yet (he hoped) but removing that particular skirt wouldn't be one even if when you got the clothes off the too tall too thin ones sometimes they surprised you. And just as well; evidently his soul or whatever it was had improved some in the three years and a bit; anyway he knew now that if such had been his fate to get this particular one off, what would happen to him might, probably would, have several names but none of them would be surprise. (352)

Charles later speculates that perhaps Gavin once actually has got the clothes off "and couldn't stand it, bear it, and ran, fled back those eighteen or twenty years to Melisandre Backus (that used to be), where he would be safe. . . . A little of terror maybe at how close the escape had been, but mainly relief that it had been escape under any condition, on any terms" (359). It is in this fashion, speculating almost idly on the proper word—surprise, relief, terror—to describe the result of getting involved with Linda, that Charles leads up to his most intemperate and frightening sexual metaphor, the image of man's fear of the spider:

> You know: the spider lover wise enough with age or cagey enough with experience or maybe just quick enough to spook from sheer timid instinct, to sense, anticipate, that initial tender caressing probe of the proboscis or suction tube or whatever it is his gal uses to empty him of his blood too while all he thinks he is risking is his semen; and leap, fling himself free, losing of course the

semen and most of the rest of his insides too in the same what he thought at first was just peaceful orgasm, but at least keeping his husk, his sac, his life. (360)

It must be admitted that Charles *is* attracted to Linda. He seems to show his mixed motives for viewing her pejoratively and for trying to shock his uncle when he tacitly admits that he could not succeed with Linda sexually. In chiding his nephew's cruel and intemperate language, Gavin definitely gets the better of Chick, but his own sentimental defense of Linda does not completely negate Chick's not-disinterested perceptions:

"Is it all right with you if I try to lay her?" His uncle didn't move. Then he closed the brief and sat back in the chair.

"Certainly," he said.

"So you think I cant," Charles said.

"I know you cant," his uncle said. He added quickly: "Dont grieve; it's not you. Just despair if you like. It's not anybody."

"So you know why," Charles said. (353)

"She's frigid."

"Well, that's as good a Freudian term as another to cover chastity or discretion," his uncle said. . . .

So it was more than that, and his uncle was not going to tell him. And his uncle had used the word "discretion" also to cover something he had not said. (354)

Linda's sexuality is devalued by several comparisons to Eula. At first Linda is definitely seen as a decline from her magnificent mother. In *The Town* Charles Mallison says he must "grieve because her daughter didn't have whatever it was that she had" (74). In *The Mansion* he repeats that "Linda didn't have that quality; that one was not transferable. So all that remained for her and Gavin was continence. To put it crudely, morality" (212). But within pages he is contradicting himself: "evidently it was transferable" (219). To this he attributes the fact that "Barton Kohl saw her once when she was nineteen years old, and look where he was now." He thinks he had better take Gavin aside and say, "Look here, young man. I know how dishonorable your intentions are." This must be considered a confession of his own sexual attraction. But evidently the favorable comparison to Eula is intended also to express the dangerous effect Linda can have on men. The only time Linda is connected to the Helen imagery associated with Eula is in Charles's spider image, where Gavin is seen as a less adroit spider lover than Paris and De Spain, "assuming that whatever made Helen was transferable or anyway inheritable" (360). Linda seems to have been belatedly elevated to Eula's sexual stature only out of Charles's fear, only to share with her mother the role of dangerous and emasculatory spider. Linda herself seeks to fill the common role with her mother when she offers herself to Gavin and reminds him that Eula once did the same: "That word you didn't like. My mother said that to you once too, didn't she" (241). Gavin does not answer directly, but Linda's statement is an invitation to the reader to remember the earlier scene, in chapter 5 of *The Town* (88–96). Linda has clearly misread her mother's character. For all her lack of subterfuge and her refusal to overvalue sex, Eula is never crude. Her pity for Gavin is not, like Linda's, harshly expressed. The answer is that Eula did not use "that word."

Linda's admirers have preferred to ignore or excuse the invidious imagery and the unfavorable comparisons. She has been described as a "natural aristocrat," an ideal coincidence of Faulkner's authorial ideology and "social vision" (Railey 165, 160–61), and as a "newly configured space of desire, autonomy, and freedom" (Kang 22).[6] Gavin, for once, does not sentimentalize. He does not spare himself the harshest words, primarily because he is characteristically hard on himself. He tells Ratliff he has just committed murder, and though Ratliff acts unimpressed, he does agree: "'Oh, that,' Ratliff said. 'I decided some time back that maybe the only thing that would make you safe to have around would be for somebody to marry you. That never worked but at least you're all right now. As you jest said, you finally committed a murder. What else is there beyond that for anybody to think up for you to do?'" (427). Gavin does not delude himself about Linda either. Speaking from Gavin's point of view, the narrator sees that her eyes are "not secret, not tender, perhaps not even gentle"; Gavin notes the possibility that "someday perhaps he would remember that they had never been really tender even" (424). He recognizes "the fact that she had ordered the car from New York or London or wherever it came from, the moment she knew for sure he could get Mink the pardon" (425). But he also recognizes that "she believed she had been in love with him all her life" (425), implying his continuing ability to credit her good intentions toward him, though she might be mistaken even about her belief. Ultimately Gavin accepts everything, which can only include love by including much else also. He accepts Linda, like her eyes, from a position of total knowledge: "the dark blue eyes that whether they were gentle or not or tender or not or really candid or not, it didn't matter" (425). We are guided to make the same complicated response to Linda that Ratliff and Gavin make, a knowledgeable response based on a long period of evaluation of quite contradictory effects.

The suspension of judgment is part of the general tone of the last pages of the novel, the saddened recognition "So this is what it all come down to" (428). Gavin does not judge Mink either, and goes to take him money out of pity, knowing that, as Ratliff says, "He's free now. He wont never have to kill nobody else in all his life" (432). Gavin has not "troubled to rationalize his decision of the amount" (433); clearly neither has he bothered to rationalize his original decision to take the money in the first place. Ratliff's hope that there will be no more Eula Varners implies also that, for these two old veterans, there can be no more major campaigns: "I dont know if she's already got a daughter stashed out somewhere, or if she jest aint got around to one yet. But when she does I jest hope for Old Lang Zynes's sake she dont never bring it back to Jefferson. You done already been through two Eula Varners and I dont think you can stand another one" (434). When Gavin, in the car with Ratliff, begins to struggle against his earlier lucidity, it is clearly as a sort of pity for Gavin, and not as a serious exoneration of Linda, that Ratliff creates the myth of the rebuke Eula would have given Linda if she had gone to heaven without "reveng[ing] me and my love" (431). If Ratliff is willing to end with a fantasy, it is not from a desire to defend Linda, but rather from a sense that all conflicts have ceased, that the opposing forces have canceled each other, that an epoch of striving is over. For once, Faulkner encourages a total relaxation of tensions, a belief that the past *is* past.

Our knowledgeable suspension of judgment on Linda is guided by rhetorical effects, but of course imagery does not exist in a vacuum. Our contemplation of Linda and other characters takes place through the "non-events" of the narrative episodes that are told as exposition, the preparation and orientation of characters toward the main event. These episodes can rarely be said to constitute "events." The experiences they detail do not distract the main characters from their central preoccupations, and each main character's will remains stable *relative* to the other major characters. But the narrative intricacies of these episodes may call forth willed interchanges between the characters they do contain. Mink, for instance, is fixed in relation to Flem (and Linda), but his financial situation on his picaresque journey forces him into significant relations with Goodyhay—his own decision not to steal Goodyhay's pistol, Goodyhay's charity in replacing Mink's stolen ten dollars. Simply as revelations of the central characters these uneventful expository episodes receive a large part of our attention; it is essential that they carry and preserve us until we arrive at the central event.

It is unsettling, then, that Faulkner does seem to belabor excessively the more overtly expository events, those which derive from his other novels. Faulkner means well in attempting to provide enough exposition for readers who have not read the earlier volumes, who begin the trilogy with *The Mansion*. But he inevitably creates difficulties for readers who have followed the chronicle from the beginning. Some compromise seems necessary between exposition and repetition. In *The Mansion* there is far more repetition than in *The Town*. The refurbished summary of past actions is never quite new enough to justify its length to old readers; nor is it quite long enough to disguise its role as summary from new ones. Chapters 3 (on Montgomery Ward) and 6 (on Eula and the rise of Flem) are almost completely old material, though chapter 6 is divertingly told by Ratliff as conjecture. Several other chapters have capsule summaries of past events, such as the story of the Snopes Indians (298); some of these are not from the trilogy, such as the story of "Knight's Gambit" (255) and the story of *Sartoris* (188–92).

As the novel marks time on the way to its major event, there is a fair amount of new narrative material, both filling out old stories (the stories of Mink and Montgomery Ward) and developing new episodes (the elimination of Clarence and Orestes Snopes). The subtly disconcerting thing about the novel is the failure of invention in much of this new material, the insistent repetition of narrative *motifs* from many earlier novels, including the earlier novels of the trilogy. Mink's new character as a simple convict who simply wants to abide by the rules recalls the tall convict of the "Old Man" sequences of *The Wild Palms*. His desire to pay off his debt to Houston by working at night repeats Jewel Bundren's night labor in *As I Lay Dying*—Jewel works to earn a horse, Mink to regain a cow. Orestes Snopes's use of a hog to intimidate and anger Old Meadowfill seems a repetition of I.O. Snopes's similar animal intimidation in the Mule in the Yard episode of *The Town* (which itself has much in common with the stampede sequence of the Spotted Horses episode of *The Hamlet*). The reappearance of Virgil Snopes and Fonzo Winbush is the direct repetition not of a motif but of an actual narrative, the rubes-in-the-whorehouse sequence of *Sanctuary*. The narrative is continued and expanded, but it suffers from the derivativeness of much of the "new" narrative of *The Mansion*. Only with Jason Compson does Faulkner successfully introduce both an old character and a new story—the account of Jason's attempt to sell the golf course to Flem for an airfield.

The contemplations of character that depend on the following of narrative incidents are inevitably handicapped by the lack of inventiveness in some of the minor expository episodes. But Faulkner does manage a major effort in his treatment of characters. The exposition of *The Mansion* contains not only simple revelation of character but also substantial *reconsideration* of at least one major character. As the pace of the trilogy slows at the end, the final volume emphasizes the contemplation through time of the depth and pliability of characters, including above all their complex ability to win our compassion.

Perceiving the emphasis Faulkner places on events, many of his readers have assumed that such pliability is precisely what Faulkner has denied himself. André Malraux deduces from Faulkner's plots both a general method of composition and a consequent structural strain: "I should not be surprised if he often thought out his scenes before imagining his characters, if the work were, in his eyes, not a story whose unfolding determined tragic situations, but contrarily that the plot was created from the dramatic opposition or crushing of unknown characters, and imagination merely served to bring forth characters for this preconceived situation" (273). Faulkner essentially acknowledged the validity of Malraux's intuition about his genetic method, yet he affirmed his ability to *find* a character who would *not* be crushed by the necessity of performing the action: "There's always a moment in experience—a thought—an incident—that's there. Then all I do is work up to that moment. I figure what must have happened before to lead people to that particular moment, and I work away from it, finding out how people act after that moment" (*Lion* 220). He also expressed faith in the pliability of human beings, affirming it as the last stage of maturity: "There is the first stage . . . when you believe everything and everybody is good. Then there is the second, cynical stage when you believe that no one is good. Then at last you realize that everyone is capable of almost anything—heroism or cowardice, tenderness or cruelty" (*Lion* 32). Here his human experience undoubtedly joined with his experience as a writer, for he frequently testified to the freedom his own characters exacted from him: "Because with me there is always a point in the book where the characters themselves rise up and take charge and finish the job—say somewhere about page 275. Of course, I don't know what would happen if I finished the book on page 274" (*Lion* 244); "When the book is finished, that character is not done, he still is going on at some new devilment that sooner or later I will find out about and write about" (Gwynn and Blotner 78); "They teach [the writer], they surprise him, they teach him things that he didn't know, they do things and suddenly he says to himself, Why yes, that is true, that is so" (Gwynn and Blotner 96).

Malraux's criticism implies an inherent difficulty in any emphasis on events, particularly complex ones; more immediately it is an indictment of the writer's forcing of the individual action at the expense of the characters. Yet Faulkner's multiple published versions of any given story sometimes give evidence of his ability to maintain one event while plausibly affecting us in a variety of ways about the characters who undergo that event. Ratliff in *The Hamlet* and his predecessor Suratt in "Lizards in Jamshyd's Courtyard" both fall prey to a salted gold mine, but Suratt's relation to us and to his community is much more tenuous, his fall into greed more predictable and less frightening. He is thus for all practical purposes a different character. The narrator observes dispassionately of Suratt that "He was believed to be well fixed" (*Uncollected Stories* 138). The narrator more explicitly guides our feelings in showing Suratt "once a year" telling himself again that the gold is "bound to be there": "Then he would drive on . . . , having carried away with him something of that ancient air, that old splendor, confusing it though he did with the fleshly gratifications, the wherewith to possess them, in his peasant's mind" (140–41). This is not Ratliff. Faulkner also has Suratt lie in the bushes and watch Flem for two nights before alerting Vernon and Henry Armstid:

> "Ain't I watched him?" Suratt said. "Ain't I laid here in these weeds two nights now and watched him come out here and dig?" (142)

. . . They glared at each other, their faces strained with sleep-
lessness and weariness and lust. It was Suratt's fourth night without having removed his clothes; Vernon's and Henry's second. (144)

In *The Hamlet,* Ratliff does not initiate the scheme but is lured into it by
Henry Armstid (384).

The I.O. Snopes in "Mule in the Yard" (1934) is missing the primary
characteristic of the I.O. in *The Hamlet* (1940), namely the profusion of
garbled proverbs. In order to accommodate one version of the character
to another, Faulkner must use subterfuge, having Ratliff explain why I.O.
is talking out of character: "Ratliff said he didn't sound like I.O. Snopes
anyway because whenever I.O. talked what he said was so full of mixed-
up proverbs that you stayed so busy trying to unravel just which of two
or three proverbs he had jumbled together that you couldn't even tell just
exactly what lie he had told you until it was already too late. But right
now Ratliff said he was too busy to have time for even proverbs, let alone
lies" (*T* 242). Such subterfuge is part of the craft Faulkner referred to
when he said that the material in *The Town* was "reworked around the
joints, you might say, the suture, to make it join and not show a rough
place" (Gwynn and Blotner 120).

We have noted that Faulkner was careful to forestall any impression
of determinism, the forcing of character, within *The Mansion.* But *The
Mansion* also makes clear Faulkner's use of the trilogy *as a whole* to develop, and even reconsider or reconceive, his human actors. The mere
length of the chronicle makes possible a gradual change and growth in
character. Faulkner creates such a growth for Eula from the vegetable
adolescent to the passionate adulteress to the self-sacrificing mother. He
also later offered an interpretation of Eula's offer of herself to Gavin as
an acquired compassion: "By that time she had learned something of
compassion for people through her determination to protect that girl,
and to see someone that anguished over the need for a particular woman
to her seemed foolish. That hers was more of a Hellenic attitude. That
wasn't important enough to be frustrated about, and if that was going to
make him feel any better she was perfectly willing to help him" (Gwynn
and Blotner 118). In the later volumes of the trilogy, a definite development takes place in Charles Mallison. Charles comes more and more to
ape his uncle, but with a cynicism that Gavin rebukes:

"I'm sorry," I said.

"Dont be," he said. "Just remember it. Dont ever waste time re-gretting errors. Just dont forget them." (230–31)

Charles becomes so talkative that Gavin must say "Hush and let me talk awhile now" (207). Yet for all his lack of tact, Charles does not duplicate Gavin's folly. Ratliff explicitly calls his attention to the process of matur-ing he is undergoing: "Someday you're going to outgrow him" (219).

But Faulkner uses the length of the chronicle to show more than de-velopment. He is able to exploit the retelling of stories as a means of correcting his own misunderstanding of his characters, those forcings of character of which he may have in fact been guilty. For the reader requires some sense of the stability of character, as W. J. Harvey explains: "Our sense of identity is in part defined by the *kind* of choices we have made in the past. It is on the basis of such history that we make predictions of the form, 'He is the sort of chap who will do such-and-such'" (131). Any readjustments or expansions of the conception of a character must pro-ceed from some original coherence. The character, as William H. Gass says, "must be unique, entirely himself, as if he had a self to be. He is required, in fact, to act *in character,* like a cat in a sack" (37).

The story of Mink Snopes's marriage in *The Hamlet* (271–74) does seem out of character, and Faulkner allows the episode to drop quietly out of the subsequent volumes of the trilogy. It is difficult to accept such a totally extraordinary event as marriage to "not a nympholept but the con-fident lord of a harem" (*H* 272), a woman who has satisfied herself with a hundred convicts. Faulkner convincingly shows how a murder draws Mink inevitably into its bizarre consequences; but the sexual encounter, let alone the marriage, seems a random and gratuitous event. It seems improbable that, even given this grotesque situation, such a man as Mink would accept such a tainted woman as his wife. Faulkner himself permits this objection on sociological grounds by his observation: "He had been bred by generations to believe invincibly that to every man, whatever his past actions, whatever depths he might have reached, there was reserved one virgin, at least for him to marry; one maidenhead, if only for him to deflower and destroy" (*H* 272). Faulkner attempts to forestall any objec-tions on these grounds by emphasizing the extraordinary nature of the event, the bizarre compulsion by which Mink becomes addicted to the "opium" (*H* 273) of the woman's sexuality. But the strategy fails to dispose of the one otherwise infrangible element of Mink's personality: his ruthless pride. Pride keeps Mink's consciousness fierce, and that fierceness is nowhere more evident than in his dealings with his wife, whom he is shown threatening or beating almost as a reflex action. Nor does the woman in her capacity as Mink's wife show any sign of "the habit of success—that perfect marriage of will and ability with a single undiffused object" which we are asked to believe she has originally shown (*H* 272). The only thing in common with her old character is the readiness with which she presumably prostitutes herself. We must conclude that her character is a forced attempt by Faulkner to make us accept an example of obsessed male sexuality confronted by an abstract female sexuality that is voracious but ultimately indifferent, detached, even utilitarian. In *The Mansion,* where Mink is not only more sympathetic but also much more the representative of a class, he is no more tormented by sex than by lust for money. The wife who appears in *The Mansion* is a more conventional and less important annoyance, nagging and whining because Mink goes out shooting but does not bring back a rabbit (38–39). Faulkner has allowed a past extravagance to be forgotten. He begins to show the pliability of his conception of Mink by doing justice to the basic stability of the character.

Faulkner also uses his retellings as a means of comprehensively re-seeing his characters, of showing his own growth in understanding major events. Events need not be deleted, as is the "nympholept" episode, for the character to be reconsidered. In practice, this means a growing sense of compassion and sympathy for even his most vicious characters. Such reconsideration is first undertaken sentimentally by Gavin Stevens in chapter 17 of *The Town* and is roundly discredited by both Ratliff and the sequence of events. In his early review of the novel, Stephen Marcus too denounces Gavin Stevens's interpretation of Flem: "By apologizing for or denying their animality, he not only misunderstands the Snopeses but dehumanizes them too. It is this misunderstanding and dehumanization that Ratliff tries to withstand, insisting that Flem's motives will not be understood if they are sociologized, that his desire for respectability is simply another form of his desire for power" (390). Somehow, though, while Marcus notes Ratliff's resistance of Stevens, he mysteriously suggests that Stevens somehow demonstrates "the central imbalance in Faulkner's art." Surely Faulkner does not endorse the sentimentality of

Stevens. Stevens's rhetoric is clearly set aside and contrasted with the more knowledgeable and restrained near-pity of Eula, Flem's last major antagonist in the novel. Ironically, Eula warns Gavin against pity on the grounds that pity would *hurt* Flem: "He's—what's the word?—impotent. He's always been. Maybe that's why, one of the reasons. You see? You've got to be careful or you'll have to pity him. You'll have to. He couldn't bear that, and it's no use to hurt people if you dont get anything for it. Because he couldn't bear being pitied" (*T* 331). Eula is just discovering that "people are really kind" (*T* 329), and her warning against sentimentality is her own act of kindness to her antagonist, a warning against pity that in itself enacts a more encompassing pity. Eula's awareness does not prevent her resoluteness for death, a sacrifice designed not to thwart Flem but to protect Linda. Faulkner clearly reinforces the substance of her discovery when he has Charles Mallison echo her words: "Because I know now that people really are kind, they really are; there are lots of times when they stop hurting one another not just when they want to keep on hurting but even when they have to" (*T* 340). Gavin, too, has been feeling in practice the substance of Eula's message, when he feels shame at having "spoiled supper and ruined sleep" for old Mr. Garraway by defending Eula and De Spain: "the old man who in his fashion, in a lot of people's fashion, really was a kindly old man who never in his life wittingly or unwittingly harmed anyone black or white, not serious harm" (*T* 315). Flem successfully resists pity by reaffirming, in his gratuitous cruelty, his own personal viciousness. But the sense of the basic kindness of people causes *The Town* to end on a general note not of sentimentality but of a very chastened pity.

Pity is a major element in the tone of *The Mansion* as well. The expression "son of a bitch" becomes through repetition not a curse but an irreverent refrain of general sadness, of sardonic human sympathy. Montgomery Ward Snopes explains his present to Mink as a desire "to make a present of forty dollars to the poorest son of a bitch I can find" (79). Mink is thus presented as only the extreme case of a general condition, and Reba later makes the sentiment explicit:

"The poor son of a bitch," she said.
    "Which one are you talking about now?"
    "Both of them," she said. "All of us. Every one of us. The poor son of a bitches." (82)

Montgomery Ward later proudly affirms his membership in mankind after seeing Mink's dignity and valor when betrayed: "I was proud, not just to be kin to him but of belonging to what Reba called all of us poor son of a bitches" (85). Then Montgomery Ward uses the expression in its more conventional, pejorative sense to describe his family; but the term inevitably carries even for Snopeses much of the pitying tone it has had in the preceding usages, particularly when Montgomery Ward emphasizes how each Snopes actually *fails* at being a supervillain:

> *Every Snopes will make it his private and personal aim to have the whole world recognize him as THE son of a bitch's son of a bitch.*
> But we never do it. We never make it. The best we ever do is to be just another Snopes son of a bitch. (87)

The phrase appears twice in the prayers of the preacher Goodyhay, with his "coldly seething desert-hermit's eyes" (271, 282). Inevitably, it is applied to Flem as well, when Ratliff points out the fear, the loneliness, and the basic weariness of the bank president in his role of materialist automaton: "The pore son of a bitch over yonder in that bank vault counting his money because that's the one place on earth Mink Snopes cant reach him in, and long as he's got to stay in it he might as well count money to be doing something, have something to do" (374). Ratliff seems genuinely sad after Flem's death that "this is what it all come down to. All the ramshacking and foreclosing and grabbling and snatching, doing it by gentle underhand when he could but by honest hard trompling when he had to" (428). In suspending judgment, Ratliff and Stevens return to this well-established refrain of the novel:

> "So maybe there's even a moral in it somewhere, if you jest knowed where to look."
> "There aren't any morals," Stevens said. "People just do the best they can."
> "The pore sons of bitches," Ratliff said.
> "The poor sons of bitches," Stevens said. "Drive on. Pick it up."
> (429)

> " . . . Yes!" Stevens said. "The poor sons of bitches that have to cause all the grief and anguish they have to cause! Drive on!" (430)

The most thoroughgoing single reconsideration of *The Mansion* is Faulkner's treatment of Mink, the "only mean Snopes" (*T* 79).[7] Compassion for Mink is not completely new. In *The Hamlet* Faulkner quite frequently depicts Mink's poverty:

> . . . the paintless two-room cabin with an open hallway between and a lean-to kitchen, which was not his, on which he paid rent but not taxes, paying almost as much in rent in one year as the house had cost to build; not old, yet the roof of which already leaked and the weather-stripping had already begun to rot away from the wall planks and which was just like the one he had been born in which had not belonged to his father either, and just like the one he would die in if he died indoors . . . (*H* 251)

> . . . the yellow and stunted stand of his corn, yellow and stunted because he had had no money to buy fertilizer to put beneath it and owned neither the stock nor the tools to work it properly with and had had no one to help him with what he did own . . . (*H* 252)

Mink is allowed also to express his inner anger at "that conspiracy to frustrate and outrage his rights as a man and his feelings as a sentient creature" (*H* 251). But even in the moments of greatest privilege Faulkner occasionally manages significant dissociations from Mink's point of view, implying that though Mink thinks one thing the opposite might be true: "Although he paid rent on this one *he was unalterably convinced* that his cousin owned it and he knew that this was as near as he would ever come to owning the roof over his head" (*H* 251–52, emphasis added). Mink is in *The Hamlet* beset by one of even less dignity than he—his cousin Lump, who blames him for not having robbed Houston's body. But significantly, Lump is *not* Mink's victim, so that even if we sympathize with him in his desire to be free of Lump, this sympathy does not really change our attitude toward the murder. Furthermore, there is at last a vicious end to Mink's forbearance, as he twice strikes Lump down; and the narrator expresses even the forbearance as a lapse from Mink's usual *ruthlessness:* "It was as though . . . ruthlessness likewise had repudiated the disciple who had flagged for a moment in ruthlessness; that it was that humanity which had caused him to waste three hours in hope that the cousin would tire and go away instead of striking the other over the head . . . , which had brought him to this" (*H* 287). Though Faulkner emphasizes Mink's deprivation, he also notes that a "negro" with a cabin "smaller and shabbier than his" has raised corn "better than his" (*H* 286).

The end of the Hound episode moves away from the privileged point of view of most of the chapter. There is no explanation of any thought processes in the pages before Mink's attempted suicide (*H* 292–94). In the jail his voice erupts out of a mental vacuum: "I was all right . . . until it started coming to pieces. I could have handled that dog. . . . But the son of a bitch started coming to pieces on me" (*H* 296). What the voice says is so misguided, so near insanity, as to prevent any understanding or pity. Mink has become not only just another prisoner, but one whose mind we cannot follow anymore. The one private thought we have from him in the jail is a stock response so inadequate to the situation as to be grotesque: "Are they going to feed them niggers before they do a white man? he thought" (*H* 296).

In *The Mansion* the compassion for Mink is not undercut, is allowed to contribute a greater part of our full response. The key to the revaluation is the first chapter, the murder of Houston. Faulkner redeems the character of Mink at its seemingly most indefensible, his commission of a vicious murder. But Faulkner does not intend to sentimentalize his character. At first Mink appears as almost gratuitously coarse: thinking of the hullabaloo Eula has caused since "the first hair on her bump"; envying Flem's "right to fumble his hand every time the notion struck him under that dress that rutted a man just thinking even about somebody else's hand doing it"; imagining a flock of women as "trading" with a hungry preacher, "filling his hole in payment for getting theirs plugged" (4, 5). He is also ludicrously self-righteous, getting angry at his victim because of the "injury which Jack Houston in the very act of dying, had done him: compelled him, Mink, to kill him at a time when the only person who had the power to save him . . . was a thousand miles away; and this time it was an irreparable injury because in the very act of committing it, Houston had escaped forever all retribution for it" (5). We are familiar with the outrageous form Mink's desire for his rights can take, the absurdity of Mink's thought processes. But in *The Mansion* Faulkner uncovers, behind the sense of outraged rights, a new and more fundamental premise, Mink's actual belief in justice: "He meant, simply, that *them—*

they—it, whichever and whatever you wanted to call it, who represented a simple fundamental justice and equity in human affairs, or else a man might just as well quit; the *they, them, it,* call them what you like, which simply would not, could not harass and harry a man forever without some day, at some moment, letting him get his own just and equal licks back in return" (6). The *belief* in the hostile integrity of Them issues in behavior that may be in radical contrast to the sense of outraged rights, the mere *desire* for justice. This belief entails a scrupulosity alien to Mink in *The Hamlet,* a willingness to abide by the rules of conduct, a conviction that retaliation comes only after the limits of human endurance. So strongly does Mink believe in fundamental justice that he refuses human charity, insisting on abiding by the letter of a court judgment which he believes to be profoundly unjust. When Will Varner and Jack Houston attempt to give him the cow or buy the cow, merely to prevent trouble, he refuses in a "gentle" voice: "That cow's under a court judgment. I cant accept it until that judgment is satisfied" (20). The acceptance of any extralegal kindness would be a violation of the rules of his forbearance: "Because he knew the trick of it . . . that a man can bear anything by simply and calmly refusing to accept it, be reconciled to it, give up to it. . . . Because patience was his pride too: never to be reconciled since by this means he could beat Them; They might be stronger for a moment than he but nobody, no man, no nothing could wait longer than he could wait when nothing else but waiting would do, would work, would serve him" (21–22). Faulkner thus shows that from a certain point of view Mink can be shown to be actually a restrained and disciplined character. In fact Mink recognizes that rage is his greatest worry: "[They] could beat him only by catching him off balance and so topple him back into that condition of furious blind earless rage where he had no sense" (24).

At the same time Faulkner shows the antagonizing behavior of Mink's victim. Mink's forbearance toward Houston before the murder changes the character of the murder as his brief forbearance toward Lump could not. Houston's lack of "decency" in buying another stallion just like the one that killed his wife (7), and his arrogance in running Mink off the road (8), infuriate Mink long before the incident of the cow. Mink's attempt to get revenge by getting his cow wintered for free is actually an attempt to secure justice in a "prolonged and passive" way (12). Houston is identified with the forces of ultimate power in the universe, the powers that are trying the limits of Mink's endurance: "And They—Houston—were still watching him" (30).

So Mink is in a sense himself a victim, and it is in this chapter that Faulkner begins the imagery of Mink as a child: "as forlorn and defenseless as a child" (36). Houston's personal arrogance can be seen also as the arrogance of riches, so that Mink becomes a prototype of a poorer class: "not being a rich man like Houston but only an independent one, asking no favors of any man, paying his own way" (8). In the words he would like to say to Houston as he kills him, Mink stands up for himself and also for all poor men: "All you rich folks has got to stick together or else maybe some day the ones that aint rich might take a notion to raise up and take hit away from you" (39). No longer a man constitutionally alien and alone, Mink is now seen as having been at one point capable of going to Memphis with "companions of his age and sex" (33). A shift in the point of view, a filling in of new but not incompatible details, makes it possible to see Mink compassionately as both victim and spokesman for other victims. These new effects from chapter 1 are accentuated throughout the novel. Mink continues to be representative of "people of his kind," people who are owned and held in perpetual "thralldom" by "the land, the earth itself" (91). And he continues to be victimized, not only "sold" (85) by Flem and Montgomery Ward but cheated by a grocery clerk (259–63) and robbed by a fellow worker (273).

In his compassionate willingness to see complexities in Mink, Faulkner occasionally does not resist the temptation to change the unpleasant facts of Mink's behavior in *The Hamlet*. Mink's sense of dignity and his representative role lead Faulkner to depict Mink as a hardworking farmer. *The Mansion* shows for the first time Mink at labor. The new Mink is not a man of lazy subterfuge but a man willing to work around the clock, beyond human endurance (21). Therefore, Faulkner now allows him to have the best corn anywhere. He notices "the planted fields standing strongly with corn and cotton, some of it almost as good as his own small patches (obviously the people who planted these had not had the leisure and peace he had thought he had to sow in)" (26). Here Faulkner does not expand the character but instead blatantly changes him. A much subtler modulation is effected in Mink's treatment of his wife. Three times in *The Hamlet* Mink either beats his wife or offers convincingly to do so (*H* 85, 253, 276). In *The Mansion* Faulkner takes the edge off this viciousness. Only his language is now "nasty":

. . . using the quick hard unmannered word when she said, "Where you going? I thought Jack Houston warned you,"— adding, not for the crudeness but because she too would not let him alone:

"Lessen of course you will step outside and do it for me." (24)

But Mink does not strike his wife in *The Mansion*—even though he does raise the possibility: "[H]is wife and daughters were at the table, which at least saved argument, the necessity to curse them silent or perhaps even to have actually to strike, hit his wife, in order to go to the hearth and dig out the loose brick and take from the snuff tin behind it the single five-dollar bill" (30). The Mink of *The Mansion* is actually better behaved in every way, but here the threat of outbursts of cruelty remains present.

In fact, considering the growth of sympathy for Mink, it is surprising how successfully Faulkner controls and balances our judgments of the events of chapter 1. Houston and Varner do not do everything possible, but they do try to forestall trouble. Having won his symbolic legal victory and having presumably crushed Mink's pride by making him dig post holes for three days, Houston actually offers Mink $18.75 for the cow, more than it was worth when he began to feed it (18). Varner, "afraid for the peace and quiet of the community which he held in his iron usurious hand" (19), buys the cow from Houston and tries to *give* it to Mink (20). The curious point in Houston's behavior, however, comes after Mink has worked off the full court judgment. Thinking to get an extra night's feed out of Houston, Mink leaves the cow in Houston's lot until morning. When he goes to collect the cow in the morning, Houston tells him about the one-dollar pound fee (26). There is no indication why Houston adds this one last—and crowning—insult to long-standing injury except for the supposition that he has been provoked to it by Mink's little strategy the previous night. Varner himself is frightened at the possible consequences of Houston's act: "'Wait,' Varner said. 'Dont you go back there. Dont you go near Houston's place. You go on home and wait'" (29). In the absence of guidance, we cannot be sure whether or not Houston has a good enough reason for further victimizing Mink. This means that we, like Varner, must simply be appalled by the incorrigibility that has prevented both these antagonists, each with strong arguments on his side, from avoiding violence. Each man is so intent on his own rights that he loses all common sense, let alone diplomacy. The key to the conflict is each man's inability to conceive of the consequences of his actions for another. Houston has no idea of the feelings of Mink; as Mink prepares to kill Houston, he is thinking of himself: "He must drain this cup too. . . . This same cup also contained Houston's life but he wasn't thinking about Houston" (37).

Nevertheless, the depiction of Mink as the Good Convict and the tenant-farmer's Everyman is in constant danger of falling into sentimentality. Mink is permitted to ponder the ravages of "the hard ineradicable land" against the "tender and elfin innocence" of "*the children of our passion*" and against "not just his body but that soft mysterious one he had touched that first time with amazement and reverence and incredulous excitement the night of his marriage" (90). This last sexual sentimentality is really only the reverse of the nymphomania in the superseded episode of *The Hamlet*. Faulkner also falls into an uncertainty of tone in making symbolism of Mink's youthful adventures with "women not only shaped like Helen and Eve and Lilith, not only functional like Helen and Eve and Lilith, but colored white like them too, where he had said No not just to all the hard savage years of his hard and barren life, but to Death too in the bed of a public prostitute" (290). The constant immanence of such moments detracts from the intention to investigate with compassion a major character. Chapter 1 is an expository episode beset, as has been noticed, by some failures of invention. It appears that the failure of invention and the sentimentality here coincide, for the noted failure of imagination in the chapter—Mink's night labor—is closely related to Mink's fairly sentimental new status as hard worker and good farmer. But the revaluation of Mink is in general remarkably restrained, a thorough reorientation that is both convincing and, in itself, an exciting feat of writing.

Martin Kreiswirth draws large significance from the inconsistencies in the accidentals of Faulkner's characters. These intertextual "instabilities," he argues, create a slight displacement that makes Faulkner's universe more like the world of history than the completely stabilized world of prose fiction. The texts thus "project a self-contradictory plenitude that denies ultimate coherence." These apparent discrepancies are not discrepancies but "performatives": "And what they perform is transgression—textual, semiotic, and generic—which calls on the reader to engage in a certain kind of transgressive interpretative activity" ("Paradoxical and

Outrageous Discrepancy" 176–77). These may be conclusions too grand to draw from Faulkner's freedom from detail. It seems important to distinguish between situations where Faulkner has simply forgotten details and those where he has reformulated characters so that they can be looked at differently. As to the latter condition, the explanation in the prefatory note to *The Mansion* that "life is motion" points to a real intention; in the former case, it amounts to an alibi. On the other hand, like the multiple narrators' freedom from fact, minor inconsistencies do suggest that there are whole areas of stories where the details simply are not important to the teller. As in the narrator's comment on Quentin and Shreve's speculation about a New Orleans lawyer, if the details are "probably true enough" (*AA* 335), then that will do.

Kreiswirth's textual "instabilities" might be an important impact of the texts if we were to rigorously exclude any notion of a producer of the texts. Then the texts as a group might seem curiously ragged, as if the facts had been compiled from different and unreconciled sources. Given, however, the insistent sense of a teller of the tale, these "instabilities" are more likely to create a sense of just what that teller is like. In this case that means a teller who is both careless about details and free to reimagine the characters of the chronicle.

It is a fairly hazardous thing for writers to offer their second thoughts in lieu of their first and invite posterity to approve their increased wisdom and judgment. But *The Mansion* surely preserves the basic storytelling mode of *The Hamlet,* and makes its alterations less from the perspective of an abstract and condescending "wisdom" than as an act of humility and tolerance appropriate to the tone of the whole novel, in which without rationalization the major characters are brought to an ending and a relaxation, even while wolfish Snopeses promise to keep appearing.

In an argument bolstered by biographical evidence from some of Faulkner's letters, some have suggested that *The Town* and *The Mansion* are the work of an aged and tired writer.[8] What the texts assert instead is that although in these late novels Faulkner takes as his subject old men and the inevitable detachment and objectivity of old age, it by no means follows that he seeks out serenity as an escape from "girls' weather and boys' luck" (*T* 317), from "your native land proffered for your perusal in ring by concentric ring like the ripples on living water above the dreamless slumber of your past" (*T* 316). In these novels equanimity does not mean flight, understanding does not mean passivity or relativism, and age does not mean inaction. In fact, even Flem's immobility does not mean inaction, only a disguised intention.

Faulkner's readjustments are a mark of his faith in his own ability to readjust events, to combine contemplation and conflict, with minor conflicts never ceasing while the major action is marking time. Series of local conflicts that give pattern and plot to a massive chronicle; causation, and unrelated actions; collision and recoil, and continuous strategies—Faulkner uses all these tools. Despite some flagging in the invention of minor exposition, he demonstrates that in *The Mansion* the game is still on. He continues to demonstrate the storyteller's multiple ways of telling the almost-infinite things people do to other people.

6
Faulkner the Teller
Humor and Magic

The act of storytelling involves the generation of structures of conflicts, the development of chronological systems wherein people do things to other people. We have examined both the variety of ways in which Faulkner develops such story structures, and the manner of coexistence of story structures with periods of static contemplation. Yet the plot, and the coexistence of plot and non-plot, do not constitute the whole continuity of stories. In the work of Faulkner we are made to feel the presence of the teller, an immediate and omnipresent coherence. The teller is in part implied by the form of plots. There is a reciprocal and central relationship in narrative between the plot and the implied teller, between the embodied *fabula* and the implied embodier.

In 1954, Paul Goodman formulated an aperçu that expresses the interplay between all the things that tie stories together: "In narrative works it is the narrator who convinces, and in principle we ought to be able to demonstrate this in the details of the work. A talking horse does not make sense, but Homer makes sense of Achilles' talking horse, and 'Homer' is a certain rhythm, diction, selection, and arrangement of episodes" (76). To vary the terminology somewhat, "Faulkner" is made up, among other things, of a certain diction, a certain extradiegetic narrator, and a certain selection and arrangement of episodes. The implied author is the storyteller that encompasses all structures, all the things that ultimately are the work. How these continuities coexist, or whether they coexist at all, is the issue that determines an implied "Faulkner."

D. H. Lawrence's famous dictum "Never trust the artist. Trust the tale" (2) could be expressed as "Trust the plot, not the narrator." "Never trust the artist. Trust the tale" recognizes the presence in the text of interpretive, intentional designs that compete for authority with other, more instinctive or autonomous elements of the discourse—elements that "should" be privileged because more emotionally authentic or more aesthetically pleasing or of greater verisimilitude. But even this is over-simplified, because within the "tale" or the plot itself, incongruities can imply the presence of a disturbing intention. The reader infers that although the narrator blames the "President of the Immortals" for sporting with Tess, it is really "Hardy" who is forcing the plot. The fact is that the text may have more than one kind of design on the reader, and not only one but more than one may be infelicitous.[1]

"Faulkner" is implicit not only in the selection and arrangement of episodes but also in the famous Faulknerian language itself. In a full account of a given act of storytelling, we ought to be interested in knowing whether the speaking of the stories augments, tempers, or counteracts the effects implicitly generated in the stories' form. We should correlate the implications of "Faulkner" the speaker with those of "Faulkner" the maker.

The following of plot and non-plot as they are shaped through time should raise the question of how events mean, what plots signify. At the very least, the form of action constitutes a statement about action itself. Genette demonstrates in the case of Proust how the usurpation by the iterative makes a definite statement about the significance of event in Proust: Proust implicitly denies that events are the armature of his text, or of life. Genette helps locate the uniqueness of Proust in the way he places his focus on a series of states and not on the events that connect them: "In Proust the event—any event—is only the transition, evanescent and *irretrievable* . . . from one habit to another" (*Narrative Discourse* 73); Proust treats "every story . . . as a *succession of states* ceaselessly substituted for each other, with no communication possible" (142). Proust's own distinctive vision is thus found in part in "the spontaneously established link between narrative inspiration and repetitive event, that is, in one sense, the absence of event" (126). Robert Caserio distinguishes texts on the basis of the writer's ability or willingness to imagine "teleological" or "purposive" action in human affairs; the significance of event thus becomes its role as a measure of a text's affirmation or denial of the ability of individuals to make willed assertions.[2]

Faulkner's structures have broad implications that have already frequently asserted themselves in these readings. Formally, Faulkner's plots reflect the implied author's ability to conceive of event structures that are of different kinds, and also his preference for complex shapes. Faulkner displays a masterful sense of different varieties of action and inaction, of forms of encounter and forms of failure. The plots certainly embody action and value it, purposive or not. The author's interest in intricacy requires of his readers a mental agility and concentration; as he is not himself passive, so he does not seem to value passivity in readers. The implied maker, we have seen, is also a restless improver of stories, manifestly complicating them with each retelling. He implies a confidence in his ability to tell something better with each retelling. Above all he implies a confidence in the independence, vitality, and growth of the characters themselves. For Faulkner, the illusion of agency is central to the imagination embodied in the texts.

Molly Hite has suggested that (at least in American hands) any notion of willed action reflects a bourgeois concept of masculinity, one subject in our age to unraveling, "agency panic," a "sensation of potency suddenly draining away": "U.S. theories making the individual the autonomous origin of action, judgment, and even identity—the subject practicing Self-Reliance, the self-made man—deal implicitly with male personhood, and moreover with male persons who have the social status and privileges that make it *rewarding* to claim responsibility for themselves" (63). Whatever the accuracy of this generalization, the notion of "potency" is appropriate to use in discussing agency in Faulkner. In *Intruder in the Dust,* Chick expresses his sense of his capacity for action with just that word: "a sense a feeling not possessive but proprietary, vicegeral, with humility still, himself not potent but at least the vessel of a potency like the actor . . . himself in himself nothing and maybe no world-beater of a play either but at least his to finish it, round it and put it away intact and unassailable, complete" (211).

In his public discourse the Faulkner-no-longer-at-the-writing-desk continually described his work in terms of autonomous characters. Despite the obvious pitfalls in taking these statements as authoritative, they may in fact reflect the way the craftsman thinks he thinks. It is as if the craftsman thinks of writing not in terms of putting together semes but in terms of holistic people. Perhaps this does reflect the way the creative process works in the brain. Perhaps in the semi-trance in which the writing brain works, the craft of writing through codes and the independent characters exist separately and simultaneously as if in two separate processors accessing each other at will.

Faulkner's plot structures also convey through their multiple actors a referential statement about the complexity of human interaction, the range of actions available to human beings, and the likelihood of multiple independent people to be engaged in relations with each other. There can finally be no doubt that Faulkner's interest is not in abstract shapes but in events as an expression of characters, in events and characters as a reflection of human capabilities and possibilities. What is important is for us to develop a resuscitated and retheorized mimesis that allows us to distinguish language which is referential from language which is not, and to determine precisely which ground rules of referentiality each text sets up.[3] For instance, *The Sound and the Fury* certainly includes the techniques of literary modernism, but that does not mean the book is representationally expressionist or cubist.

When we learn to "read" painting, we learn to experience shapes—triangles, inverted curves, parallelograms—that have nothing to do with referentiality. We learn to read the shapes in terms of our own experience of them, the movement of our own "reading eyes." Yet in addition to this perception of abstraction and this foregrounding of our own subjectivity, we do not cease to simultaneously register referentiality. Nor do we have any difficulty distinguishing different kinds of referentiality, the difference between the details in a portrait of Napoleon by David, the stylized portraiture of Botticelli, and the characters of *La Grande Jatte* of Seurat. In fact, we without difficulty assimilate the abstract and the particular and the way the shape is used to create narrative "point" about the human figures, for instance the way Raphael creates a triangular shape to give attention and prominence and to group forcefully together the three most important people in the world in his *Alba Madonna*. In the same way we should both acknowledge referentiality in Faulkner's writing and try to delineate the particular shapes and forms with which it coexists.

The nature of discourse is that it leaves hermeneutic gaps. Narrative is words on a paper. Interpretation makes the words into "people." In this respect an exhaustive enumerative description is ontologically no different from an impressionistic sketch, however much they were traditionally thought to be extreme opposites on the continuum of "mimesis." But the acknowledgment of Faulkner's interest in human people as opposed to semes or to literary "actants" permits us to see that one major implication of his plots is an expression of what the implied author thinks human action is like, what people are capable of.

It is essential to assert that Faulkner conveys through plot an implied conviction of the spectrum of things real people do to other people. It is a spectrum of agency that includes brutality, combat, inadvertence, and all kinds of incapacity. There are the good intentions that pave the way to hell, and a fantastic conception of the way to acquire hell itself. Sometimes there is "death in it" (*T* 301). The fact that there is such variety means more than technical versatility; it means that Faulkner asserts formally that people are capable of anything. This holds whether or not we are persuaded that "people just do the best they can" (*M* 429). We see the implied author act out his empathy for his human actors by becoming temporarily one of them, speaking like a male astounded by Eula; on the other hand, we see the characters become one with the implied author, as Ratliff is permitted to appropriate the Faulknerian voice.

It seems appropriate to consider these effects of Faulkner's stories as the revelations of a personality. "Homer" may be known only by diction and structure, but nevertheless it is as "Homer" that we know "him." This is true even of those writers most publicized—both praised and denounced—for developing techniques of impersonality by which the author might be said to be "refined away." In *The Nature of Narrative*, Kellogg and Scholes write that while James does not speak in his own persona, the reader can always hear him breathing. They make their observation with the implication that James has been caught in an inconsistency, a violation of his own theory. Yet James, despite his exhortation to "dramatize it, dramatize it" (e.g., *AN* 251) and his concentration on a human center of consciousness (e.g., *AN* 67), makes it very clear that the watcher at the window of the house of fiction is the writer. It is always the view from the writer's personal window that is given the reader. "The spreading field, the human scene, is the 'choice of subject'; the pierced aperture, either broad or balconied or slit-like and low-browed, is the 'literary form'; but they are, singly or together, as nothing without the posted presence of the watcher—without, in other words, the consciousness of the artist" (*AN* 46). This essentially repeats what James had written twenty years earlier in "The Art of Fiction":

[The ways of being interesting] are as various as the temperament of man, and they are successful in proportion as they reveal a particular mind, different from others. A novel is in its broadest definition a personal, a direct impression of life. (*Future of the Novel* 9)

Experience is never limited, and it is never complete; it is an immense sensibility, a kind of huge spider-web of the finest silken threads suspended in the chamber of consciousness. (12)

The deepest quality of a work of art will always be the quality of the mind of the producer. (26)

Late in his career James returned to these themes in explicitly speaking about the personal temperament in a particular novel. In his essay "The New Novel" he praises Conrad's *Chance* for reasons quite other than the perhaps over-rigorous "objective" method, because Conrad offers the reader "the bribe of some authenticity other in kind . . . and . . . equally great if not greater, which gives back by the left hand what the right has . . . taken away. What Mr. Conrad's left hand gives back then is simply Mr. Conrad himself" (*Future of the Novel* 283). James seems eager to recognize the artist's breathing as an inevitable and invaluable presence. In this he does not differ from his predecessor Flaubert, who wrote, "The artist must be in his work as God is in creation, invisible yet all-powerful; we must *sense him everywhere* but never see him" (emphasis added).[4] We too need to recognize the ways in which we sense "Mr. Faulkner himself."

We need to distinguish more closely the elements of a writer's personality, the ways in which a writer dramatizes himself both explicitly and implicitly. Some writers dramatize themselves more personally than others; some are even said to have "negative capability." Mann's presence is stolid and pedantic, Flaubert's visually observant, Trollope's voluble and decorously playful. Claude-Edmonde Magny distinguishes the "creative vivacity" of Stendhal from "Balzacian 'hustling'" and "Faulknerian 'sorcery'" (202–3).

The boldest criticism of Faulkner has always sought to define Faulkner's essential qualities. The critics who wrote about Faulkner in his own lifetime provide an illustrative panoply of attempts to characterize the writer's temperament: Wyndham Lewis denounces Faulkner's cruelty;[5] Sartre criticizes what he calls a "metaphysic," but which might better be called a tendency of temperament—the tendency to face toward the past rather than the future (87–93); Magny is awed by the "theological inversion" of Faulkner as an Old Testament God in anguished yearning for salvation; Walter Slatoff attacks Faulkner's self-punishing "quest for failure." Whether insightful, unsubstantiable, or even simply outrageous, criticism of this kind prods us to our own assessment of the nature of Faulkner's presence.

Of course, James's formulation "Mr. Conrad" predates the "death of the author" and the widespread deep distrust of the concept of authorial volition.[6] Critical orthodoxy has allowed the author to be disenfranchised, usurped by the text. The term "implied author," coined by Wayne Booth, offers a vehicle for characterizing the author's "second self" (*Rhetoric of Fiction* 71), but Booth tends to confine himself to the ascertainment of the ethical norms by which a writer influences the reader. When he moves beyond norms to talk about a "failure of character" in an author, he does so principally apropos of narrators who are presumed to express the character of an implied author (219). Many of those who have followed Booth have described the implied author only in terms of ethics, explicit values, or mind systems.[7]

Mary Thomas Crane, moving to "re-theorize authorship" (10), compares herself to Dr. Johnson kicking the stone, the famous commonsense refutation of relativistic Idealism. Obviously it is at one level perfectly ridiculous to have to assert that someone produced the text, that no two people would produce the same text, that no monkey has ever written *Hamlet* nor any Pierre Menard the *Quixote*. But Crane gives a local habitation for authority by locating the place of production in the brain of the writer, a place where the conscious and the subconscious play, and where polysemous words are generated without the need for intention or consistent definition. In the patterns of language, the maker's brain leaves traces of itself and its activity.

> The metaphors that in a deconstructive reading seem to disrupt the surface logic of the text could also be interpreted as traces of basic cognitive structures. These seemingly contradictory metaphors are present in a text because thought, from a cognitive perspective, is able to accommodate contradiction and recursivity. (24)

> Shakespeare (i.e., Shakespeare's language-processing functions) causes us to notice these connections—which in turn reveal information about his culture and also about the organizational tendencies of the brain. (25)

The following of unusual connections in Shakespeare's language permits the description of "the organizational features of his mental lexicon" (27).

A different line of defense of authorship is speech-act theory as developed by Susan Lanser.[8] The speech act implies a speech-actor, "a 'generative authority' behind textual speakers that emanates from the authorial persona him- or herself" (114). The extradiegetic, or "public," narrators may in fact not be differentiated at all from the ultimate tellers: "Ordinarily, the unmarked case of narration for public narrators is that the narrating voice is equated with the textual author (the extrafictional voice or 'implied author') unless a different case is marked—signaled—by the text" (151).[9] As a narrator has a voice and personality,[10] so the implied authority of which the narrator is partly constitutive has a voice and personality, the natural foundations of the speech act. Because only humans have speech, the author implied is inevitably implied as human, an anthropomorphic figure.[11] The notion of an implied author constituted only of norms and values without a persona would thus be a logical inconsistency. The fact that this concept of the implied author virtually requires anthropomorphic characterization is what makes some theorists reject it altogether. Mieke Bal, for instance, rejects the entire speech-act rationale as a reversion to "intentionalism": "I cannot agree with this pre–New Critical intentionalism which Lanser passes off as speech-act theory" (*On Story-Telling* 15).

Ruth Ginsburg and Shlomith Rimmon-Kenan, rediscovering and rehabilitating Wayne Booth in the light of Bakhtin, have revalidated both an implied author and its anthropomorphic personalism. What they do not want to concede is that the author function, or "author-version" (75), is a stable or unitary persona. They insist that "author" be discontinuous, reflecting a subject that is fragmented:

> Not a "character," and certainly not "ideal," no moral value or norm is attached to this "author." Nor do we conceive of it in terms of a constant self. It is rather thought of in terms of a continuously changing subjectivity. . . . "Author"—in particular as "subject in process"—is not a constant but a becoming, in and by the interaction with the other participants. Booth, on the other hand, describes a process of discovery, where both the author and the reader gradually find out about the given particular implied author. (77)

There seems to be no reason, however, that a variable and various implied author should not be consistent with some fundamental stability and continuity, or be sufficiently unique to be differentiated from other implied authors in *other* texts. The multiple narrators of Morrison's *Jazz*, cited by Ginsburg and Rimmon-Kenan, do seem intended to create an implied author that is unstable and that overtly questions its own authority. But another implied author, like Fielding or Faulkner, might act out several narratorial roles and still imply a coherent persona. All implied authors are by nature gapped, interstitial, and inferred because of the medium of language in which they are created. But that is not inconsistent either with the presence of continuous threads of characterization or with the creation of differentiating characteristics that are unique to a given implied author. As David Lodge concludes in discussing cognitive psychology, human self-consciousness, and the fiction (and narrative) of human personality, however much indeterminacy and fluidity we build into the model, the fiction of human personality is unavoidable and the best we have (91). We should be able to describe an anthropomorphic author-persona without reverting to biographism and intentionalism.

Certainly the implied "Faulkner" is nowhere more explicitly characterized —and complementary to the implied maker of eventful plots and evolving retellable stories—than in the speech acts of the extradiegetic narrator and in the language which that narrator shares with the characters. The Faulkner language makes all the extradiegetic narrative voices variants of one voice. Whether the narrator is "unmarked" or whether the narrative voice is intermittently detached from its authoritative status, the insistently unique voice requires us to consider it as the creation or revelation of personality.

In *The Hamlet* there are several major narrative stances. The first narrator is seemingly all-knowing and detached, able to crisply sum up the panorama of an entire culture: "They took up land and built one- and two-room cabins and never painted them, and married one another and produced children and added other rooms one by one to the original cabins and did not paint them either, but that was all" (5). The voice moves from the deadpan to the eloquent, but we are always reminded that it is a voice, telling us a story, saying narratively, "Then in September something happened" (67).

Another narrative stance in *The Hamlet* is assumed when the narrator inhabits the mind and point of view of a character, a "he." For each of these characters—Ike, Houston, Mink—the diction and tone of voice is a little different, but basically, as for Ike, the narrator speaks for "him who had been given the wordless passions but not the specious words" (224).

Here too we must be reminded that this is a narrative act, for Faulkner conspicuously shifts his camera from inside to outside: "Now the dog shouted at him. It did not move yet, it merely shouted once; . . . and, still moaning, trying now to talk to the man with his blasted eyes, he moved on toward the still-open gate" (191). "Shouted" is a sensation Ike might express as a word if he could talk. The adjective "blasted," however, tells us that we are now watching Ike from *outside.*

Faulkner actually seems to insist on his narrator's presence in all the narrative stances of the book. For instance, we would normally expect the authoritative narrator to efface himself when his characters are conversing in a nonliterary sort of folk diction or when a character tells his own story in the first person. Is there a Faulknerian persona implied in this dramatic technique? Or are we limited to inferring the values and ethical norms of the implied author, who makes up Ratliff making up a story so much like one of his own? Surely the form of Fool About a Horse, although told by Ratliff, implies an ultimate storyteller who is the same one as the narrator of the goat-trading episode, with not only the same sympathies but the same unique delight in intricacies.

But Faulkner seems to go out of his way to make the *voice* of this ultimate narrator present in Ratliff's voice as well. A strange antimimetic marriage is present in Ratliff's Flem in Hell fantasy, between the Faulknerian high style and Ratliff's folk grammar: "*In a flash the sybaritic indolence and the sneers was gone*" (*H* 174). Ratliff is speaking, but where did he get a phrase like "sybaritic indolence"? The antimimetic mixture of voices is present throughout Faulkner's career, and by no means only for comic purposes. The speakers of *Absalom, Absalom!* seem to some degree to be variations of a common voice. Warwick Wadlington has observed that in *As I Lay Dying* every voice is a composite voice (*Reading Faulknerian Tragedy* 126). What Warren Beck calls the "imperial and opulent use of words" is present, allowing Faulkner to move beyond "colloquial verisimilitude." And as Beck also notes, what this means is the abiding presence of a "dominating temperament" ("Faulkner's Style" 45, 43). We can certainly say that the eccentricity of the "Faulknerian" style notably calls attention to a voice that does not belong to one of the characters. Faulkner transforms a technique that normally effaces the writer's persona, so that instead the writer's persona takes a high profile, through style.[12]

Many commentators have contributed to the list of linguistic traits that we associate with the Faulkner voice. Again the earliest writers on

Faulkner offer an illustrative range of attempts to interpret stylistic features. Among the stylistic signatures noted are inclusive sentences, iteration, the use of trailing clauses, the incantation of favorite words, the delayed revelation of meaning (Aiken); the cumulative effect of sentences, the suspension of time for reflection and musing speculation, the lyric style that transcends colloquial verisimilitude (Beck); the sentences that are designed to keep the reader moving (Zoellner); the combination of distance with emotionally moving rhetoric (Swink); the use of paradox and oxymoron (Slatoff); the barrage of adjectives (Magny); and the variation in speeds, "sometimes slow-motion, sometimes double-time" (Welty, "In Yoknapatawpha" 597).[13] But what is difficult is moving from stylistic traits to their significance for the overall tone and impact of a writer's language.

We may agree as to the presence of a verbal signature without agreeing on the significance of that signature. The work of Walter Slatoff provides a cautionary example. Slatoff sees the style of Faulkner as "governed," to a greater degree than that of other novelists, by a personal temperament: "that is, by the particular compound of intellectual and emotional inclinations, tendencies, and responses that characterize his mental life and shape his reactions to experience" ("Edge of Order" 198).[14] Yet Slatoff finds the temperament to be one unable "to set limits on abundance" (198) or to commit itself to choices. These traits Slatoff deduces from Faulkner's use of oxymorons. He begins by arguing that not all of Faulkner's oxymorons are "mechanical or excessive," that the important thing is "their remarkable frequency and variety" (176). He seems to want to argue that by its very nature the oxymoron renders a sort of mental paralysis, an inability to resolve opposites:

> Like Faulkner's writing in general, the oxymoron involves sharp polarity, extreme tension, a high degree of conceptual and stylistic antithesis, and the simultaneous suggestion of disparate or opposed elements. Moreover, the figure tends to hold these elements in suspension rather than to fuse them. . . . One's recognition that the contradiction is apparent rather than real does not eliminate the tension between the terms, for the conflicting elements remain. Neither negates the other. The oxymoron, on the one hand, achieves a kind of order. . . . On the other hand, it moves toward disorder and incoherence by virtue of its qualities

of irresolution and self-contradiction. . . . It does not so much explore or analyze a condition as render it forcefully. Traditionally it has often been used to reflect desperately divided states of mind. (177)

But Slatoff cannot really argue that the oxymoron always implies a mind at sea. What of Webster and Donne?

> Whatever the tensions and opposing suggestions, explicit or implicit, in a poem by Donne or a play by Webster, one feels behind them, I think, a governing mind which never really doubts the validity of its own ideas and perceptions or the possibility[,] if not the existence, of a moral universe in which such ideas and perceptions are relevant, which never abandons the effort to order its thoughts and emotions. Like many modern artists Faulkner has no such certainty. (197)

What this must mean is that Faulkner's oxymorons *are* an unusually "excessive" sort of oxymoron after all, that they register a kind of self-punishing irresolution and moral paralysis, that they are "especially insoluble suspensions" (177). It does matter whether Faulkner's oxymorons are brilliant or mechanical. It becomes clear that Slatoff has rigged the question of proof; he has argued that he does not need to prove his most debatable argument. In fact, if we look at the oxymorons he actually cites—many of them from *The Hamlet*—we see some of Faulkner's most perceptive paradoxes. The description of Ratliff as having "a sort of delicate robustness" (*H* 78) expresses perfectly the way Ratliff's humorous vitality survives even while he treats himself gingerly after his operation. The paradox does ask us to see, to visualize a complicated combination of frailty and natural heartiness. And is it a gratuitous paradox that Eula is "at once supremely unchaste and inviolable" (*H* 131)? Quite the contrary. Faulkner humorously expresses the feeling of every male that Eula is by nature a goddess of illicit love, but that for *him* she is too fine, too hopelessly unreachable. We reconcile the apparent incongruity and recognize that the writer has urged us to see, like him, to the point where the opposites can be subtly reconciled. It would seem that the evidence shows Faulkner's "governing mind" to be as poised, witty, and humorous as those of Webster and Donne.

John Matthews makes a valuable distinction between "language which searches tirelessly but vainly for a full expression of truth" (39) and writing which constitutes "serious play" dedicated not to "the capture of truth" but to the "rituals of pursuit, exchange, collaboration and invention" (16). Matthews thus refuses to devalue Faulkner's later work because of its concentration on the rituals of "writing." He declines to accept those "biases against language [which] encourage us to esteem fiction that denigrates or suppresses its own medium" (44). For this reason he cites Slatoff as having reached a particularly "morose" view of Faulkner based on his mistaken assumption that the writer is trying and failing to make language achieve a "realization" of "the ideas it signifies" (39).

Others besides Slatoff have taken their view of Faulkner from his famous—and heavily qualified—praise of Thomas Wolfe: "I rated Wolfe first, myself second. I put Hemingway last. I said we were all failures. All of us had failed to match the dream of perfection and I rated the authors on the basis of their splendid failure to do the impossible. I believed Wolfe tried to do the greatest of the impossible, that he tried to reduce all human experience to literature."[15] Wolfe clearly does impress us with a feeling of a yearning for the ineffable. Yet Faulkner does not write like a failure in this sense, or any other. As much as any other writer, his persona calls attention to the incredible virtuosity of his voice, the manifold ability to make us experience radically various extremes of "human experience."

Some commentators, perhaps because of Faulkner's obvious understanding of human pain and anguish, have seen his writing as a perilous assertion of identity or as a therapeutic act to relieve personal anxiety.[16] Hugh Kenner, for instance, speaks of the "aesthetic discomfort that commenced to alleviate itself as he visualized the muddy seat of a little girl's drawers" (199). But Kenner also describes the way in which Faulkner reached a confidence that makes him not a modernist at all but instead "the Last Novelist": "His was our last mutation, anyhow, of the procedures that dominated the novel for many decades. They stemmed from the nineteenth century's confident positivism, from the belief that what was *so* was the writer's province, that he was the supreme generalist, to be trusted by the literate for the reports they needed" (212). The difficult question, perhaps, is at what point preverbal anxieties and needs become authorial confidence. How do we assess the relative balance of "need" and authority? Brent Harold neatly walks the tightrope, saying that Faulkner's sentences are "filled with a sense of rhythmic re-creation of the world moment by moment, object by object, word by word, and, at the same time, . . . tense with the possibility of failure" (225).

To describe Faulkner's art in terms of tensions, a perilous balance of violent contraries, may be to take the part for the whole, the sensations of the characters for the virtual voice of the implied storyteller. In this respect, Faulkner's art shows an intriguing similarity to sixteenth-century mannerist art, which has traditionally been described as an art of strain, an art of "aggression, anxiety and instability" (Shearman 15). The critic John Shearman, however, has added another dimension to our sense of this art. He has pointed out the role in the mannerist aesthetic of "the notion of difficulty, that is to say of difficulty overcome" (21). Faulkner might be said to share just this feature with mannerism: behind the strain, the sense of "those kinds of complexity and invention that are the result of deliberately raising more difficulties, so that dexterity may be displayed in overcoming them." Shearman cautions against the modern "priggish attitude" toward this overt "virtuosity." Faulkner shares with the mannerist artists the love of complexity, and his invention implies for us what invention implied for Vitruvius: "the solving of difficult problems and the treatment of new problems achieved by a lively intelligence." Quintilian's attitude toward novelty of this kind in effect anticipates the Russian Formalists' praise of the art that "makes it new": "The very novelty and difficulty of execution is what most deserves our praise. A similar impression of grace and charm is produced by rhetorical figures, whether they be figures of thought or figures of speech. For they involve a certain departure from the straight line and have *the merit of variation from the ordinary usage*" (84–85). The style with the high profile is meant to be seen as artistic, as an act of pride and control. Among the sixteenth-century mannerists, one went so far as to advise: "You should introduce at least one figure that is all distorted, ambiguous and difficult, so that you shall thereby be noticed as outstanding by those who understand the finer points of art" (86). Shearman emphasizes that the mannerist artist assumes a "god-like relation to his material," an attitude that is all the more remarkable considering the referential nature of the subject matter: "If the material were abstract, the achievement would still be remarkable; that it is figurative increases its 'difficulty' immeasurably" (88). Shearman's critical scrutiny and his research into the aesthetic of the period reveal dexterity rather than distortion, control instead of imbalance. Similarly, Faulkner's own apparent strains should be seen as ultimately resolved and encompassed by a voice and a personality both poised and exuberant.

In his noted essay on the first paragraph of *The Ambassadors,* Ian Watt has used the word "humor" to describe the implications of a narrative stance. Watt notes in James, too, the primacy of the relation between the narrator and the reader. The virtuosity of the prose, particularly its abstract diction, he argues, permits "the presentation of life as a spectacle" (263) from which the narrator stands partially detached. Watt writes: "One could, I suppose, call the aesthetically perfect balance between distance and involvement, open or positive irony: but I'm not sure that humour isn't a better word, especially when the final balance is tipped in favor of involvement, of ultimate commitment to the characters" (267). Faulkner exhibits this same involvement: his humor is never merely comic or merely anguished; his serenity is never merely serene.[17] Faulkner's mannerism takes the form of a combination of poise and virtuosity, of humor and what Claude-Edmonde Magny calls "magic" (198).

One stylistic signature as pervasive as the oxymoron in Faulkner's writing is the Faulknerian parallelism. Faulkner's parallelisms embody a voice both capricious and controlled, both careless and authoritative.

> If she were looking at the man,
>   they could not tell it;
> if she were looking at anything,
>   they did not know it. (*H* 419)

> He was the largest landowner and beat supervisor in one county *and* Justice of the Peace *in* the next *and* election commissioner *in* both, *and* hence the fountainhead if not of law at least of advice and suggestion to a countryside *which* would have repudiated the term constituency if they had ever heard it, *which* came to him, *not* in the attitude of *What must I do* but *What do you think you would like for me to do if you was able to make me do it.* (*H* 5, emphasis added)

The balance of even the longer sentence is obvious. It is based on four predicate nominatives, joined by the word "and." And yet even here there is not a simple parallelism, because within the last of the series there is a balance of two clauses, and within the second of these there is a pair of long alternative phrases. Ultimately the sentence seems unbalanced, an infinitely bifurcating series that requires from the reader a sense of symmetry but also much more. This is particularly true in that the antecedent of the second "which" is not immediately clear—it might, for instance, be the entire preceding clause. The reader in this case is forced to work ahead, to grasp the idea, then to work *backward* to find the antecedent.

> He was the largest landholder and beat supervisor in one county
>   and Justice of the Peace in the next
>   and election supervisor in both
>   and hence the fountainhead . . . to a countryside
>   which would have repudiated the term constituency . . . ,
>   which came to him not in the attitude of What . . .
>   but   What . . .

It is characteristic of Faulkner that his parallelisms not only do not allow the reader to relax into a sense of easy structure but that they often are not immediately perceived to be parallelisms.

> They supported their own churches and schools,
> they married and committed infrequent adulteries
>   and more frequent homicides among themselves
>   and were their own courts, judges and executioners. (*H* 5)

Only after racing through this sentence do we see that it is actually an obscured parallelism. Its basic lucidity is disguised by what must be a cavalierly obscurantist use of "and." After "schools," the first "and" joins two verbs, but the second confuses us by doing something totally different and joining the two direct objects of "committed." Then, just when we have assimilated this false parallelism, we seem to be getting another "and" which will add something to "themselves" as another object of the preposition "among." But that, too, turns out not to be the case, for this last "and" adds another verb, "were," to parallel "married" and "committed"; so that we are again surprised by being given after all the parallelism we originally expected. The reader punctuates by hindsight. If Faulkner's balanced sentence has a certain amount of imbalance, his unbalanced sentence turns out to have a true balance capriciously concealed.

Just as we learn to find obscured parallelisms, imbalance that is a disguise for balance, so do we find apparent parallelisms that are comically spurious: "They were Protestants and Democrats and prolific"; "He was a farmer, a usurer, a veterinarian" (*H* 5). These sentences are like those test questions in which children are asked to pick out the word that does not belong with the other words. The incongruous word surprises the reader, as the narrator blandly and innocently pretends that usury is really just another profession. The parallel structure turns out to be a pretence, which is at least in part a joke at the expense of the stance of authority in the storyteller himself. Apparently, even at his most authorial and authoritative, the Faulkner narrator creates "difficulty" by refusing ever to be merely rational and controlled. The balance seems to imply an augustan equanimity and wisdom, but the imbalance implies almost the opposite—caprice, carelessness, perhaps even confusion. Yet the combination works to Faulkner's advantage, for the exuberance keeps the wisdom from ever being merely pompous or dull, while the underlying grammar of the sentences keeps the exuberance from ever seeming merely disordered. The reader is constantly being shown whimsy, and a human haste, and the restlessness of a mind that never runs out of something to add.

The apparent carelessness with which the narrator works is greatly increased when Faulkner uses his obscurantist "and" with phrases and clauses of greatly varying lengths.

> He sold it to one of the family's negro retainers, so that
>> on almost any Sunday night one whole one or some part of
>> one of his old suits could be met—and promptly
>> recognized—walking the summer roads,
> and replaced it with the new succeeding one. (*H* 8)

> He managed the store
>> of which his father was still titular owner
>> and in which they dealt mostly in foreclosed mortgages,
> and the gin,
> and oversaw the scattered farm holdings

> which his father at first and later the
> two of them together had been acquiring
> during the last forty years. (*H* 8)

The narrator makes it all too possible for the careless reader to get lost, or for the overcautious reader to get stalled. We must have the patience to wait for the end of the sentence for its structure and meaning to become clear; or to put it another way, we must have enough confidence to hasten onward in order to find the missing elements. The authorial narrator, far from being stately and pacific, goads the reader through his narrative in wind sprints. He does not strive to achieve a consistent speed, to demonstrate his authority and wisdom by soothing the reader. Instead, he might be said to make us wait and hurry up.

The sentence may be structured in balanced parallel phrases, but as it is written and punctuated, that structure is not so much disguised as obscured. The reader is given no help as the sentence runs on ahead. The reader must punctuate and picture the structure at speed but also slow down the reading process to loop back and retrospectively decipher. The complex prose thus frequently requires circling, and therefore not only greater "duration" than initial reading time but also a reading of many loops rather than one linearity. What does this imply about the voice? Apparent disorder, actual complex order; absorption in the discourse to the extent of not troubling with detail or convention; not Olympian detachment, but haste to spin out words.

The most baroque sentences of *Absalom, Absalom!* or "The Bear," those most difficult sentences that are often thought of as the purest or most exemplary "Faulknerian" sentences, exhibit this same combination of haste and retardation. Sentences that may be thought of as primarily a way to simulate streams of consciousness or the trance of intense thinking on the part of a character are also demonstrations of the virtuosity of the authorial narrator, his control over language, his demands on the reader, his intense engagement with the discourse.

The stylistic signature represented by Faulkner's characteristic use of parallelisms to create imbalance and variations in speed has, of course, a corresponding feature in Faulkner's characteristic formal structures. The long flashbacks, the attenuations of major plotlines, the lengthy irrelevancies—all tease us and force us to wait and hurry up. In *The Hamlet,* for instance, we step off the porch with Ratliff and wait forty pages to find out what he is going to see (186–224). We are tested to see whether we can wait for the final ordering to come, for the story to show how it will include everything. We are tested to see whether we have patience and confidence in the storytelling authority. The time-consuming and digressive inclusiveness that Tristram Shandy calls the soul of the narrative is nevertheless in Tristram's case an admission that the story is going to wander because Tristram will always be comically unable to keep up with his task. In Faulkner's case, we see digressions not as an admission of failure but as a handicap the writer sets himself: Let's see him get back to the subject *this* time, we think. But he always meets his challenge and demonstrates once again his authority and control over his plenitude. Children are frustrated by such roundaboutness; perhaps we demonstrate our maturity as listeners by learning to be impressed by such feats of circumnavigation.

The curious combination of balance and imbalance in Faulkner's parallelisms, and the endless vitality with which the parallels are diversified and prolonged, are signs of the narrator's sense of humor and his authority, his caprice in the midst of seriousness. The variations in pace and seriousness keep the reader active and alert and demonstrate that the narrator also is one who is active and alert. The narrator tempers equanimity with mercurial play. It seems appropriate to call this a voice of "humor."

The confident humor of the Faulkner voice is reinforced by the role played by comedy in many of Faulkner's fictions. For comedy in Faulkner's stories is not walled off from serious matters. The comedy is interstitial, matted-in in the middle of extremes. In the midst of the terrible, as in *Absalom, Absalom!*, Faulkner interpolates extremely funny riffs on a character's incongruous sense of entitlement (Miss Rosa as the "southern lady") or highly individualistic moral accounting (Mr. Coldfield). In "My Grandmother Millard" even a terrible event like the Civil War is an opportunity for farce, without ceasing to be war. Grandmother Millard, in full knowledge that she is an eccentric, insists on her right to *be* an eccentric by actually practicing the southern picturesque, the romantic tableau of silver burial by candlelight. She is a grandmother who is going to keep on being a grandmother as long as she can get away with it, war or no war. But this is not merely a form of flight from the terrors of reality. For "My Grandmother Millard" is in effect a story that debunks the terrible itself, making war an adjunct to the eccentric life carried on more or less willy nilly by one southern grandmother. War is placed in the healthy context of human character. An essential sanity is sensed, encompassing individual woes and national calamities.

Faulkner has a way also of giving his characters moments of comic insight in which they are able to see the simultaneity of the terrible and the ridiculous; and in such moments the awareness restores balance and sanity in the midst of pain. Bayard Sartoris hears of his father's death from his law professor and calmly asks him for a fresh horse for Ringo: "'By all means take mine—Mrs. Wilkins,' he cried. His tone was no different yet he did cry it and I suppose that at the same moment we both realized that was funny—a short-legged deep-barrelled mare who looked exactly like a spinster music teacher, which Mrs. Wilkins drove to a basket phaeton—which was good for me, like being doused with a pail of cold water would have been good for me" (*Unvanquished* 245).

Such comic moments should be seen as similar to other moments of insight in which characters are able to see their own anguish in a larger context. Joe Christmas, for instance, is able intermittently to see himself as if from outside, and in these moments he almost understands the degree to which he has scripted his own suffering. In such moments he is able to consider with amazement the existence of possibilities of love and belief not previously allowed in his script: "*God perhaps and me not knowing that too*" (*LIA* 98); "*Why not? It would mean ease, security*" (*LIA* 250). In Joe's case, these moments of serene insight are not perpetuated. Arguing that all he has ever wanted was peace, Joe nonetheless flings himself back into the street that can have only one ending, saying, "If I give in now, I will deny all the thirty years that I have lived to make me what I chose to be" (*LIA* 250–51).

Gavin Stevens is a character who is able to maintain for long periods of time a dual focus on himself, seeing himself as both anguished and—*because* of his exaggerated anguish—ridiculous. Reporting that he would even have shared Eula if he could have had her in no other way, he parenthetically admits, "Oh yes, it was that bad once, that comical once" (*T* 134). The bad and the comical are the same thing seen from two different perspectives, and here Stevens is able to see from both at the same time. Gowan's way of expressing his own double feeling as a spectator is that "it was like watching somebody's britches falling down while he's got to use both hands trying to hold up the roof: you are sorry it is funny" (*T* 60). But it is funny, and the redeeming thing about Gavin is that he knows it. Gavin's sister Maggie says that Gavin is "acting just like a high-school sophomore" over Eula (*T* 63). She also realizes that everyone else is, too; and unfazed by that recognition, she continues her own participation in the action. In his own perception of himself running from Linda, Gavin verifies the rightness of Maggie's view: "It was adolescence in reverse, turned upside down: the youth, himself virgin and—who knew?—maybe even more so" (*T* 208). Gavin's moments of bemused detachment precede and follow and sometimes coincide with the moments of folly and frenetic motion when he is captured by his human tendency to be sophomoric. Faulkner thus includes in his tales a sense of humor that puts in context more obvious kinds of comedy and anguish, when he gives his characters an awareness of their foolishness without forcing them to stop being foolish. In fact, Charles Mallison seems to testify to this as a necessary condition of all human existence, or of human maturity: "It's when they laugh at you and suddenly you say, *Why, maybe I am funny,* and so the things they do are not outrageous and silly or shocking at all: they're just funny; and more than that, it's the same funny" (*T* 304).

The explicit presence of such mature comedy in Faulkner's career certainly reinforces our sense of the humorous tone of his work as we have seen it in the pervasive voice of the storyteller. But even more importantly, implicit forms of humor are seen in the forms of whole novels. Eudora Welty was perhaps the first to discuss the presence of comedy in the whole texture of one of Faulkner's books, and that in a seemingly serious one—*Intruder in the Dust.* As Welty says, "The complicated and intricate thing is that his stories aren't decked out in humor, but the humor is born in them" ("In Yoknapatawpha" 597). Welty implies the paradoxical way that books can be funny and very serious in different ways at the same time. The furious motion of anguish is also as hilarious as the Keystone Kops, and as Welty says, the abused victim Lucas Beauchamp is "gorgeously irritating" ("In Yoknapatawpha" 596). If it comes to a choice, the implicit tone is more gorgeous than it is disturbing.

In the rhetoric of his novels, Faulkner fosters the notion of a hope that succeeds despair: "[the age of] five is still too young to have learned enough despair to hope" (*LIA* 132). Faulkner never does dramatize the emergence to hope for Joe Christmas, and the triumphant return to life of Hightower turns out to be only temporary. The writer's refusal to fully enact or demonstrate the paradigm of rebirth reinforces the reader's sense of the difficulty of hope, the power of despair; the rhetorical push of the narrative in this case seems to endorse a Dostoyevskian anxiety which has as yet imperfectly struggled its way through despair.

But even in *Light in August* this balked grasping for hope is "sweetened" (Flint 293) a great deal by the very form of the novel. We are given a humorous distancing from the most terrible aspects of our experience. We are, for instance, meant to be as moved by Joe's crucifixion as are those who watch it; we too are meant "not to lose it" (*LIA* 440). But the distress and guilt permanently etched in the witnesses are mixed with a feeling of Joe's escape from the harm of man. And this mixed discontent is then itself pulled back into the body of the novel. The reader is temporally distanced from the apparent climax of the crucifixion, first by Hightower's own relapse into sterile romanticism and then by the comic anguish of Byron Bunch, still in pursuit of Lena. By the end of the novel, we are a long way from the emotional pitch of Joe's death. The end of the novel has its own pathos, but at that point we are associated with the furniture dealer and are not permitted to be undistanced even from Byron's pathos. Even if Byron's anguish will not pass, it is something he—and we—can live with. Byron's pathos becomes comedy, and that comedy effectively brackets and encloses Joe's pathos.[18] We are left with characters in motion, characters who are not bound by the conventional shape of a novel or of a tragedy. Life with its frustrations goes on humorously.

A similar distancing is embodied in the form of *The Sound and the Fury*, but with a very different effect. The novel reaches a climax in the most explicitly dramatized mystical escape from human despair and the fragmentation of the human community that can be found anywhere in Faulkner's writings. The narrative moves toward—though afterward, characteristically, also away from—an experience that places all Faulkner's divided possibilities in context. Dilsey's human love and mystical sense of God's love represents an ordering that almost denies us the ability any longer to experience the impotence and inarticulateness to which we have been so completely given over in the "Quentin" section. We are then drawn back into normal life, as if to demonstrate how fragile and temporary is the reconciling vision of Dilsey's Christianity. For this reason, many commentators have resisted Dilsey's experience on the grounds that it is demonstrably not available to the other human beings in the novel. But that is precisely the point: the desperate condition of the Compsons comes to be measured by their inability to be moved by a momentarily transforming experience. The return of the Compsons in their quotidian pattern of living shows how each of the Compsons—including Benjy—is hopelessly committed to an end rather than a beginning. The fact that life goes on in this novel signifies a continuation of drift, decay, and doom—and makes Dilsey's vision all the more worth striving for. The implicit humor in this book is thus known primarily, but not exclusively, in humor's loss. Warren Beck has written that in Faulkner the tragedy is the constant, the comic a "shaped echo" (*Man in Motion* 200); but it would seem more correct to say that humor envelops the tragedy, whether the last word is explicitly given to sanity, as in *Light in August*, or whether, as in *The Sound and the Fury*, the last words remind us of the limitations of the humorless and unaspiring. As Warwick Wadlington writes, "[F]undamentally the contest is not that of nihilism and belief but of empowering hope set against, and poised upon, its potentially enervating opposite" (*Reading Faulknerian Tragedy* 25).

Not only the speaking voice of the narrator, then, but other means explicit and implicit contribute to a sense of the humorous temperament of Faulkner's implied artistic personality. The humor includes a certain relation between anguish and detachment in which the anguish is fixed in the context of a larger vision, an encompassing equanimity that is never sanctimonious. Faulkner seems to be speaking of his goal for his own persona when in *The Town* he describes "a sanctuary, a rationality of perspective, which animals, humans too, not merely reach but earn by passing through unbearable emotional states like furious rage or furious fear" (27). In that sanctuary Tom Tom and Turl can see beyond their own antagonism and combine against their true antagonist, Flem. On Faulkner's own part we feel the serenity as an elevated wisdom, almost, toward the end of his career, as age. Faulkner describes Gavin as experiencing such an authorial elevation when he stands on top of a hill looking "from Jefferson to the world": " . . . yourself detached as God Himself for this moment above the cradle of your nativity and of the men and women who made you . . . ; you to preside unanguished and immune above this miniature of man's passions and hopes and disasters . . . all bound, precarious and ramshackle, held together by the web, the iron-thin warp and woof of his rapacity but withal yet dedicated to his dreams" (*T* 316). At that moment Gavin feels himself to be "the old man"; the implication is that in Gavin's case serenity is restful, but also that time has cut him off from "the spring dark peopled and myriad, two and two seeking never at all solitude but simply privacy, the privacy decreed and created for them by the spring darkness" (317). But the Faulknerian narrator manages his detachment without losing empathetic understanding for the Laboves and Houstons and Minks for whom he provides language.

Paradoxically, the authority and self-control of the performer is nowhere more evident than in his confidence in temporarily abdicating that self-control—a phenomenon we have already noted in such phrases as "a farmer, a usurer, a veterinarian"—for in this way he shows what Watt calls an "ultimate commitment to the characters" and a sense of humor about "himself" as narrator. The characterization of Eula represents such an abdication. Many readers have been bothered by this mythic, possibly symbolic, outrageously antimimetic character, who seems to belong in a tall tale or *One Hundred Years of Solitude* rather than in the same novel with Ratliff; and even more have been outraged by Faulkner's rehabilitation of Eula in the role of a serious and finally self-sacrificing matron in *The Town*. Faulkner claimed the intention of showing growth in the character, but many readers would reply that the character is originally of another order altogether, too extravagantly comic to be made the victim of such serious growth. Another possibility, however, is that Faulkner expects us to see the exaggeration as being not in the tale but in the teller. The Faulknerian storyteller becomes involved in the story through self-exaggerations, performances in which "he" shows his enjoyment at playing the fool—or, more precisely, the eternal adolescent male.

The narrator of the "Eula" section begins with the same voice later used in the Mink passages, where he provides words for Mink in an understanding but definitely detached voice.

> It was as though the very capacity of space and echo for reproducing noise were leagued against him too in the vindication of his rights and the liquidation of his injuries. (*H* 250)

> And here again, for the third time since he had pulled the trigger, was that conspiracy to frustrate and outrage his rights as a man and his feelings as a sentient creature. (*H* 251)

> Now, though not yet thirteen years old, she was already bigger than most grown women and even her breasts were no longer the little, hard, fiercely-pointed cones of puberty or even maidenhood. On the contrary . . . (*H* 107)

She seemed to be not a living integer of her contemporary scene,
but rather to exist in a teeming vacuum in which her days followed one another as though behind sound-proof glass, where
she seemed to listen in sullen bemusement . . . (*H* 107)

These last two sentences, like the preceding two from the Mink section,
are crisp, their diction precise. In the first, only "fiercely" betrays any emotion. In the second the "not . . . but rather," the scientific "integer," and
the attempt at explanatory simile implied by "as though" all contribute to
a sense of decorum and control, and only the word "teeming" gives a hint
of what is to come. For each of these two sentences plays a trick on the
reader. The voice, apparently so dignified, seems to abrupt into phantas-
magoric extravagancies of passion:

> . . . maidenhood. On the contrary, her entire appearance sug-
> gested some symbology out of the old Dionysic times—honey in
> sunlight and bursting grapes, the writhen bleeding of the crushed
> fecundated vine beneath the hard rapacious trampling goat-hoof.

> . . . to listen in sullen bemusement, with a weary wisdom heired
> of all mammalian maturity, to the enlarging of her own organs.

Suddenly the narrator seems obsessed by sex. His frustrations are those
of a fantasy of pornographic sadism, a scene of violence: "crushed," "hard
rapacious trampling," "bursting," "writhen bleeding." That the narrator
just as abruptly gets himself under control helps us to see that the frustrations and excesses are comic ones. In fact, the obsession with grapes
and the mammalian organs sounds like nothing so much as the voice of a
harmless male adolescent amazed by the build of the teenage sex goddess.

Of course, Faulkner uses Labove to embody these feelings in what is
not only a more frenzied but ultimately a crazed form. As with Mink, the
narrator is simultaneously involved with and detached from Labove. He
tells us "He was mad. He knew it" (*H* 135); but he also voices for us the
strange compulsion to be "drawn back into the radius and impact of an
eleven-year-old girl who, even while sitting with veiled eyes against the
sun like a cat on the schoolhouse steps at recess and eating a cold potato,
postulated that ungirdled quality of the very goddesses in his Homer and
Thucydides" (128). We are unable to say whether it is the thought of

Labove or the narrator that Eula brings into the schoolroom "a moist blast of spring's liquorish corruption, a pagan triumphal prostration before the supreme primal uterus" (129). When Labove gets sick looking at a sweet potato we laugh, but we are not distanced enough not to know what he is going through. The comedy in his crazed frustration is his attempt to deal with "priapic hullabaloo" by clinging to maleness and to the book knowledge of which Eula's very existence makes a mockery: "He moved as quickly and ruthlessly as if she had been a football or as if he had the ball and she stood between him and the final white line which he hated and must reach" (137); "He held her loosely, still smiling, whispering his jumble of fragmentary Greek and Latin verse and American-Mississippi obscenity" (138). But along with comedy there is the poignancy of Labove's sad perception of "the now deserted room in which there were still and forever would be too many people" (140). There is also a sense of the alternative to adolescence—a sympathetic awareness that frustration is after all a striving for glory, and that the end of adolescence is not really maturity but the beginning of death. The narrator speaks of the failure of two of Eula's three suitors: "[T]hose two would thus be relegated also to the flotsam of a vain dead yesterday of passionate and eternal regret and grief, along with the impotent youths who . . . had conferred upon them likewise blindly and unearned the accolade of success. By fleeing too, they put in a final and despairing bid for the guilt they had not compassed, the glorious shame of the ruin they did not do" (160).

The most important thing to recognize, however, is that the narrator voices the male hysteria over Eula not only from the characters' point of view but in his own voice as well. The extravagant conceits come from both the characters and the narrator:

"At the rate she's going at it, there aint a acorn that will fall in the next fifty years that wont grow up and rot down and be burnt for firewood before she'll ever climb it." (*H* 109)

She might as well still have been a foetus. (109)

The three of them would be seen passing along the road—
Mrs Varner in her Sunday dress and shawl, followed by the negro man staggering slightly beneath his long, dangling, already indis-

putably female burden like a bizarre and chaperoned Sabine rape. (108)

These comparisons are not only "bizarre" but amazed, and hilarious partly because of the amazement they express. The "Eula" section is the story of the common experience of men with inaccessible female goddesses.

The whole section, especially the Eula-Labove story, with its resemblances to one of the most famous in our folklore, becomes in its own right a tall tale, a sort of Sleepy Hollow legend. It becomes apparent at some point that not only the tone and the descriptions but even the dialogue and the supposed facts are fabulous. After the excesses of the first paragraph of the section, we may well suspect that we are being told a whopper when we reach the deadpan statement "She was late in learning to walk" (*H* 107). Certainly the famous response of Mrs. Varner to Eula's pregnancy suggests that the narrator's extravagancies have transformed his emotional telling out of the realm of the mimetic altogether: "I'll fix him. I'll fix both of them. Turning up pregnant and yelling and cursing here in the house when I am trying to take a nap" (163). We also find that the football hero Labove is leveled by Eula, who stands over him "breathing deep but not panting and not even dishevelled" (138). Faulkner's comically emotional self-dramatization leads to a distortion of the story—and reminds us that tall tales too are within the range of narrative conventions available to the teller of this novel of multiple stories.

Eula is a phenomenon so foreign to male minds that she must always be approached obliquely—through metaphors—by both the characters and the narrator. Ratliff thinks of her as a heifer wasted as bait for a rat (*H* 182) and as an "unscalable sierra, the rosy virginal mother of barricades" (181). And even her father, who thinks himself above any concern with what he thinks of as the fiction of female chastity, speaks of Eula as "pure liver" (180). But the lack of objective treatment should not be viewed—here any more than elsewhere in Faulkner—as a tacit admission either that Eula is a myth rather than a character or that Faulkner is more interested in fiction-making than in the characters of the fiction. On the contrary, just as the multiple possibilities of stories free storytellers from mere fact, so do those possibilities leave characters free of our ability to talk endlessly about them. We should see that while Faulkner is having fun at his own expense, he also creates a Eula free of the idealizations and pseudo-facts generated by male legend-makers. We see in the comic role of the storyteller the same faith in the imagined world implied by the intentional unreliability of the narrators of *The Town*.

This is possible because for one thing Ratliff raises for us some serious words that we might have thought inapplicable to a sex goddess. Is Eula a tragic victim? Is she "another mortal natural enemy of the masculine race" (*H* 171)? In "The Peasants" the narrator seems to endorse this view by describing "the mask not tragic and perhaps not even doomed: just damned" (349). But more importantly, the events of the story reveal in Eula an aptitude for unexpected action that fails to fit the myth of her gargantuan passivity. According to one of the victims, it is Eula herself who defends McCarron with a buggy whip: "*springing* from the buggy and with the reversed whip *beating* three of them back" (157, emphasis added). Appropriately enough, it is Will Varner who makes the biggest miscalculation of Eula's capabilities: "the father . . . who, regardless of what error he might have made in the reading of the female heart in general and his daughter's in particular, had been betrayed at the last by failing to anticipate that she would not only essay to, but up to a certain point actually support, with her own braced arm from underneath, the injured side" (159–60).

Finally, after fifty pages of the male viewpoint, Faulkner suddenly stops, starts a new section (chapter 2 of book 2), and bluntly offers us a sudden vision of *Eula's* point of view: "She knew him well" (*H* 167). That sharp sentence punctures the male illusion of her mindlessness and reveals a new dimension in the character. The narrator goes on in a kind of litany to affirm the new idea of Eula's knowledge: "She knew him so well that . . . She had known him ever since . . . " (167). In fact, it is from Eula that we get the most effective disregard of Flem in the whole novel: "Without rising or even turning her head she would call toward the interior of the house: 'Papa, here's that man,' or, presently, 'the man,'—'papa, here's the man again,' though sometimes she said Mr Snopes, saying it exactly as she would have said Mr Dog" (167). The comic role-playing of the narrator does not finally prevent a belief in the essential reality of the character, does not prevent a mimetic intention from being implicitly present. We do gain a sense of Eula's human character, the reality imperfectly seen somewhere in the teenage sex queen.

This method of character revelation is actually continued in *The Town*.

There, the male perspective is perpetuated in the chivalric buffoonery of Gavin Stevens, "talking (I presume I was; I usually am)" (216). Gavin sees Eula as a "Lilith: the one before Eve herself whom earth's Creator had perforce in desperate and amazed alarm in person to efface, remove, obliterate, that Adam might create a progeny to populate it" (44). And as Charles Mallison says, "If I had been there and no older than Gowan was, I would have known that if I had been about twenty-one . . . I not only would have known what was going on, I might even have been Uncle Gavin myself" (46). As the reader identifies with Gavin, Charles, et al., seeing Eula from the outside, he shares with the male characters their surprise at the moments of sudden insight that make clear Eula's existence not as a goddess but as a person. Like a child trembling with terror, Gavin realizes "*Why, she can't possibly be this small, this little . . .* too small to have displaced enough of my peace to contain this much unsleep" (90). In that moment Gavin realizes too that Eula has understood him more than he has understood her, that her gaze is an "envelopment," "one single complete perception to which that adjective complete were as trivial as the adjective dampness to the blue sea itself" (90). Gavin's fear is similar to that which Charles intuits on the part of Manfred de Spain: "I reckon there was a second when even he said Hold on here; have I maybe blundered into something not just purer than me but even braver than me, braver and tougher than me because it is purer than me, cleaner than me?" (74). De Spain, according to Charles, must have felt "amazement and unbelief and terror too at himself because of what he found himself doing without even knowing he was going to—dancing like that with Mrs Snopes" (74). Man is led against his expectation into the awareness of Eula's existence and into the orbit of that unforeseen volition and willingness to act. Paradoxically, the revelations that make Eula suddenly real to De Spain actually reinforce the old feeling that there is something superhuman there after all—"that splendor, that splendid unshame" (75).

Once we have accepted the necessity of seeing through comic narrative conventions, we can see that the line of Eula's character is actually rather consistent from *The Hamlet* to *The Town*.[19] She begins by being mythically passive but capable of surprising acts of exertion, and becomes a saddened advocate of passivity, capable of surprising, violent self-sacrifice. In *The Town* her arguments are no more rational than is the character of the seemingly mindless goddess of *The Hamlet;* but here, too, Faulkner manages to suggest an instinctive knowledge that puts to flight all reason and book learning: "Nobody needs to have a scene to get what you want. You just get it" (*T* 321). Eula offers herself to Gavin in a way that affirms the ultimate identity, in her case, of action and passivity: "Dont expect. You just are, and you need, and you must, and so you do. That's all. Dont waste time expecting" (94). In short, Eula's character has a consistency and makes sense, in spite of the fact that the response of the narrator of *The Hamlet* is as male and sophomoric as is that of Gavin Stevens in *The Town*.

Other readers have spoken of Eula as a product of male discourse, but principally either to imply a weakness in characterization or to condemn the limitations of all male language. John Matthews argues that the "overstatement of her body reminds us that Eula is a figure of speech" (200). Evelyn Jaffe Schreiber calls Eula "an empty space on which community members project their desires" (88). Deborah Clarke discusses the way the language of male law and the male language of Ratliff and the narrator constrain Eula, leave her "vulnerable to narrative violation" (81). Richard Gray writes that "what we are offered . . . is an account of male reactions to her" (258). He cites the "feverish, excited idiom" deployed to describe Eula not only by "other, male characters" but also by the narrator (259): "The voice of the narrator collaborates with the voice of the community, and the voice of the author, however implied, seems to be in there cooperating as well. The lip-smacking, tumescent prose used to describe her indicates that author and narrator, just as much as the male characters, are talking about Eula rather than talking with her" (261). Elizabeth Rankin describes Eula as "a product of the male imagination," but with the conclusion that "in a way, Eula is not a character at all" (148). But in itself this filter of language makes Eula ontologically no different from any other character, for as Matthews points out by quoting Derrida, "imitation, principle of art . . . having to be a *discourse*, . . . has always already broached presence in differance" (31). All character-presences are products of someone's words. Acknowledging that characters can only be created through language, we must distinguish those characters that seem to be *only* projections of other people's language, and whether that is caused by failure on the part of other speakers in the language community, failure of the author's own conception, or something else altogether, like narratorial humor.

Faulkner's manifest faith in the reality of his imagined world is a major indication of the control and confidence of what I have called his humorous temperament. The character of Eula escapes the comically limited male versions of her. And though Faulkner must improve the story of Mink, he does so with an almost apologetic tone. Speaking as the extra-fictional writer "W.F." of the foreword to *The Mansion,* he says that he has failed to understand the characters in the earlier versions, as if the characters have an existence independent of the creator. Faulkner does not celebrate himself at the expense of his characters or call attention to his own act of making them up. Rather, he takes delight in stories already beyond the point of making-up. Like the narrators in *The Town,* Faulkner as narrator implies a limitless source of material in characters and situations that have a life independent of his discourse. As we have seen, this gives a basic orderliness and security that permits the improvisation of all the storytellers in his stories—both the authorial persona and the character/narrators. And this is true both inside and outside the novels. For the reader comes to share the belief in the power of the act of telling to order Faulkner's world without exhausting it. Like the narrators in *The Town,* the reader acts as listener only while waiting a turn as teller. The story becomes accessible to us, not to make up but to embroider and retell. I suspect that this is not only theoretical, rather that in fact we readers of Faulkner often do retell Faulkner's stories to our own listeners.

Claude-Edmonde Magny sees Faulkner's conviction of the reality of his own creation as a major reason why the books are so demanding. Faulkner not only insists that the reader work as hard as *he* has; he even assumes the reader has already been successful: "His eyes are so fixed on the universe within him that he comes to believe that everything is as clear to us as it is to him, and he never ceases to treat the eventual reader like another self" (212). Faulkner's demands on the reader do not represent an abdication of authority. His violations of lucidity represent an act of confidence in the reader's ability to rise to a challenge. But at the same time they represent the writer's confidence in himself, a confidence that the word "humor" will only partly account for.

Faulkner establishes his humor in spite of the handicap of the tension and strains of anguish; the corollary is that only through virtuosity could such a humorous poise be established against such a handicap. Not only is Faulkner's art ultimately not paralyzed by its tensions, but it exhibits positive freedom through its inventive conquests over the usual. Faulkner's work must be meant, not just to demonstrate its poise, but to *impress* us with its poise. It is with Faulkner as with the mannerists: "The very

novelty and difficulty of execution is what most deserves our praise"
(Shearman 84). Faulkner's own twentieth-century mannerism manages
to insist on its own artfulness—without ceasing to be "about" the human
figures it represents. Faulkner's work asks us to see that it is ornately
made, not that it is made up.

The author's virtuosity is central in our response to a stylistic signature
like Faulkner's parallelisms. In one common form of the parallelism
Faulkner uses a series of qualifications:

> He looked like a Methodist Sunday School superintendent
> who on week days conducted a railroad passenger train
> or vice versa
> and who owned the church
> or perhaps the railroad
> or perhaps both. (*H* 6)

The narrator urges the reader through the phrases by which the joke is
capped. We see the narrator going himself one better, and the process of
telling is brought front and center along with the comedy of the joke
itself. It is the same process of retelling that we have seen embodied in
the entire shape of some of Faulkner's stories. The point is not that the
narrator is fumbling for a good way to express himself, unable to bring
himself to cut his own rejected lines. On the contrary, the joke that is
capped is *part* of the joke; the intermediary versions are used as building
blocks. Each line in itself *is* "right," but the self-confident narrator wants
us to follow with augmenting amazement as he adds one more line after
another to the joke, one more phrase after another to the sentence:

> It was as though the original nose had been left off by the
> original designer or craftsman and the unfinished job taken over
> by someone of a radically different school
> or perhaps by some viciously maniacal humorist
> or perhaps by one who had had only time to clap into the center
> of the face a frantic and desperate warning. (*H* 59)

Surely we are meant to be as amused by the virtuosity with which the
narrator can prolong the parallel structure as by the thought expressed in
the joke.

Magny provides the word *magic* to describe the quality of Faulkner's authority, when she assesses the significance of the adjectives that she sees as a central signature of his style:

> Qualifiers . . . are so many magic means by which man can appro-
> priate nature. Far from *describing* things, as common sense naively
> believes . . . , these qualifiers mark our power over things, . . .
> things that are given particularities that make no sense except in
> relation to us. . . . It is obvious that a certain kind of writer might
> use epithets to present things to the reader in a magical way, to
> *suggest* them rather than truly to describe them—in short, *to
> force them to appear,* which is the strict meaning of the word
> "evoke." (198)

The confidence and equanimity of Faulkner's humor is surpassed only by the air of triumph of his magic. We feel continuously, as Eudora Welty says, "this writer's imagination soaring like the lark" ("In Yoknapatawpha" 598). Faulkner repeatedly demonstrates that he accomplishes things un-attempted yet in prose or rhyme. The idiosyncratic verbal medium is the magical solution in which he holds his people. The final significance of the stylistic signatures is that they evidence a speaker who continuously revels in his own ability to do anything with the world verbally. Miracu-lous words are proof of a magician, a wonder-worker.[20]

Faulkner asserts himself to be among those to whom writing is not grand failure but power. To use the language of the Nobel-speech formu-lation, this is not the "endurance" of the voice of man outlasting every-thing by its unremitting and perhaps meaningless talking, but rather a demonstration that by talking in this powerful way, man has already "pre-vailed." Modernist technique and conventional modernist despair are oc-casional elements of his writing, but modernism does not hold him. He does not abide the modernist question. The full process of living is "to have learned enough despair to hope" (*LIA* 132). Despair is the necessary precursor to hope. But to voice despair in such language is already to have enabled hope. Yeats famously makes the distinction: "They know that Hamlet and Lear are gay, / Gaity transfiguring all that dread" ("Lapis Lazuli"). Hamlet and Lear are certainly not gay, but *Hamlet* and *Lear* may be gay, and "Shakespeare" may be gay. The triumph of expression is itself a transformation. Modernism in Faulkner is a fact, but it is not the whole truth, and cannot be the final formulation.[21]

The tour-de-force writing foregrounds the otherness of voice, vocabulary, even subject matter. In *The Hamlet*, what entity but "Faulkner" can not only see such things in a rain shower but put these things into words? What other subjectivity wants to express the sensations of an idiot with the vision and language of a poet, and a baroque Miltonic poet at that? Faulkner provides words that are not specious to him who "had been given the wordless passions but not the specious words" (*H* 224).

It is certainly wrong to say that the tour-de-force performance is designed to alienate, to set the teller apart in a godlike state. In responding to this tour de force, the reader is elevated as well, to an elite partnership with the performer—*if*, that is, as Warwick Wadlington says, it works: "When we feel we can make seemingly inexhaustible power like that of *Absalom* our own in some measure, it is a remarkable form of empowering" (*Reading Faulknerian Tragedy* 218). The possibility that Faulkner may "lose this audience entirely" (218) seems like a legitimate concern for the unknown writer of 1928, or even the unacknowledged and undervalued writer of 1936. Today, from the point of view of an educated audience, there seems no reason to take much notice of the reader who will not make the effort to join the partnership, who will not respond to the gambit.[22]

I have spoken of the Faulknerian temperament as if it were consistently humorous and magical in much the same fashion. Of course, it would be virtually impossible for this to be true. When Wayne Booth is reluctant to talk about the temperament of an implied author over an entire career, it is because he is sensitive to temperament and is aware that there are large, even surprising inconsistencies from one "Fielding" persona to another:

> The author of *Jonathan Wild* is by implication very much concerned with public affairs and with the effects of unchecked ambition on the "great men" who attain to power in the world. If we had only this novel by Fielding, we would infer from it that in his real life he was much more single-mindedly engrossed in his role as magistrate and reformer of public manners than is suggested by the implied author of *Joseph Andrews* and *Tom Jones*. . . . On the other hand, the author who greets us on page one of *Amelia*

has none of that air of facetiousness combined with grand insouci-ance that we meet from the beginning in *Joseph Andrews* and *Tom Jones.* . . . Though the author of *Amelia* can still indulge in occa-sional jests and ironies, his general air of sententious solemnity is strictly in keeping with the very special effects proper to the work as a whole. (*Rhetoric of Fiction* 72–73)

Over a long career, there are also inevitable variations in the tone of Faulkner's work, whether because of subject matter or theme, or simply because the temperament of authority and equanimity is difficult for any-one to maintain—even on paper. The combination of control and abdi-cation in the narrator implies the temperament of one who positively enjoys being the Faulknerian narrator. But it would be pointless to claim that Faulkner's persona is always so eupeptic. *Sanctuary,* for instance, might be seen as a work that shows by contrast what the Faulknerian narrator is usually like. For in *Sanctuary* Faulkner falls from authority not intentionally but from loss of poise; the narrator shows a hysteria any-thing but humorous over the phenomenon of adolescent female sexuality. Faulkner is unable to distance himself from his flapper character; we find him actually guilty of a cruel hounding of Temple, a perverse relish in seeing her degradation.

M. E. Bradford has said of Faulkner's "Elly" that it is "a portrait etched in acid . . . Elly is a bundle of the very traits which he utterly despises." Bradford notes that "ordinarily Faulkner's sympathetic leanings drive him to complicate and discover touches of pitiable humanity in his creations, to go inside them and 'feel what wretches feel'" (185–86). His detachment from Elly is therefore significant. But in *Sanctuary* we might say that Faulkner is anything but detached; with Temple, he is virtually on the attack. We can sense the writer rigging the plot so as to commit Temple to the furthest depravity. Not only is she brutally raped, but she is made victim of Popeye's voyeurism while she is publicly degraded further. And to cap that off, she is made to desire that very degradation; so given over is she to her lust that she ignores the voyeur, and later she pursues Red so maniacally as to cause his murder. Faulkner graphically portrays the shak-ings of her body, showing her totally the prey of sexual impulse. Actually, one of Faulkner's most compelling bits of writing is the portrayal of Temple's compulsive nervousness before the rape: her behavior is an in-distinguishable combination of her tendency to tease and a hysterical fear.

Yet Faulkner undercuts his own characterization and intentionally stunts the compassion he has generated by having the sympathetic Ruby denounce Temple: "And you, you little doll-faced slut, that think you cant come into a room where a man is without him . . ."; "'You poor little gutless fool,' the woman said in her cold undertone. 'Playing at it'"; "Afraid? You haven't the guts to be really afraid, any more than you have to be in love" (*Sanctuary* 57, 58, 59). That the town boys mimic her "My father is a judge" is an expression of their frustration and hatred of her; that in a moment of terror Temple herself uses the phrase is a reduction of the character to the level of the town boys' satire. It is a cheap shot on the part of the author.

The critical dialogue on *Sanctuary* shows many feminist critics generously unwilling to accuse Faulkner of misogyny. This involves arguing that Faulkner exhibits a profound sympathy for Temple in spite of being bound within a misogynistic "horizon of discourse" (Duvall, *Faulkner's Marginal Couple* 17). Ruby's attack on Temple has been dismissed as the voice of a woman corrupted by patriarchal values, or even of a masculinized woman. Diane Roberts describes this as "rape by language" (132). Ruby's cruel lack of sympathy to Temple does cause her to miss the ways in which Temple's frantic movements represent not exhibitionism but terror. On the other hand, Ruby herself is very sympathetic as a victim, and her angry words to Temple seem designed to have some credibility. As Richard Gray says, Ruby's "remarks are given the kind of weight and authoritativeness that is denied to those of, say, Horace Benbow or his family" (169).

Temple's fatal perjury and her apparent spiritual death in the Luxembourg Gardens have also been defended both as the legitimate effects of traumatization and as a justifiable revenge on the entire patriarchy that has repeatedly raped her. Deborah Clarke offers a more nuanced view of the character. Clarke explains Temple's "seductive poses and apparent animalistic desires as the attempt to play on expectations of masculine logic," an attempt to negotiate her captivity that is the only course left open to her. Her "behavior becomes a desperate attempt to articulate what she cannot speak verbally—a feminine discourse which will prove effective in the face of male aggression" (67). Clarke calls the perjury "appropriate," but she does not justify it: "This time her language constitutes not protective figurative fantasies but lies, the perversion of the figurative into the untrue" (68). Indeed, for most readers, it would take a quite material effort to make sympathetic an act that dooms an innocent man to a lynch mob.

In a sense both views of Temple are at least partly right: she is certainly brutalized and traumatized, but she also "enjoys it" and commits a murderous lie. If Faulkner blames the brutalizers, does he not also blame the victim? In fact, Faulkner does not love Temple, as, according to James, "Balzac loves his Valerie" ("The Lesson of Balzac," *Future of the Novel* 116).

In *Sanctuary* the urgency of the implied author is distressed, even vindictive. Richard Gray argues that "Temple's last two appearances . . . only serve to confirm the fear and anger that went into her making. She is a character who seems, in the last analysis, to have been invented to prove the equation: woman = nature = chaos/evil" (167). Gray writes of the "voyeuristic note that invariably creeps into descriptions" of Temple, and of "the aggression the narrative voice seems to feel toward her" (167). He detects a sense of "radical disturbances" deriving from Faulkner's own deeply conflicted views about women. He sees Faulkner's outrage at the rape of Temple as "contradicted not only by the narrator's voyeuristic attitude towards her—even when she is defecating—but by the violence of the language marshalled to describe her at times" (175). Kevin Railey says that "to depict reactions to a rape the way they are depicted here, as if this experience would unleash raging lust, seems particularly, and even absurdly, the perspective of a paternalist" (187). It would be easy to use a much stronger word than "paternalist" here to describe the disorder of Faulkner's vision.

In what sense is *Sanctuary* atypical? Not in the form of its plot, for both its actions and its inactions are assertive and are distributed among several agents making their own moves. There are a number of features of technique that might be said to show a form of modernism: the shape of Popeye as if two-dimensionally "stamped from tin"; the eerie slapstick of Red's funeral. But the action itself is brutally complete, only made modernistically weird by the fact that most of the violent central acts are not explicitly shown—not the murder of Tawmey, the rape of Temple, or the murder of Red. What makes *Sanctuary* atypical is simply the darkness that overpowers the implied author's own vision. This is a world where good is impotent and sick, where literal impotence is rapacious, where death has the last word. The implied author's almost malevolent manipulation of Temple shows that here, unlike in *The Sound and the Fury*, we have an implied author who is himself sickened, given over to a wasteland despair, consumed by the darkness.

The failure of temperament in *Sanctuary* should not, however, deny us a sense of Faulkner's usual control. That control itself does show significant variations from work to work. Obviously the "humor" of *Pylon*, such as it is, is differently constituted than that of *The Reivers*. *Pylon* is distinctive for the particular tenor of the unmistakably Faulknerian magic in the prose. The volubility of the narrator achieves a kind of feverishly sardonic babbling totally appropriate to the drunkenness, the Mardi Gras chaos of the setting, and the confused frustration acted out in the plot. *Pylon* cultivates an ironic shrug born of male frustration not only at women but also at the strange nonhumans that fliers seem to be. But the air of futility, which persists through the ending, is tempered, for the reader's scope is not limited to a sense of frustration. Instead, we are made to see that Laverne is a human being driven to extremity by love. We feel sorry for her, and we feel that such a feeling is an achievement of a perspective denied to all but one of the characters in the novel—including the sympathetic journalist who is the novel's unnamed central character. The exception is the unnamed newspaperman who says "Let them all rest. They were trying to do what they had to do, with what they had to do it with, the same as all of us only maybe a little better than us" (*Pylon* 290). In *Pylon*, Faulkner achieves humor both by acting out grim irony and by putting irony itself into perspective.

Yet the whole range of Faulkner's control is very different from that of Joyce, for example. In spite of all the humanism credited to him, Joyce really does give prominence to his own artistry at the expense of his characters. As Richard Poirier says, "The drama of *Ulysses* is only incidentally that of Stephen, Bloom, and Molly; more poignantly it is the drama of Joyce himself making the book" (38). Joyce is concerned more than anything with his own magic. His virtuosity, his encyclopedic learning, and his versatility are so important to him as to justify Eric Auerbach's conviction that Joyce actually shows a hostility to "reality"—that is, to human actors (551). The prose is magical, but the control is anything but humorous.

Despite Faulkner's variations in tone, we should not too quickly give in to the temptation to make simplistic divisions in his career—to say, for instance, that the "magic" of the late novels reflects the acclaim Faulkner received late in his career. The canonical version of Faulkner's career is that he began as a high modernist and became something else which represented a falling off.[23] In order to make his distinction between the ends of Faulkner's career, Philip Weinstein argues that the high modernist Faulkner engages with the Other by rendering the troubled interface of the subject and the world, while the late Faulkner makes the focus the ascendancy of the Faulkner voice itself.[24] Donald Kartiganer argues that beginning with the tour-de-force writing of *The Hamlet*

> Faulkner sets up a deliberate gap between style and event. . . .
> At least one of the results of this gap is to call attention to the author himself, for these are clearly "performances," an outrageous coupling of form and content that parades the writer's mastery both of his craft and his material. (*Fragile Thread* 120)

> In *The Hamlet* . . . [the] illusion of style as the author's desperate attempt to embrace an ever-shifting reality is reversed and becomes the illusion of an author so assured of the direction and shape of his material that he can afford every stylistic excess available to him. (125)

This general notion of the career accords with the idea that the oratorical "Faulkner" voice appears in mid-career:

> [Faulkner's] later voice is of course the one we call "Faulkner," and once we concede that it is more capacious than any summary of it suggests, it remains recognizably a *voice:* "Faulkner." (Weinstein, *Faulkner's Subject* 123)

> Our stubborn (through illusory) sense that we are hearing the writer himself, hearing his own voice, shapes decisively our reading of [*Absalom*], establishing it thus as the pivotal novel in Faulkner's career, the one in which his "signature" emerges as a rhetoric: a distinctive use of syntax and vocabulary that we are invited to take as an originating power. (141)

Stephen Ross also finds appearing in *Absalom, Absalom!* "the overwhelming consistency of an oratorical Overvoice pervading the entire text. . . . The Overvoice envelops the discourse, taking up into itself all subsidiary voices. . . . [It is] the Voice of authority that sanctions the discourse we hear. . . . This Overvoice becomes an entity unto itself" (220–21).[25]

But this is surely an unnecessary distinction. As Wadlington demonstrates, the voice of the virtuoso Faulkner is every bit as present in the period of Faulkner's modernist style: "In [*As I Lay Dying*] the shared voice that is bigger than they are is clearly that of their impersonator, Faulkner, who makes them all 'speak Faulkner.' He thus calls attention to his tour de force" (*Reading Faulknerian Tragedy* 126); "Both novels [*As I Lay Dying* and *Sanctuary*] surround these lives with a narrative rhetoric of extraordinary voice which only enters them in rare, private, furtive, or grotesque ways" (129).

The Sound and the Fury is not exclusively a novel of unresolved tension, in which the novelist acts out extreme and extremely divided possibilities. Quite apart from the role of Dilsey, there is a fundamental fact about the novel that undercuts or encompasses the fragmentation, and that is the fact that evidently these fragmented voices can be mimed by "Faulkner." It is obvious that only tremendous pride in his art, a tremendous daring, would permit a writer even to attempt the mind of an idiot—whatever the private needs and uncertainties of that writer might be. The art reveals only pride and daring, not uncertainty. But Faulkner goes himself one better here no less than in the retellings of the Snopes books. He "does" the mind of an idiot. And then, he implicitly tells us, he will do a college boy at the very point of suicide. And *then* he will do . . . From the point of view of the "speakers" themselves the voices may be totally at odds, but from our own perspective the situation can never be quite so desperate. Quentin is inarticulate but, within, sensitive and bursting with things to say; we could not know anything except the inarticulateness if Faulkner were not willing to accept the artistic challenge to voice Quentin's inward thoughts for us. We see rather triumphantly that we can be made to see, almost to understand, a mind we might have thought totally closed to us. Not only can each of these minds be "done," but they can be done within the pages of one book, by one writer. Such a magisterial ventriloquism is intended to impress us; we of necessity sense a writer who is impressively able both to render and to understand. Such a writer could never really be in danger of despair, could never be in danger of getting stuck in Quentin's narrative. The author implied by the plot contradicts but yields precedence to the author implied by the narration. Thus modernism is not the final word on *The Sound and the Fury*.

Theoretically there are as many "Faulkners" as there are texts. Yet no one feels constrained to define a hundred Faulkners. So though "Faulkner," like "Fielding," is undoubtedly a bit different in all his books, we may still feel that there is a basic continuity in his implied personality, even in his novels of the wasteland. Even in *The Sound and the Fury* there is a force of temperament that impresses us with its authority and control, its inventiveness and virtuosity, and its human aspiration to serenity.

There may be an evolution in his narratorial voice. There may be a turn, from the use of epistemological tension for anguished investigation, to its use in the improvisational retelling of stories. But the overarching role of the implied author, the dominant presence of plots, and the persistence of "potency" of agency create a continuity in Faulkner's career.

In one sense the career issue may be beside the point. The term "differentiation" used in the theory of competitive strategy (Porter 198) suggests that a disproportionate impact in creating the identity of a "person" or an institution is generated by the one feature that is unique about that entity. In Proust, the "little phrase" is characteristic of Vinteuil's music not because it is representative of all his music, or because it is the average of all the bars of music Vinteuil writes, but because it stands out, is distinctive, differentiates Vinteuil from other composers. When Proust's narrator talks about writers, he defines them by their most differentiated characteristic—a scene in Dostoyevsky, a pattern of tripled relationships in Hardy (2:642–47).

A writer is not always demonstrating his most differentiated features, but his identity is nevertheless constituted by them:

> Proust's Flaubert consists in fact of a corpus of a few privileged pages. . . . To be perfectly precise, Proust, it seems to me, has put his finger with truly surgical precision on what is most specific to Flaubert. These Flaubertisms are found in his work in relatively small but increasing and, above all, decisive quantities; they set the tone, and we know that it takes only two or three original dissonances to transfigure a score which without them would be simply correct. (Genette, *Palimpsests* 117–18)

By this logic Faulkner is not quantitative but qualitative, not diachronic but essential.

In either case, the distinctive Faulknerian notes surely include the style that makes demands on the reader, the combination of virtuosity and poise, and the character-driven plots with a fundamentally humanistic vision of independent actors making moves and living through events. The elite partnership of teller and audience forming a community through magical style comports with the emplotted autonomy of persons making moves.

The Faulknerian storyteller, with his humor and his magic, is both an implicit and explicit presence who joins with his own characters to form the medium by which we gain access to the variety of human actions in the plots of William Faulkner. The implied author and the plot reach an important symbiosis, a complementarity. The plot partly constitutes the implied author, while the implied author gives context and tone to the plot. Faulkner's magisterial teller can place in context the darkness of doomed actions by the characters. But the willfulness and freedom of the characters make it clear that for all his virtuosity and poise, the implied author cannot control all human action. There is thus a creative tension between the story and the teller. The story and the teller, the *fabula* and the implied author—together these constitute a central relationship in narrative, essential elements of the act and art of storytelling.

Notes

Introduction

1. Godzich (xvi) and Marie-Laure Ryan (149) discuss this concern.

2. Ann Harleman Stewart gives a summary of different visual models for rendering narrative schema. See also Marie-Laure Ryan, chapters 7, 8, and 10.

3. "While texts are indeed full of formal elements, a priori assumptions govern which ones we ought to analyze. . . . Whether or not a novel has an integrity that precedes context or interpretative orientation . . . is a debatable modernist proposition of textual autonomy" (Cohen 636, 637).

4. For example, in a criticism of *The Mansion* that is an argument from biography, Zender (142–52) contends that Faulkner evades addressing in the relation of Gavin and Linda the issues of sexual intimacy he himself is known from the writings of Joan Williams to have been facing in his romance with Williams. Polk (*Dark House*) deconstructs the language of the Nobel Prize speech as a diversion of its audience from the real Faulkner; the audience is seen as being asked to forget corncob rapes, incest, and suicides and listen to affirmative attitudes incompatible even with the William Faulkner of 1950, let alone the William Faulkner of 1929. In Polk's view of Faulkner, the writing act expresses, but does not resolve, a primal sense of enclosure, captivity, a dark house, isolated and frightened children. One version of the primal scene is the scene of the rejected child at the door, a structural repetition in *Absalom, Absalom!* For additional biographist criticism, see Gray, Watson (*Self-Presentation*), and Singal.

5. In one example of postmodern text processing, Polk infers a homosexual relationship between Flem Snopes and Will Varner and attributes to Ratliff an "intense sense of guilt and shame over his own sexual, doubtless Oedipal, perhaps homosexual, impulses" (*Dark House* 191): "We can reasonably suspect that some experience of his own parents' marriage is his inspiration. . . . It seems reasonably clear that that miniature house on Ratliff's buggy represents some emotional baggage from his childhood that has made him a constantly moving refugee from the feminine" (189).

6. See Duvall's introduction, and the articles by Fowler, Hite, Tebbetts, and Weinstein, in Duvall and Abadie. See also Zender xiii.

7. Cf. Matthews: "In literary texts proleptic of postmodern fiction—among

which texts Faulkner's belong—the disestablishment of truth is welcomed by the impulse to play" (24).

8. Weinstein (*Faulkner's Subject*), Kartiganer (*Fragile Thread*), and Polk (*Dark House*) have used modernist features to frame their discussions of Faulkner. Faulkner's modernism is affirmed in different ways in recent works by Minter, Millgate (*Faulkner's Place*), Watson (*Self-Presentation*), and Singal—the latter two in particular also using a pronounced biographism. In the *Cambridge Companion* (ed. Weinstein), articles by Weinstein, Moreland, Matthews, and Patrick O'Donnell also address modernism. The article by Bleikasten constitutes a good reminder of all the different features that have been ascribed to literary modernism alone. There are numerous attempts to distinguish modernism and postmodernism in Duvall and Abadie's *Faulkner and Postmodernism*.

9. George Eliot offers a classic qualification: "But you have known Maggie a long while and need to be told, not her characteristics, but her history, which is a thing hardly to be predicted even from the completest knowledge of characteristics. For the tragedy of our lives is not created entirely from within. 'Character,' says Novalis in one of his questionable aphorisms '—character is destiny.' But not the whole of our destiny. . . . Maggie's destiny, then, is at present hidden, and we must wait for it to reveal itself like the course of an unmapped river; we only know that the river is full and rapid, and that for all rivers there is the same final home" (*The Mill on the Floss*, book 6, chapter 6).

Chapter 1

1. The terms *plot* and *story* distinguished by Forster, the *fabula/sjuzhet* distinction of the Russian Formalists, and a cluster of other related definitional terms have been used in a dizzying variety of combinations. For a summary see Lowe 13–14. The variations are displayed in tabular form in O'Neill 21.

Ian Reid dissents from what he sees as a dominance in narratology of "an event-based concept of story structure": "the structure of a written narrative utterance can be seen more productively as a matter of rhetorical successivity (a substitutive shuffle of signifiers) than as a chain of actions" (14). Michael Peled Ginsburg counters that on the contrary, "the 'actionist orthodoxy' against which Reid polemicizes is a straw man" (581).

2. There has been much spirited conversation regarding precisely what "causation" means in fiction. Forster's distinction between sequence and causation is in practice hard to make. Chatman writes: "Theory must recognize our powerful tendency to connect the most divergent events" (*Story and Discourse* 47). Proust himself wrote that ultimately everything can be seen as caused and that everything eventually happens: "The laborious process of causation . . . sooner or later will bring about every possible effect, including (consequently) those which one had believed to be most nearly impossible" (1:361). Kroeber cites Hannah Arendt, writing in 1953, to the effect that cause and effect is an imposed connectivity not necessary in narrative, specifically historical narrative: "Whoever in the historical sciences honestly believes in causality actually denies the subject matter of his own science. . . . The application

of general categories . . . [and] the search for general trends which are the deeper strata from which events spring . . . extinguish the 'natural' light history itself offers and, by the same token, destroy the actual story with its unique distinction and eternal meaning" (229). Egan asserts a different kind of causality, an "affective rather than logical or rational causality" (463). Rabinowitz cites Barthes and Gerald Prince to the effect that in narrative, causality is normally assumed based on temporal sequence alone (108–9). Carroll demonstrates that the minimal causal relation is that the "earlier event in a narrative connection is *at least* a necessary or indispensable contribution to a sufficient, though nonnecessary, condition for the occurrence of the relevant later event" (28). Richardson analyzes different senses of causation in a variety of texts.

3. Dolezel distinguishes one-character and multiple-character plots (*Heterocosmica,* ch. 4, "Interaction and Power," 96–112). Marie-Laure Ryan addresses the complexity that arises in narrative from the "virtual embedded narratives" of multiple characters (156). This makes possible the continuous holding open of other possibilities than those which actually happen. The "disnarrated" creates "diversity" in the narrative (169). "The appeal of the trip depends not so much on the immediate surroundings of the road actually followed as on the glimpses it permits of the back country, and of the alternative roads it invites the reader to travel in imagination" (174). This explains why endings are dependent for their impact on the openness that precedes them (see page 12 above). Ryan also describes the "parallelism" of the "narrative machine": "More often than not, a plot is not a single line of action, but the interaction of concurrent processes. In a narrative, as in a multitasking computer, a process may start another process, interrupt it, terminate it, slow it down, or speed it up" (128).

4. Others who discuss event in terms of change of "state" include Dolezel (e.g., *Heterocosmica* 56), Chatman (*Story and Discourse* 44), Lowe (the "game-state," e.g., 63) and O'Neill (17). Quoting Von Wright, Dolezel describes a "Logic of Change": "[Event is] a change of state of the person or of its environment" (241). Marie-Laure Ryan says "the plot occurs as a sequence of states mediated by events" (127). She places emphasis on the change of "relations among the worlds of the textual universe" (126).

For very different approaches to narrative continuities, see Miller's discussion of different kinds of "line" and Tilley's positing of a universal plot line of a binding and unbinding of energy.

Kreiswirth ("Centers, Openings, and Endings") suggests that stories can be described as structured by other formal strategies such as the use of the "empty center," for instance Caddy, a "shadowy presence at the novel's core": "These figures occupy their focal positions not only because all the circumferential characters obsessively look to them as a means of evaluating themselves and each other but also because they initiate and control their texts' sequence of incidents, its proairetic elements, as well as its sustaining enigmas, or hermeneutic elements" (202–3).

5. Cf. Todorov, *Poetics of Prose* 232: "'To begin' is not an action in and of itself, it is the (inchoative) aspect of another action."

6. Dolezel speaks of events in terms of "transitive action" (55) and "intention-

ality" (*Heterocosmica* 56). In describing plots of multiple characters, he writes that "conflict is the most common mode of interacting" (107) and catalogs different types of conflict: fights, games and debates, feuds, and inner conflicts (108–9). But Dolezel also emphasizes that contest can proceed "along parallel but interlocked strains of intransitive actions" (109). Marie-Laure Ryan uses the concept of moves to distinguish different types of events, such as conflict-solving moves (132) and narratives of plan and counterplan (142). She offers this general guideline: "a good plot must represent conflict and at least one attempt at solving it" (154).

7. Eric Rabkin discusses the difficulty of determining what is and is not an event (257). In order to see an event as part of a significant "function," Kafelnos requires "disruptive change," that is, "an event that alters the external world" ("Functions after Propp" 474). Chatman, using Barthes's term *noyau*, distinguishes material events as "kernals" (*Story and Discourse* 53 ff.). See also Cohan and Shires 54. Marie-Laure Ryan makes a similar distinction in terms of narrative peaks and valleys: "A theory of tellability implicitly regards a plot as a sequence of peaks and valleys, and seeks out the formulae for building up the peaks" (151). Pavel also counsels the need for qualitative distinctions: "The proposed *Move*-grammar and its semantics are subject to this kind of intuitive evaluation. Their categorical load, abstract as it is, still has an intuitive correspondence: one 'naturally' knows when a certain action is an important *Move,* or an inconsequential one" (*Poetics of Plot* 115). Lowe makes "a strong distinction between . . . *moves,* sharp changes to the game's balance of knowledge or power, and the kind of incidental pottering that produces only gradual and incremental shifts" (63). Herman (*Story Logic*) gives a full review of theories of event and action.

The analysis of the four "events" in the comic strip *Cathy* is in Cohan and Shires.

8. Kroeber also asserts the limitations of "analyses that make a story's ending wholly determinative of its meaning" (228). See also Marie-Laure Ryan's adaptation of Stendahl's road metaphor to emphasize the importance of things along the way (174).

Frank Kermode makes a similar point regarding the effect of "pleroma" in the New Testament fulfillment of Old Testament types: "The New Testament, as 'end,' is made up of many small typological completions, little ends in themselves; and perhaps this, in some more defined form, would give us the model we seek for dispersal and supplementation of endings" ("Sensing Endings" 155).

9. R. Rawdon Wilson imagines relationships of game and play between text and reader; Reid calls for a release from the tyranny of story and a focus on the "exchanges" between text and reader.

10. The metaphor of the multi-player board game is somewhat imperfect. The players of a board game are not *on* the board except symbolically or vicariously, whereas the players in a narrative are "on" the board and not outside it, except as narrators.

11. There has been much disagreement over the role of characterization in the description of events. Early narratologists such as Greimas, Bremond, and Genette have thought it important to separate the action from the "actant." Chatman (*Story and Discourse*) and Lanser have each argued the impossibility of describing an act

without knowing the context or the motivation of the actor. Dolezel writes: "The character of an action is determined not so much by what is done as why it is done" (*Heterocosmica* 70). For his character-driven model of narrative, Ferraro argues: "In fiction the character is used as the structuring element: the objects and the events of fiction exist—in one way or another—because of the character and, in fact, it is only in relation to it that they possess those qualities of coherence and plausibility which make them meaningful and comprehensible" (252). Similarly, Pavel concludes: "My own solution, which rests on notions derived from game-theory, suggests that plots as strategic clashes cannot be reduced to sequences of anonymous actions; a proper understanding of plot includes knowledge of the person or group who performs an action, the reason for it, and its effect on the overall strategic configuration" (*Poetics of Plot* 14). Margolin, conversely, writes of the necessity of actions for the process of characterization.

12. Jean-Paul Sartre, *Nausea* (1938), quoted in Kartiganer, "Faulkner's Quest for Form" 626. See also Kartiganer, *Fragile Thread* 175–76.

13. Wadlington also comments that in *The Sound and the Fury* "the plot offers no resolution at the level of narrative action" and that essentially "Caddy's is not really a *story*" because "it cannot be spoken in the Compson world" (*Reading Faulknerian Tragedy* 78, 82–23).

14. Much of the literature on epistemology in *Absalom, Absalom!* is cited in Dalziel and in Hoffmann. Matlack's essay is an example of an emphasis on the synthetic accomplishment of the creative and deductive impulses in characters and narrator, a "movement from chaos and bewilderment to clarification and insight" (346). Kuyk continues the increasingly unfashionable view that the "plausible inferences" of Shreve and Quentin "make their account convincing," and documents ways that the "official Voice" of the third-person narrator gives authoritative support to the two characters (60). Hoffmann, Krause, Basic, and Heberden Ryan see a dominant indeterminacy, emphasizing "the suspensive or even deconstructive traits . . . rather than the integrating and constructive ones" (Hoffmann 277). Reed articulates the rejection of the idea of conceiving *Absalom* as a book about knowledge or understanding: "Once we see that mystery-solving will bring us no closer to the heart of the novel, we move not so much through the book as we do down into it" (149); "The confusion remains confusion only so long as the reader assumes that he must solve the puzzle. To accept this assumption that the book is driving toward completion or solution is to be happy in the dark" (150). Batty, by contrast, seeks a new way of solving the "riddle" of the novel.

Further, it is possible to describe *Absalom* as a book that poses an ontological doubt about the world itself or which liberates the storyteller from a search for truth. On the other hand, recent critics have found ways to describe the product of Quentin and Shreve's thinking as an achievement that goes beyond "historical" truth and is achieved by means beyond ratiocination. Molly Hite reaches a judicious formulation that describes something more than play for play's sake: "The transgressive 'Let me play now' with which Shreve takes over the narration . . . signals a different approach to recounting history, one in which eyewitness accounts, physical evidence, and conjecture are reinterpreted or even replaced by virtuoso fabulation. In engaging in narrative 'play,' Shreve is concerned not with historical truth but with narrative integrity and effect" (69). Kreiswirth describes this process as "a pragmatics of transgression and transference" ("Intertextuality" 120). He calls Faulkner's story a "modernist blueprint . . . one based on recuperation through transference" (111).

Zender voices a sense that the whole topic of knowledge in *Absalom* has been thoroughly exhausted: "Some of the issues that had formerly seemed central to the interpretation of Faulkner's fiction—all that talk about epistemology in *Absalom, Absalom!*, for example—now seem stale in comparison to the issues being raised by the new wave of Faulkner critics" (41–42).

Chapter 2

1. The three stories have received limited treatment. Only "Mountain Victory" appears on Skei's list of Faulkner's best stories. Ross (88–90) includes a discussion of voice in "That Will Be Fine." James Ferguson describes "the child-narrator" as "a monster of greed" and says that the story "suggests the figurative reality of Original Sin" (59). Of "My Grandmother Millard," Ferguson says: "It can even be argued that the *fabulae* underlying some of Faulkner's less successful works of short fiction . . . are marvelous tales, even though he was unable to bring them to life because of the diminution of his narrative drive late in his career" (127). "Mountain Victory" has received more attention lately, in both Skei and Johnson.

2. In this chapter, *Collected Stories* is cited in the text without abbreviation, by page numbers only.

Chapter 3

1. Reed calls the trilogy "predominantly a progress sequence" (274), a world of "true flux" (224): "The form beneath the formlessness affords a better explanation of the fictions. I think the governing principle of this underlying form is plenitude. . . . An aim of plenitude provides that everything attached to the structure is of equal relevance and that the structure can sustain the addition of any number of incidents or characters. . . . Nothing is irrelevant once attached because its attachment to the chronicle . . . constitutes its relevance" (269). Essentially he is saying that "the form is the formlessness."

2. In this chapter, *The Hamlet* is cited in the text without abbreviation, by page numbers only.

3. Toliver 243 and ch. 6, "Narrative Stress Systems," 221–96.

4. Cf. Rabkin, especially 267–70.

5. Godden asserts a "latent sense that Flem is black" ("Earthing *The Hamlet*" 78) on the part of the inhabitants of Frenchman's Bend. But this reading is somewhat weakened by his assertion that in Ratliff's fantasy of Flem and Eula's wedding night, "he gives Flem 'long black stockings'" (97). Surely the point is not that Flem is metaphorically black but that Ratliff thinks Flem can only perform in the store with the black field hand. In Ratliff's conjecture it is actually Eula who must be dressed up in black tights in order for Flem to be able to encounter her sexually.

6. William Faulkner, "Father Abraham," MS fragment, Arents Collection, New York Public Library; discussed in Millgate, *Achievement* 24, 180–83, 326.

7. In the critical literature of patriarchy, Ratliff has often figured as a different form of masculinity. Rogers describes him as "a composite of both the active (male) and passive (female)" (147). Barnett writes that Ratliff "can . . . escape through language as genuine self-expression and verbal play," that he "is the only character to use language non-transactionally to a positive end" (403). Dale describes Ratliff as "an alternative to the Southern patriarch" (336). Railey suggests that Ratliff has "the potential to become a natural aristocrat" but is defeated by his lack of vision (155).

Inevitably, revisionist views of Ratliff have arisen. Polk argues that Ratliff fears women and deals with his customers cold-bloodedly, expressing a world in which woman is "contained . . . not by his [i.e., man's] love but by his economic power" (*Dark House* 194–5). Godden questions Ratliff's role in and his interpretations of Flem's rise, and also the authority of the narrator who appears to accept unquestioningly the "Ratliffian" reading of *The Hamlet* ("Earthing *The Hamlet*"). Urgo sees Ratliff as a voyeur with "the most actively immoral imagination" (*Faulkner's Apocrypha* 175) in the novel, one whose voyeurism in a sense enables the Snopeses: "Ratliff . . . has acted to turn Snopeses . . . to potential community leaders. He teaches them the all-important first lesson of a suppressed love of the body" (177). Urgo calls into question Ratliff's interpretive credibility as well, particularly in *The Town*, where he sees Ratliff's attitude toward the Snopeses as "incipient fascism" (188), an abuse of words to create a public ideology, a politics of knowledge (189–90). Kang also sees Ratliff as speaking for the patriarchy. When at the end of *The Mansion* Ratliff expresses the hope that there will be no more Eula Varners, Kang says that "his fearful wish reveals his fantasy for the exclusively male and perhaps homosocial 'utopia' devoid of the devouring and dismembering presence of woman and of her sexual Difference" (38).

8. The critical literature on patriarchy in Faulkner is large. Dunn emphasizes the way men are imprisoned by the "'man's world' of rules and rituals through which they assert their dominance over others and ironically create new bonds for themselves" (422). Kang represents Eula as "silenced 'within' the patriarchal discourse" (23). Schreiber disagrees, emphasizing Eula's "sense of agency over her sexual drive" (89) and her ability to rebel against imposed role models "by her sheer immobility" (88). Dale sees Eula as "bartered" by her father (330). She asserts that "Faulkner . . . radically challenges patriarchy itself" (323). But, rather differently, Dale also focuses on the central patriarch in the text itself, Flem Snopes: "The Snopes trilogy [is a] patriarchal narrative in that the patriarch is the focus of the multiple narrators" (336). Clarke observes that Eula, when married off to Flem, is not an "exchangeable commodity" (89) but instead reflects "the de-humanization of humanity which results from the denigration and de-sexualization of women" (90). It may overstate the case to suggest that Eula is desexualized for anyone but Flem. Trouard describes Eula as part of a different "economy," the "patriarchal economy" (281) which is constituted by "male discourse" (284). Subsequently she appears to use the word "economy" literally and argues that Eula is commoditized. She writes that Eula is Faulkner's "bitterest illustration of the patriarchal subjugation of women in American culture" (281).

9. The issue of Eula's victimization raises the question of whether she has any

role as agent in *The Hamlet*. Snead writes that "the narrative voice makes her into an emblem of centrality, purity, origins, power, even as it consigns her to social subordination and separation" (166). Others see a definite agency in Eula. Polk writes that "Eula's challenge to Will's centrality . . . lies . . . in the complete indifference to masculine hierarchy and tradition" (*Dark House* 168). Urgo also emphasizes Eula's passive resistance (*Faulkner's Apocrypha* 174). Others have pointed out Eula's unexpected activity in both the Labove and McCarron incidents (see Rankin 151; Clarke 72–73). Clarke is disturbed by the presentation of Eula as "only half human, a barely sentient womb," but she concludes that Eula has the "capability to bear herself" and thus has "far greater creative potential" than Ratliff, the narrator, or Flem (74). Schreiber sees Eula as rebelling against her mother's role model by "sheer immobility" but as having a "sense of agency over her sexual drive" and as achieving full and "final subjectification" through her suicide in *The Town* (88, 89, 90).

10. Duvall (*Faulkner's Marginal Couple*), Crews, and Kartiganer ("Faulkner Criticism") give detailed readings of Brooks. Brooks intuits a folk community of health and wisdom and cohesion, a sort of Silent Majority that includes Lena Grove and the furniture dealer but not Doc Hines or McEachern or Percy Grimm. In *The Hamlet* such an attribution of a folk community would have to affirm a basic sanity and "humorous poise" (*H* 79) in the same people who are at critical moments inert, angry, detached, or corrupted by greed. Yet in a certain sense Brooks's extrapolation may be no less a presumption than the postmodern inverse—bigoted, oppressive, patriarchally exploitative, even implicitly anti-Semitic—described by those who see Brooks as imposing an Agrarian fantasy on the Faulkner text. The warmth and irony of the coffee shop; the angry integrity of Mrs. Littlejohn; the dreams of all those who remember Eula: these could be adduced to balance the view of a society that exploits and wastes everybody.

Recent attention to Brooks's inferred folk community has obscured the influence of his work on the moral valuation of individual characters, which has continued to be central in Faulkner criticism, and on close engagement with the ambiguous facts of the texts. In *Fictions of Labor*, Godden mocks "the detectives" like Brooks: "Watching the detectives skirt an epistemological void has its pleasures, but these are limited. Detection seems stymied on an undenied lack of 'direct evidence'" (135). Godden's response to Brooks is not to seek for words that are "missing" but to infer words that are "obstructed by other words that constitute their hiding place": "I offer in evidence key words that are systematically marked by what they don't quite say" (135). In practice, this means an engagement with facts, but facts that cannot be verified.

11. Many indictments of the patriarchy do not limit themselves to gender issues. Snead writes of "the surrender of self" that results "upon entry into society's vicious exchange systems" (155); "Frenchman's Bend has made the act of exchanging much more valuable than either the particular items exchanged or the equity of the exchange. . . . Someone's gain is always someone else's loss" (152). Railey's focus is Faulkner's own political "paternalism": "Faulkner can never, it seems, break from a deep allegiance to paternalism and the social stratification it requires" (45). Godden

("Earthing *The Hamlet*") also analyzes the relation between the established society and the Snopes outsiders.

In "Faulkner's Real Estate," Urgo connects talking and trading in *The Hamlet* in an interesting way, relating the buying of land to "buying" a story, since buying a story about land is what actually leads to the buying of the land. If stories are commoditized as land is commoditized, it would follow that stories are as infected by the meanness of bourgeois capitalism as the cash transaction itself.

12. Readers who view Flem as a victim of or a rebel against an oppressive social structure include Urgo (*Faulkner's Apocrypha*) and Kang. Godden ("Earthing *The Hamlet*") argues that "Ratliff's account of Flem as the rapist of a work force is finally self serving. . . . Flem, as Ab's son, retains class continuity with the political violence of a resistant tenantry" (103). Godden says Flem is not "capital's epitome" (113). Others have seen Flem as the ultimate conformist, not a "symbol of pure rapaciousness" but "the perfect bourgeois" (Polk, "Idealism in *The Mansion*" 115). Flem can be seen as one who completely embraces the power structure, as essentially no different from Will Varner. This position is taken by Gregory, by Schreiber, and in his own way by Raymond Wilson. Snead sees Flem as the "revolutionary who shatters not by destroying the system, but by taking it to its extremes (indeed, this is an adequate definition for all 'parody')" (159); this view is compatible with Schreiber's view that by taking materialism to an extreme, Flem offers the community a "carnivalesque reflection of its values" (88).

Railey sees the assimilation of Flem to Varner's world as a parallel to Mississippi history: "the coalition between the Redeemers and the redneck Progressives defeated all challengers" (155). Gray offers a balanced view in which Flem is both insider and outsider: "Flem is neither the outsider, the stranger who brings an alien virus into an otherwise whole and stable body politic; nor is he the victim, the symptom of an established disease who is mistaken somehow for the cause. He is, quite simply, another if radical step in the continually unfolding history of the community: an agent of a transformation that comes from within. . . . [It is a change] by which both trading and talking are stripped down to a functional minimum" (255). Barnett sees Flem simply as "an allegorical monster, a personified abstraction of Acquisition" (405).

13. Godden deconstructs the text of the Flem in Hell episode, evoking words the text cannot say: "soil" and its unspeakable cognate "soilure." The "smear" that was once Flem's soul connects to the "suption" in a chew of tobacco, which connects to "rectal dirt" to evoke "the labor/credit relations to which the collateral, or '*smear*' heard as 'soil,' alludes." Without applying these seemingly free associations to unmask the tale Ratliff "cannot quite bring himself to tell," Godden argues, the story makes no sense: "Unless the story is 'about' the teller, its resolution makes no sense, the Devil having no reason to be dethroned by what amounts to confirmation of his authority." The hidden subject matter, which Ratliff himself does not understand, is "mourning for the resistant class victims of agricultural modernization" ("Earthing *The Hamlet*" 108–11).

14. A similar notion of multiplicity within novels is explored by Toliver, whose "mixed modes" of the novel include "the added complications of verse units, cine-

228 / *Notes to Pages 93–113*

matic technique, descriptive pauses, static portraiture, and the logic of authorial essays" (216).

15. What is troubling about the plot of *Intruder in the Dust* is not its improbabilities but that it is so perfunctory. The unraveling is reduced to Gavin talking. It has no urgency or intensity and does not really seem to matter. The unraveling of motive and the actual sequence—why Crawford dug up Vinson, when he killed Jake, why he buried him—are only dealt with in two pages of conjecture from Gavin. The actual apprehension of the killer, his incarceration, and his suicide are all offstage, mentioned and summarized as a kind of offhand afterthought. Morris contends that the deviation into a plot of fratricide represents both an evasion of racial violence and a failure of fundamental invention: "In order to construct the mystery which is at the heart of the plot of his detective story, Faulkner reproduced, in order to dismantle, the dominant narrative of Southern white male society; what he did not or could not construct for us was a genuinely alternative story. . . . It is safer, one might say, for a white male Southerner to forget about the story of class bias . . . and racism while pursuing a story of mythological dimensions (the foundations of society in the taboo against fratricide)" (146, 147). But the fratricide is in fact as superfluous as the rest of the murder plot, moved aside for another plot that does matter. The plot that matters is one action, Chick's, and his "potency" and inclination for future action, and the strange nature of his vicarious acting *on behalf* of the community that otherwise or perhaps simultaneously contemplates other actions of its own—namely lynching (*Intruder* 211).

16. *Sartoris* actually adds one incidence of the wen (85) not found in the earlier *Flags in the Dust*. The sequence in *Flags in the Dust* falls on pages 84, 87, 93, 98–109, 245–47, 252–53, 257, 262–63, and 266–69.

Chapter 4

1. In this chapter *The Town* is cited in the text without abbreviation, by page numbers only.

2. There has been some discussion about the way in which society constrains Eula's agency in *The Town*. Railey writes that Eula "settles the matter in the only way she can: she sacrifices herself on the altar of respectability, masculine power, and economic lust" (160). Schreiber sees the suicide as forcing the community "to cede its 'desire' for her" and as paving the way for Linda to "alter the dominant culture" (90). Trouard also looks for ways in which Eula's action has meaning, despite the narrow options open to her: "When she clumps up those stairs to his office, she violates both commodity laws: she is not supposed to speak (express desire or choice) and she has come to market on her own"; "Her emotional reserves . . . enable Eula to offer herself *practically*, despite sanctions—including Gavin's—prohibiting her exercise of freedom and power"; in her final exit "she leaves . . . the male-dominated territory for good" (288–89), but her suicide demonstrates "just how few possibilities" are open to her (290). Rankin sees the suicide not only as a sacrifice but as a sign that Eula "is a woman capable of dramatic action" (150).

3. Gavin Stevens has been a constant critical target. This is due partly to his

overelaborate rhetoric (more pronounced in some novels than others) and partly to the critical perception that at least occasionally Faulkner is using him as a spokesman for retrograde views on civil rights (in *Intruder in the Dust*). Snead sees Stevens's "excesses" as unintended self-caricature by Faulkner, "a kind of unconscious literary kitsch" (217). Polk calls him "mouthy" (*Dark House* 162) and elsewhere describes him as an unreliable narrator, a filter who obscures the fact that there is actually "no evidence whatsoever to support the accusation that Flem regularly steals and cheats, forecloses on widows, or does any of the reprehensible things we have come to think of him as doing" ("Idealism in *The Mansion*" 116). In fact, Polk argues, Stevens himself "does more scheming and cheating than Flem does" and lives on the "ill gotten gains" of his wife's first husband (116). Urgo describes Gavin's logic as applied to Mink Snopes as "the logic of bigotry" (*Faulkner's Apocrypha* 200). Trouard finds that Gavin, in failing to accept Eula's offer of herself, "aligns himself with Flem and De Spain. He becomes an economic winner, rejecting the currency, refusing the transaction" (289). Kang views Gavin's sexual restraint toward Linda in *The Mansion* as the sign of a "deep, romantic horror toward woman's sexuality": "In his fantasy of embracing a child instead of Linda, Gavin shows his defense mechanism to convert his shame and guilt and thus to free himself from [the] moral burden and responsibility of Flem's death" (35, cf. *M* 423–24).

4. There are many exceptions to this observation, the most notable being *The Black Sheep* (*La Rabouilleuse*), *Cousin Pons*, and *Cesar Birotteau*. In these the financial transactions are not only important but followable.

5. Another analysis of "point of view" in the Centaur episode appears in Creighton 50–52.

6. Reed compares the unusual drama of *The Town* to a minstrel show: "We think we've been given a dramatic situation when we haven't. The book at this point seems to be a front porch or a minstrel show, each character listening to the others, taking up his story where the preceding narrator left off, listening patiently while another talks, then talking himself, giving us the information he's gathered or been given, while the others listen" (245).

7. Reed suggests that unlike *The Hamlet*, the first-person narrative method of *The Town* requires a process of selection that inhibits the variety of the novel: "If Ratliff, Mallison, or Stevens sees something being done, . . . it tends to be seen to some purpose, noticed to some end; it is not just there for its own sake. It is a natural result of the first-person technique that each individual narrator must select details because they are relevant to his particular narrative, and this, of course, eliminates the grandeur of the suspended world" (241). This notion of first-person selectivity contrasts with James's famous observation of the "terrible *fluidity* of self-revelation" (*AN* 321).

8. William Faulkner, "Spotted Horses," *Scribner's Magazine* June 1931: 585–97; "The Hound," *Harper's Magazine* Aug. 1931: 266–74; "Centaur in Brass," *American Mercury* Feb. 1932: 200–210; "Lizards in Jamshyd's Courtyard," *Saturday Evening Post* 27 Feb. 1932: 12–13, 52, 57; "Mule in the Yard," *Scribner's Magazine* Aug. 1934: 65–70; "Fool About a Horse," *Scribner's Magazine* Aug. 1936: 80–86; "Barn Burning," *Harper's Magazine* June 1939: 86–96. "Barn Burning" is a special case because it is a ver-

sion originally intended for the novel itself but found to be more appropriate for independent publication. It is an alternative version, not a more rudimentary one. All the stories are reprinted in either *CS* or *Uncollected Stories*.

9. This revision is also discussed in Creighton 54. In her discussions of the revisions of "Centaur" and "Mule in the Yard," Towner emphasizes how the stories have been expanded to focus on Flem and to create expectations about Flem's goals or about what Flem will do next. She sees Faulkner as consistently blunting the humor of the original stories (97–101).

10. Montgomery Ward argues that he has not violated the federal law against sending obscene material through the mails, that no one can prove he has even been making money from obscene materials, and that in any case there is no federal officer present to make an arrest. But clearly Gavin and Hub intend to send him before the federal judge anyway (165); whether or not he is actually guilty of any violation, it is certain that Judge Long will convict him. The fact that no federal officer is present makes it necessary to hold him temporarily under the obsolete anti-automobile law. Montgomery Ward argues that the automobile law is a city law and Hampton a county sheriff, but Hampton makes the arrest anyway (164).

In all this, Faulkner appears to endorse a certain arrogance in Gavin, an authoritarian willingness to manipulate the law for presumably moral ends: "You're like me. . . . You don't give a damn about the truth either. What you're interested in is justice" (176). Cf. also *Knight's Gambit* III: "In my time I have seen truth that was anything under the sun but just, and I have seen justice using tools and instruments I wouldn't want to touch with a ten-foot fence rail."

11. In *The Mansion*, Faulkner belatedly supplies Flem with an additional motive: the different prisons (Atlanta and Parchman) that would result from different crimes. Flem wants Montgomery Ward at Parchman so he can tempt Mink into an escape attempt. In *The Mansion*, the dirty-picture charge is never spelled out and is simply assumed to involve a real crime.

Chapter 5

1. In this chapter, *The Mansion* is cited in the text without abbreviation, by page numbers only.

2. Mink's financial history forms a counterpart to his agony over money in chapter 1 (e.g., 15, 17). Leaving prison, he begins with a ten-dollar bill and $3.85 left from the money sent him by Montgomery Ward (103, 259). He is cheated of fifty cents at the grocery store and left with a total of $13.03 (263). He is robbed of the ten dollars (273) but gets ten more from Goodyhay (282). He is given fifty cents by a policeman, whom he confuses with the "W P and A" (287). He spends twenty cents on animal crackers (290) and $12.10 on a pistol and three bullets (292). He now has $1.23.

3. Robinson discusses Flem's conversion into a rigid "monument" in *The Mansion*. Gray sees Flem's immobility as part of an overall "metaphysical quietism" in which "all are seen as victims . . . ultimately impotent and deserving of our pity" (353). Flem's detachment and passivity are "shared by everyone else"; "most of the

characters . . . subside from action into anonymity, allowing themselves to unwind from 'all the grief and anguish,' the anxiety of having to desire and act" (354).

4. See, e.g., Bakhtin, *Dialogic Imagination* 324: "Heteroglossia . . . is *another's speech in another's language,* serving to express authorial intentions but in a refracted way. Such speech constitutes a special type of *double-voiced discourse.* . . . In such discourse there are two voices, two meanings and two expressions." Bakhtin has been an influence in recent Faulkner criticism. Dalziel and Kidd offer readings based on the concept of "dialogic form," and Bakhtin is also used extensively by Lockyer, Wadlington (*Reading Faulknerian Tragedy*), Weinstein (*Faulkner's Subject*), Ross, and Gray.

5. Dolezel (*Heterocosmica*) emphasizes the importance of "nonactional events," specifically natural events and accidents. Cf. Faulkner's "Old Man": " . . . existing now, as he did and had and apparently was to continue for an unnamed period, in a state in which he was toy and pawn on a vicious and inflammable geography" (*Wild Palms* 162).

6. In the evaluation of the moral stature of individual characters that has absorbed much of the critical history of the Snopes trilogy, Linda Snopes has been thoroughly contested. Early defenders were Beck (*Man in Motion* 160–63, 171–73) and Watson, who praises Linda's "ideologically based love," her "philosophical orientation to love," her "transcendent humanistic love" (*Snopes Dilemma* 178, 228). On the other hand, Kang's praise of Linda is for rage and revenge against "the father" (25) and the "specular phallocentric structure" (28) and for her "rebellion and deliberate betrayal of Gavin" (34). Schreiber considers whether Kang's praise of Linda's manipulations shows Linda to be like Flem, but she concludes that "Linda differs in her honesty and her insight into the flaws of the society she rejects" (93). Others have judged Linda more coldly. Towner writes that Linda is "finally a profoundly immoral character—cold-blooded where even Mink has a few regrets, and more deviously 'respectable' than even Flem in his heyday in *The Town.* . . . The girl's father might have been the wild Hoake McCarron, but Flem is indeed father to the woman" (111, 113). Rankin says that "Linda seems more perverse than Mink himself, because we have seen her ideal potential as a daughter of Eula destroyed" (151). Dale struggles with the rhetorical poles of "revenge" and "murder," terms introduced in the novel by Ratliff: "It is hard to fault Linda for avenging her mother on the despicable Flem; nevertheless, she is an accomplice to the murder of her putative father, and her voice is compromised" (334). In my view the novel does not really grant the rhetorical license not "to fault" Linda for vengeance; Ratliff himself introduces the idea only as a way of cheering Gavin up after the fact.

Snead focuses on the originality of the characters, seeing Linda's character as a characteristic failure of Faulkner's late career, a typical "kitsch offprint," in this case of Eula (225).

7. Like the other principal characters, Mink has been interpreted with a remarkable range of sympathy and judgment. Cleanth Brooks dignifies Mink's "sense of honor" (*Yoknapatawpha Country* 184). Railey sees Mink as an "instrument of justice" (164) with an admirable value system: "Mink's value as a character stems from . . . his recognition of the natural ties and responsibilities between people" (163). Urgo, with-

out denying Mink's criminality, offers Mink as typical of "individuals who do become conscious of their oppression" (*Faulkner's Apocrypha* 204): "Mink's attitudes and actions have their basis in a deep-seated but barely articulated class antagonism" (205). Polk applies a higher standard of conduct: "Can we condone Mink's—anybody's—taking the law into his own hands? . . . Must not we, finally, repudiate him? . . . If violence, if murder, is the only way we can deal effectively with Snopesism, if the world has to depend on the likes of Mink Snopes to save it, then we are in sorry shape indeed" ("Idealism in *The Mansion*" 125).

8. Faulkner's letters provide biographical evidence that Faulkner was (occasionally) a tired man. The letters, during the writing of *The Town* in particular, document the writer's fears that he might no longer have passion for his work and perhaps no longer can judge whether his work is good or not (see Gray 335–36 and Towner 158 n. 9). Gray argues that *The Town* and *The Mansion* in particular are tired books. In *The Town* he detects an "elegiac feeling" that betokens an "impulse of absence and departure," a search for a "God-like view" that implies aloofness from his work. In *The Mansion* he sees a need to dissipate narrative tensions too quickly, a metaphysical quietism, and a mood of equanimity which in this case represents a slackening of energy (345, 346, 352, 353, 357).

Snead summarizes and recapitulates many of the traditional reasons for devaluing the late Faulkner: repetition of ideas, a prolix and bombastic style, and reliance on a Gavin Stevens character whose excesses are like a parody of Faulkner (216–17). Another argument has been that Faulkner depends on overt expressions of uplifting values. Gray is concerned that "much of the later writing from *Go Down Moses* on is vitiated by Faulkner's apparent need to strike the public pose and make the public statement, that this often diverted him from where the real strengths of his fiction lay . . . , and that, ironically, it was this diversion and its consequences that attracted many of his first critics" (276).

Among alternative valuations, Urgo argues that Faulkner's insurgent and radical "apocrypha" reaches its masterpieces in *A Fable* and the Snopes trilogy. Towner sees the late novels as offering a host of new characters and a new focus on the act of telling stories: "The meaning of *Snopes* exists in its evolution, its amplification of narrative 'facts in evidence'" (138).

Chapter 6

1. Genette speaks of the phenomenon in Proust of the "invasion of the story by the commentary, of the novel by the essay, of the narrative by its own discourse" (*Narrative Discourse* 259). This may be an extreme phenomenon and distinctive of Proust, but as Miller points out, "Any novel already interprets itself. It uses within itself the same kind of language, encounters the same impasses, as are used and encountered by the critic. The critic may fancy himself safely and rationally outside the contradictory language of the text, but he is already entangled in its web" (23). By Miller's logic, then, contradictions are inherent, and any reader must reach an impasse, an aporia. But surely it is worthwhile to distinguish between that which is

innately multivalent and polysemous and that which is incoherent and fundamentally confused.

Chambers argues that the reader has the "responsibility to free the text from its own limitations. In other words, one should not allow one's own mode of reading to be determined exclusively by the text's situational self-reflexivity—that is, by the ideology of art to which the text happens to subscribe" (27). From the perspective of the reader in the narrative exchange, Reid raises the issue of the text's resistance to the "totalizing force" of privileged voices and calls attention to the "ways in which [the] story resists its own main ideological current" (127). The point here is not that even Barthes's "readerly text" has indeterminacies and hermeneutic gaps but rather that even the most overdetermined text can escape the designs programmed into it.

2. Dolezel ("A Thematics of Motivation and Action") suggests ways in which the nature of the action implies thematic meaning, for instance the many responses generated in the struggle between individuals and a "modally circumscribed world" (64). Lowe writes: "Above all, classical plotting is teleological: it asserts the deep causality and intelligibility of its world even where it denies human access to direct apprehension or control" (260). Leitch speaks of a range of possible implications of events: "The variety of relations between action and meaning . . . corresponds to a range of attitudes toward the human subject: from person as agent to person as object or spectacle to person as consciousness" (147); "Action is a trope for human existence: It equates being alive with a sequence of purposive, discrete, consequential, morally significant decisions. . . . However, it is not a privileged trope; that is, it is one way among others of imaging human experience" (143).

3. Monica Fludernik formulates a revived mimesis of "experientiality" in her concept of a "natural" narratology.

4. Gustave Flaubert to Mlle Leroyer de Chantepie, February 19, 1857. Reprinted in Allott 271.

5. See also Thompson and McCole.

6. Although "pre–New Critical intentionalism" (Bal, *On Story-Telling* 15) has long been by consensus critically unthinkable, some have sought legitimate ways to speak of manifestations of intention in the text. Boardman looks for "the overdue reinstatement of individual volition as a serious subject of inquiry" (18). See also Alter, *Pleasures of Reading* 142.

7. The term "implied author" has been contested. Narratologists such as Mieke Bal have considered the notion of "implied author" to be beyond the concerns of narratology (*Narratology* 18). The common alternative is to treat the text as having its own identity. Thus Peter Brooks and Chambers metaphorize the text, Brooks emphasizing the text's desire to subjugate the reader (61), Chambers speaking of an attempted seduction performed by the text (214). Rabinowitz focuses on the role of the "authorial audience," the audience prepared to accept the "conventions" and "rules" assumed in the text. This is consistent with other attempts to remove a personalized implied author from the critical terminology. It also generally accords with concepts of narrative contracts (e.g., Chambers) or narrative "exchanges" (e.g., Reid).

Lowe has an excellent description of the way the reader learns the rules of a text (22–27).

Among those who have endorsed the concept of implied author are Chatman (*Coming to Terms*), Lanser, O'Neill, Darby, and Kearns. Preston has looked for contradictions in the implied author of *The Great Gatsby*. O'Neill has raised the logical possibility of an unreliable implied author, arguing that there are as many implied authors as there are real readers. Others drop the word "implied" completely. Genette argues in *Narrative Discourse Revisited* that to the extent the concept has merit, it should simply be called "the author" (148). Walsh, like Genette, simply speaks of "the author." Lowe also speaks of "authors—not the real author, but a phantom figure projected by the reader"; he describes "the author" as wearing "the mask of a control-level presence built into the story universe" (75). Ginsburg and Rimmon-Kenan, wary of a unitary subjectivity, are unwilling to use the definite article before the word "author."

The explicit formulation of implied authority as only a set of implied norms which is inferred by the reader is made by Chatman (*Coming to Terms*) and continued by Fludernik and Darby. Fludernik speaks of "the entire novel's frame of values" (183), of "an abbreviation for the narrative's overall meaning structure" (381), and of "the world view that the reader constructs for the text as a whole" (395). Darby sees this as an important extension beyond formalist poetics, a bridge between "two traditions' contrasting understandings of narrative as either communicative process or intellectual product" (847).

The relations of author, implied author, character, reader, and other related entities are presented diagrammatically in the introduction to Onega and Garcia Landa, in Maclean, and in Lanser.

8. Kearns draws heavily on Lanser in creating a "rhetorical narratology"—his own synthesis of Booth, of Phelan's character-centered narratology, and of narratology in general. Others who discuss the textual speech act as the creation of a "display text" include Leitch (esp. chapter 2), Kroeber, Onega and Garcia Landa (26), and Walsh.

9. The relation between "author" and "narrator" is problematic. Certainly on occasion, Suzanne Ferguson says, "It is reasonable to identify the narrator as the 'implied author,' or simply as the 'author,' with the tacit understanding that he is a fictional persona, not a real person, a critical task easy for most readers" (233). But as Ginsburg and Rimmon-Kenan observe, "It may be worth noting that even in classical narratology the neatness of the category of 'narrator' is sometimes disturbed. While personified character-narrators could be clearly distinguished from authors, nonpersonified, third-person ones potentially put the distinction in doubt. First-person narrators are equally problematic" (75). Graesser et al. show experimentally that "the impersonal, omniscient, third-person narrator" is an "invisible agent" to the reader (266).

10. Bal wants not to only to dispose of the implied author ("pre–New Critical intentionalism") but to de-anthropomorphize the narrator as well: "I shall rigorously stick to the definition of 'that agent which utters the linguistic signs which constitute the text'" (*Narratology* 15). Ronen notes that "focalization and its associated concepts

are inherently *anthropomorphic*" but asserts the possibility of "impersonal narration": "In this case the subject holding the ability to narrate the story is attributed a zero degree of individuation and no psychological foundation" (183).

11. Chatman wants to "resist the anthropomorphic trap" and describes the "career-author" as "the subset of features shared by all the implied authors (that is, all the individual intents) of the narrative texts" (*Coming to Terms* 88). Darby cites Rimmon-Kenan and Chatman as having redefined the implied author as "depersonified," not the "anthropomorphic entity . . . originally conceived by Booth" (838–39). Walsh responds to Chatman that "If we want to talk about intent in fiction, we should accept that in doing so we are necessarily invoking the author" (510). Walsh is willing to speak in terms of "authorial personality": "Authorial personality can be regarded as an intertextual phenomenon to be abstracted from a writer's whole corpus; but there still remains the unwarranted assumption that this personality is uniform. . . . Personality, after all, is not monolithic, not timeless, not unitary, not even necessarily coherent. Indeed novelists, who are perhaps rather less straightforward than academics, are likely to attitudinize in diverse ways in their writing" (506). The writings of Bakhtin show that the language of anthropomorphism is compatible with a focus on "semantic instantiation": "It is in fact out of this stratification of language, its speech diversity and even language diversity, that [the novelist] constructs his style, while at the same time he maintains the unity of his own creative personality and the unity (although it is, to be sure, unity of another order) of his own style" (*Dialogic Imagination* 298–99); "It is as if the author has no language of his own, but does possess his own style, his own organic and unitary law governing the way he plays with languages and the way his own real semantic and expressive intentions are refracted within them" (311). Lanser argues that it is not "naively anthropomorphic to say that there is an author, or any person, speaking in or through the text": "Many fictional elements are designed precisely to carry out this naturalizing function, and almost all structures of narrative are subjected by writers and readers alike to this naturalizing process. . . . Textual personae are anthropomorphized and given voice through the process of textual production. In Western fiction that is 'readable,' there is indeed a voice that 'speaks' and another, usually silent consciousness that 'hears'" (112–14).

Kearns interprets speech-act theory to mean that "because of the ur-convention of authorial reading, readers will always infer an authorial presence" (94), and that "because a reader must cooperate with someone, she or he constructs that someone to account for the existence of the communication, the text" (100).

O'Neill speaks of the implied author as constituted by the "positions and values the text is inferred to espouse" (73), yet he also says that the narrative "necessarily presupposes a presenting instance, a consciousness that selects and orders" (17). He also characterizes the implicit author as "the 'director' behind the narrative" (68), a clearly anthropomorphic metaphor. Speaking of *The Hamlet*, Bruss wonders, "Is there personality or impersonal force behind a narrative process that weaves its way through the desires of one consciousness and the fears of another . . . ?" (165). Marie-Laure Ryan thinks it right to say that "Faulkner impersonates" his characters, leaving open the possibility for some description of the impersonator (71).

12. Others have written about mixed voices. Matthews argues that the speakers of *Absalom, Absalom!* are not completely differentiated, so that there is the effect of "interpenetrations of voice": "There is an essential sameness to the baroque prolixity, the nightmarish breathlessness, and the Latinate polysyllabism of the novel. . . . In addition . . . the reader is occasionally presented with passages that have no identifiable source" (121). Ross writes that because of the common features of the voices of the narrators, we have in *Absalom* "the overwhelming consistency of an oratorical Overvoice pervading the entire text" (220). Ross offers nuanced readings of numerous voices and combinations of voices in Faulkner, including the mingling of narratorial language and the language of Mink Snopes in *The Mansion*. Minter sees a "medleyed voice" in the final section of *The Sound and the Fury:* "It is not so much Faulkner's own voice that we hear as it is a medleyed voice created out of the discrete voices that together define the imaginative context" (147).

Guerard also surveys the shifts of tone among various voices in *The Hamlet*. Cf. 213–20. An analysis of narrative voices in *Requiem for a Nun* appears in Ruppersberg.

Gray describes the effect of different voices—"the voice of Will Varner, the voice of folkloric wisdom, the voice of a more sophisticated narrator, and the 'voice' of nature"—engaging each other: "As a result, [the] event is no longer perceived as stable, a scene from provincial life recollected in tranquility by a cosmopolitan narrator for the benefit of an audience just as cosmopolitan as himself. It is seen, rather, as a collision" (51). Oddly, writing of *The Town*, Gray sees the interchange of vocabularies between the characters there as an indication of the entire book's "uncertainty of speech and instability of explanation" (334): "What was a creative use of confusion in the earlier writing, or at least some of it, becomes, simply, confusion" (345).

By contrast, Kinney defines Faulkner's "poetics" in terms of the "phenomenological" process of the reader's formation of a "constitutive consciousness" out of the partial cognitions of characters. He claims that narrative of this kind cannot be told through "omniscient narrators," because a voice insufficiently dissociated from the author inhibits the reader's role. He finds the Snopes novels in varying degrees untypical of Faulkner—and flawed (5, 30, 242, 254).

13. Other stylistic analyses in more recent years include Matthews's discussion of the ambiguities and evasions in a sentence in *The Hamlet* (200–202) and Bunselmeyer's division of Faulkner's writing into a "contemplative" style of negatives and appositives and a comic style of "right-branching kernels." Others who relate style to voice are Brumm and Gresset. Like Welty, Guerard also moves from style to temperament.

14. Matthews disagrees with Slatoff's search for "temperament," a search that "emphatically underlines our common assumptions about texts. The text looks not only toward manifest meaning, but also toward its manifested author" (39). But Matthews continues that "stories may mean without signifying, constitute selfhood without expressing it" (40). In this sense he agrees that Faulkner creates an implied temperament in writing, rather than expressing a previously existing personality from the biographical world. The distinction appears to be the same as that between the biographical and the implied author.

15. Interview with Harvey Breit, *New York Times Book Review,* January 30, 1955. In *Lion* 80–83. Quoted by Slatoff in Hoffman and Vickery 184.

16. Lockyer follows Polk in emphasizing the importance of the character of Horace Benbow as an important expression of the "unresolved anxieties about language that mark the flowering of Faulkner's writing life" (10). She says the narrator of *Light in August* "perpetuates the dialectic by uncovering the emptiness of words and then turning around to underscore their power" (95).

17. Moreland also uses the word "humor" in this way, deriving the term from Faulkner's own description of Ratliff's "humorous poise" (*H* 79).

18. Guerard also observes the "modulations" by which the reader is permitted to "disengage himself gently" from *Light in August* (209). Wadlington refers to the ending of *Light in August* in terms of "closure by comic buffers" (*Reading Faulknerian Tragedy* 163). On the multiple plotlines of *Light in August,* see Kreiswirth's excellent article "Plots and Counterplots."

19. Gray sees a central inconsistency in the conception of Eula, between "the preternatural creature of Stevens's and other people's occasional imaginings" and the "frustrated woman who eventually kills herself rather than be branded a whore": "The two versions of Eula, Lilith and Bovary, the 'incandescent shape' . . . and the pathetic victim of the boredom of provincial life: these do not go together, any more than the narrative idioms to which they belong do" (341).

20. Cohen writes that the "earlier modernist versions of Faulkner portrayed him as an invisible magician orchestrating the illusion of objectivity and detachment in his novels" (639). The "magic" I am suggesting is anything but invisible; it is a style of virtuosity, a high-profile presence.

21. The relation of gaity and dread has been a lasting theoretical concern. In his preface to *Samson Agonistes,* Milton insists on the pleasurable emotions generated by tragedy. Boardman cites Hume on the "unaccountable pleasure" of tragedy, the way terrible things are "converted into pleasure" by the "delightful movements" of dramatization (144). Alter sees reading as directed toward determining the distinctive pleasures of the writer (*Pleasures of Reading* 91) and focuses on "the high fun of literature" (228).

22. Ross posits a relationship of struggle and dominance. He comments that Faulkner's "silent readers confront a dominant rhetoric that they must both accept and resist. . . . Faulkner's prose would seem to try to overpower or overwhelm doubt with its sheer prolixity" (197).

23. One variation to this is Moreland, who sees Faulkner as escaping from the repetitive and confusing "vacillation between nostalgia and irony" that characterizes his modernism (7). Matthews, on the other hand, sees in the new departures of Faulkner's late career not an abandonment of his central career but a new form of postmodern play.

24. Weinstein also sees an evolution in Faulkner's subjectivity: "By 1942 . . . he had lost the capacity (or perhaps the desire) to dramatize through reader disorientation and immersion the traumatic entry of the individual subject into the culture's maturational field: a traumatic entry at the core of the great Modernist texts. At the

level of the writing the hurt had ceased, the subject had sutured" (*Faulkner's Subject* 9). For Weinstein the pivotal text is *Absalom, Absalom!* The voice of later "Faulkner" does constitute an "identity limned by a certain deployment of language" (123).

25. Stonum (*Faulkner's Career*) sees Faulkner's career as a series of transformations, not of identity but of subject and theme. Moreland describes the essential shape of Faulkner's career, the escape from modernism, in terms of the transformation of repeated scenes. He asserts that in *The Hamlet* Faulkner works through the scene of the rejected child at the door from *Absalom, Absalom!* with repetitive reimagining, a "revisionary repetition" (7) in which Ab Snopes angrily tracks manure through De Spain's front door, a scene which for Moreland is filled with "potential poetry and humor" (135).

Selected Bibliography

Abbott, H. Porter. *The Cambridge Introduction to Narrative.* Cambridge: Cambridge UP, 2002.

Aiken, Conrad. "William Faulkner: The Novel as Form." *Atlantic Monthly* November 1939: 650–54. Reprinted in Warren 46–52.

Allott, Miriam. *Novelists on the Novel.* New York: Columbia UP, 1959.

Alter, Robert. *A Lion for Love: A Critical Biography of Stendahl.* New York: Basic Books, 1979.

———. *The Pleasures of Reading: In an Ideological Age.* 1989. New York: Norton, 1996.

Arpad, Joseph L. "William Faulkner's Legendary Novels: The Snopes Trilogy." *Mississippi Quarterly* 22 (Summer 1969): 214–25.

Auerbach, Eric. *Mimesis: The Representation of Reality in Western Literature.* Trans. Willard R. Trask. Princeton: Princeton UP, 1953.

Bakhtin, Mikhail M. *The Dialogic Imagination: Four Essays.* Ed. Michael Holquist. Trans. Caryl Emerson and Michael Holquist. 1975. Austin: U of Texas P, 1981.

———. *Problems of Dostoevsky's Poetics.* Trans. R. W. Rotsel. Ann Arbor: Ardis, 1973.

Bal, Mieke. *Narratology: Introduction to the Theory of Narrative.* 2nd ed. Trans. Christine Van Boheemen. 1980. Toronto: U of Toronto P, 1997. Orig. trans. 1985.

———. *On Story-Telling: Essays on Narratology.* Ed. David Jobling. Sonoma, CA: Palebridge Press, 1991.

Balzac, Honoré de. *The Black Sheep* (*La Rabouilleuse*). Trans. Donald Adamson. London: Penguin Books, 1970.

———. *Cousin Bette.* Trans. Anthony Bonner. New York: Bantam Books, 1961.

———. *A Harlot High and Low* (*Splendeurs et miseres des courtisanes*). Trans. Rayner Heppenstall. London: Penguin Books, 1970.

Barnett, Louise K. "The Speech Community of *The Hamlet.*" *Centennial Review* 30 (Summer 1986): 400–414.

Barthes, Roland. "The Death of the Author." Trans. Richard Howard. *The Discontinuous Universe.* Ed. Sallie Sears and Georgianna W. Lord. New York: Basic Books, 1972. 7–11.

———. "Introduction to the Structural Analysis of Narrative." *Image, Music, Text.* Ed. and trans. Stephen Heath. 1966. New York: Hill and Wang, 1977. 79–117.

———. *S/Z.* Trans. Richard Miller. 1970. New York: Hill and Wang, 1974.

Basic, Sonja. "Faulkner's Narrative: Between Involvement and Distancing." Hon-nighausen, *Faulkner's Discourse* 141–48.

———. "Faulkner's Narrative Discourse: Mediation and Mimesis." *New Directions in Faulkner Studies: Faulkner and Yoknapatawpha, 1983.* Ed. Doreen Fowler and Ann J. Abadie. Jackson: UP of Mississippi, 1984. 302–21.

Batty, Nancy. "The Riddle of *Absalom, Absalom!* Looking at the Wrong Blackbird?" *Mississippi Quarterly* 47 (Summer 1994): 461–88.

Bayley, John. "Against a New Formalism." *Critical Quarterly* 10 (Summer 1968): 69–71.

———. "The Flexner Sonata." Review of *The Sense of an Ending,* by Frank Kermode. *Essays in Criticism* 26 (April 1968): 208–18.

Beck, Warren. *Man in Motion: Faulkner's Trilogy.* Madison: U of Wisconsin P, 1963.

———. "William Faulkner's Style." *American Prefaces* 6 (Spring 1941). Reprinted in *Faulkner.* Madison: U of Wisconsin P, 1976. 34–51.

Bentley, Eric. *The Life of the Drama.* New York: Atheneum, 1964.

Bleikasten, Andre. "Faulkner from a European Perspective." Weinstein, *Cambridge Companion* 75–95.

Boardman, Michael M. *Narrative Innovation and Incoherence: Ideology in Defoe, Goldsmith, Austen, Eliot, and Hemingway.* Durham, NC: Duke UP, 1992.

Booth, Wayne C. *The Company We Keep: An Ethics of Fiction.* Berkeley: U of California P, 1988.

———. *Critical Understanding: The Powers of Limits of Pluralism.* Chicago: U of Chicago P, 1979.

———. *The Rhetoric of Fiction.* Chicago: U of Chicago P, 1961.

———. "*The Rhetoric of Fiction* and the Poetics of Fiction." *Novel* 1 (Winter 1968): 105–17. Reprinted in *Now Don't Try to Reason with Me: Essays and Ironies for a Credulous Age.* Chicago: U of Chicago P, 1970. Reprinted in Spilka 77–89.

Bowen, Elizabeth. "The Search for a Story to Tell." *Highlights of Modern Literature: A Permanent Collection of Memorable Essays from the New York Times Book Review.* Ed. Francis Bacon. New York: New American Library, 1954. 30–32.

Bradbury, Malcolm. "Towards a Poetics of Fiction: 1) An Approach Through Structure." *Novel* 1 (Fall 1967): 45–53. Reprinted in Spilka 3–10.

Bradford, M. E. "Faulkner's 'Elly': An Exposé." *Mississippi Quarterly* 21 (Summer 1968): 179–87.

Bremond, Claude. "The Logic of Narrative Possibilities" (1966). Trans. Elaine D. Cancalm. *New Literary History* 11 (Spring 1980): 387–411.

Brooke-Rose, Christine. "Whatever Happened to Narratology?" *Poetics Today* 11 (Summer 1990): 283–93.

Brooks, Cleanth. *William Faulkner: The Yoknapatawpha Country.* New Haven: Yale UP, 1963.

———. *William Faulkner: Toward Yoknapatawpha and Beyond.* New Haven: Yale UP, 1978.

Brooks, Peter. *Reading for the Plot: Design and Intention in Narrative.* 1984. Reprint, New York: Vintage Books, 1985.

Brumm, Ursula. "Theme and Narrative Voice in Faulkner's 'Old Man.'" Honnighausen, *Faulkner's Discourse* 242–47.

Bruss, Elizabeth. "The Game of Literature and Some Literary Games." *New Literary History* 9 (Autumn 1977): 153–72.

Budd, Louis J., and Edwin H. Cady, eds. *On Faulkner: The Best from American Literature.* Durham, NC: Duke UP, 1989.

Bunselmeyer, J. E. "Narrative Styles" (1981). Budd and Cady 143–61.

Burke, Sean. *The Death and Return of the Author: Criticism and Subjectivity in Barthes, Foucault, and Derrida.* 2nd ed. 1992. Edinburgh: Edinburgh UP, 1998.

Cary, Joyce. "The Way a Novel Gets Written." *Harper's Magazine* Feb. 1950: 87–93.

Carroll, Noel. "On the Narrative Connection." Peer and Chatman 21–42.

Caserio, Robert L. *Plot, Story, and the Novel: From Dickens and Poe to the Modern Period.* Princeton: Princeton UP, 1979.

Chambers, Ross. *Story and Situation: Narrative Seduction and the Power of Fiction.* Minneapolis: U of Minnesota P, 1984.

Chatman, Seymour B. *Coming to Terms: The Rhetoric of Narrative and Film.* Ithaca: Cornell UP, 1990.

———. *Story and Discourse: Narrative Structure in Fiction and Film.* Ithaca: Cornell UP, 1978.

Clarke, Deborah. *Robbing the Mother: Women in Faulkner.* Jackson: UP of Mississippi, 1994.

Cohan, Steven, and Linda M. Shires. *Telling Stories: A Theoretical Analysis of Narrative Fiction.* London: Routledge, 1988.

Cohen, Philip. "Faulkner Studies and Ideology Critique in the 1990s." Review of *Faulkner and Ideology: Faulkner and Yoknapatawpha, 1992,* ed. Donald Kartiganer and Ann J. Abadie. *Mississippi Quarterly* 49 (Summer 1996): 633–54.

Cowley, Malcolm. —*And I Worked at the Writer's Trade: Chapters of Literary History, 1918–1978.* New York: Viking Press, 1978.

———. *The Faulkner-Cowley File: Letters and Memories, 1944–1962.* New York: Viking Press, 1966.

———. "Introduction." *The Portable Faulkner.* Ed. Malcolm Cowley. New York: Viking Press, 1946. Reprinted in Hoffman and Vickery 94–109.

———. "Storytelling's Tarnished Image." *Saturday Review* 25 Sept. 1971: 25–27, 54.

———, ed. *Writers at Work: The Paris Review Interviews.* New York: Viking Press, 1958.

Crane, Mary Thomas. *Shakespeare's Brain: Reading with Cognitive Theory.* Princeton: Princeton UP, 2001.

Crane, R. S. "The Concept of Plot and the Plot of *Tom Jones.*" *Critics and Criticism.* Ed. R. S. Crane. Chicago: U of Chicago P, 1952. 616–47.

Creighton, Joanne V. *William Faulkner's Craft of Revision.* Detroit: Wayne State UP, 1977.

Crews, Frederick. "Faulkner Methodized." *The Critics Bear It Away: American Fiction and the Academy.* New York: Random House, 1992. 113–42.

Critical Inquiry 7 (Autumn 1980). "On Narrative."

Culler, Jonathan. "Fabula and Sjuzhet in the Analysis of Narrative: Some American Discussions." *Poetics Today* 1.3 (1980): 27–37.

Dale, Corinne. "*Absalom, Absalom!* and the Snopes Trilogy: Southern Patriarchy in Revision." *Mississippi Quarterly* 45 (Summer 1992): 323–37.

Dalziel, Pamela. "*Absalom, Absalom!* The Extension of Dialogic Form." *Mississippi Quarterly* 45 (Summer 1992): 277–94.

Darby, David. "Form and Context: An Essay in the History of Narratology." *Poetics Today* 22 (Winter 2001): 829–52.

Diderot, Denis. *Jacques the Fatalist and His Master.* Trans. David Coward. World's Classics. Oxford: Oxford UP, 1999.

Dolezel, Lubomir. *Heterocosmica: Fiction and Possible Worlds.* Baltimore: Johns Hopkins UP, 1998.

———. "A Thematics of Motivation and Action." *Thematics: New Approaches.* Ed. Claude Bremond, John Landy, and Thomas Pavel. Albany: State U of New York P, 1995. 57–66.

Dunn, Margaret. "The Illusion of Freedom in *The Hamlet* and *Go Down, Moses.*" *American Literature* 57 (October 1985): 407–23.

Duvall, John N. *Faulkner's Marginal Couple: Invisible, Outlaw, and Unspeakable Communities.* Austin: U of Texas P, 1990.

———. "Postmodern Yoknapatawpha: William Faulkner as Usable Past." Duvall and Abadie 39–56.

Duvall, John N., and Ann J. Abadie, eds. *Faulkner and Postmodernism: Faulkner and Yoknapatawpha, 1999.* Jackson: UP of Mississippi, 2002.

Egan, Kieran. "What Is a Plot?" *New Literary History* 9 (Fall 1978): 454–73.

Erlich, Victor. *Russian Formalism: History and Doctrine.* The Hague: Mouton, 1965.

Fadiman, Regina K. *Faulkner's* Light in August: *A Description and Interpretation of the Revisions.* Bibliographical Society of the University of Virginia. Charlottesville: U of Virginia P, 1975.

Farmer, Norman, Jr. "The Love Theme: A Principal Source of Thematic Unity in Faulkner's Snopes Trilogy." *Twentieth Century Literature* 8 (Oct. 1962–Jan. 1963): 111–23.

Faulkner, William. *Absalom, Absalom!* New York: Random House, 1936. Reprinted 1964.

———. "Barn Burning." *Harper's Magazine* June 1939: 86–96. Reprinted in *Collected Stories* 3–25.

———. "Centaur in Brass." *American Mercury* Feb. 1932: 200–210. Reprinted in *Collected Stories* 149–68.

———. *Collected Stories of William Faulkner.* New York: Random House, 1950.

———. *Doctor Martino and Other Stories.* New York: Harrison Smith and Robert Haas, 1934.

———. *Flags in the Dust.* New York: Random House, 1973.

———. "Fool About a Horse." *Scribner's Magazine* Aug. 1936: 80–86. Reprinted in *Uncollected Stories* 118–34.

———. *The Hamlet.* New York: Random House, 1940.

———. "The Hound." *Harper's Magazine* Aug. 1931: 266–74. Reprinted in *Doctor Martino and Other Stories* 52–71 and in *Uncollected Stories* 152–64.

———. *Intruder in the Dust.* New York: Random House, 1948.

———. *Knight's Gambit.* New York: Random House, 1949.

————. *Light in August*. New York: Harrison Smith and Robert Haas, 1932. Reprint, New York: Random House, 1966.

————. "Lizards in Jamshyd's Courtyard." *Saturday Evening Post* 27 Feb. 1932: 12–13 ff. Reprinted in *Uncollected Stories* 135–51.

————. *The Mansion*. New York: Random House, 1959.

————. "Mountain Victory." *Collected Stories,* 745–77. Revised and reprinted from "A Mountain Victory," *Saturday Evening Post* 3 Dec. 1932: 6–7 ff. Reprinted from *Doctor Martino and Other Stories* 315–54.

————. "Mule in the Yard." *Scribner's Magazine* Aug. 1934: 65–70. Reprinted in *Collected Stories* 249–64.

————. "My Grandmother Millard and General Bedford Forrest and the Battle of Harrykin Creek." *Story* 22 (Mar.–Apr. 1943): 68–86. Reprinted in *Collected Stories* 667–700.

————. *Pylon*. New York: Harrison Smith and Robert Haas, 1935. Reprint, New York: Random House, 1967.

————. *The Reivers*. New York: Random House, 1962.

————. *Sanctuary*. New York: Jonathan Cape and Harrison Smith, 1931. Reprint, New York: Random House, 1958.

————. *Sartoris*. New York: Harcourt, Brace, 1929.

————. *Selected Letters*. Ed. Joseph Blotner. New York: Random House, 1977.

————. *The Sound and the Fury*. New York: Jonathan Cape and Harrison Smith, 1929. Reprint, New York: Random House, 1964. Random House edition includes "Appendix. Compson: 1699–1945," originally published in *The Portable Faulkner*. Ed. Malcolm Cowley. New York: Viking Press, 1946. 403–27.

————. "Spotted Horses." *Scribner's Magazine* June 1931: 585–97. Reprinted in *Uncollected Stories* 165–83.

————. "That Evening Sun." *Collected Stories* 289–309. Revised and reprinted from "That Evening Sun Go Down," *American Mercury* Mar. 1931: 256–67, and from "That Evening Sun," *These 13* (1931).

————. "That Will Be Fine." *American Mercury* July 1935: 264–76. Reprinted in *Collected Stories* 265–88.

————. *These 13*. New York: Jonathan Cape and Harrison Smith, 1931.

————. *The Town*. New York: Random House, 1957.

————. *Uncollected Stories of William Faulkner*. Ed. Joseph Blotner. New York: Random House, 1979.

————. *The Unvanquished*. New York: Random House, 1938.

————. *The Wild Palms*. New York: Random House, 1939.

Fehn, Ann, Ingeborg Hoesteray, and Maria Tatar, eds. *Neverending Stories: Toward a Critical Narratology*. Princeton: Princeton UP, 1992.

Ferguson, James. *Faulkner's Short Fiction*. Knoxville: U of Tennessee P, 1991.

Ferguson, Suzanne. "The Face in the Mirror: Authorial Presence in the Multiple Vision of Third-Person Impressionist Narrative." *Criticism* 21 (Summer 1979): 230–50.

Ferraro, Fernando. "Theory and Model for the Structural Analysis of Fiction." *New Literary History* 5 (Winter 1974): 245–68.

Fiedler, Leslie A. *Love and Death in the American Novel.* New York: Criterion, 1960. Revised, New York: Stein and Day, 1966. Reprint, New York: Dell, 1969.

Flint, R. W. "What Price Glory?" *Hudson Review* 7 (Winter 1955): 602–6.

Fludernik, Monika. *Towards a "Natural" Narratology.* London: Routledge, 1996.

Forster, E. M. *Aspects of the Novel.* New York: Harcourt, Brace, 1927.

Fowler, Doreen. "Revising *The Sound and the Fury: Absalom, Absalom!* and Faulkner's Postmodern Turn." Duvall and Abadie 95–108.

Friedman, Norman. "Criticism and the Novel." *Antioch Review* 18 (Fall 1958): 343–70.

———. *Form and Meaning in Fiction.* Athens: U of Georgia P, 1975.

———. "Forms of the Plot." *Journal of General Education* 8 (1955). Reprinted in *The Theory of the Novel.* Ed. Philip Stevick. New York: Free Press, 1967. 145–66. Revised as chapter 5 of *Form and Meaning in Fiction* 79–101.

———. "What Makes a Short Story Short?" *Modern Fiction Studies* 4 (Summer 1958): 103–17. Revised as chapter 9 of *Form and Meaning in Fiction* 167–86.

Gable, Harvey L., Jr. "Hightower's Apotheosis in *Light in August.*" *Mississippi Quarterly* 49 (Summer 1996): 425–40.

Gass, William H. "The Concept of Character in Fiction." *Fiction and the Figures of Life.* New York: Knopf, 1970. 34–54.

Genette, Gerard. *Fiction and Diction.* Trans. Catherine Porter. 1991. Ithaca: Cornell UP, 1993.

———. *Narrative Discourse: An Essay in Method.* Trans. Jane E. Lewin. 1972. Ithaca: Cornell UP, 1980.

———. *Narrative Discourse Revisited.* Trans. Jane E. Lewin. 1983. Ithaca: Cornell UP, 1988.

———. *Palimpsests. Literature in the Second Degree.* Trans. Channa Newman and Claude Doubinsky. 1982. Lincoln: U of Nebraska P, 1997.

Gerrig, Richard J. *Experiencing Narrative Worlds: On the Psychological Activities of Reading.* New Haven: Yale UP, 1993.

Ginsburg, Michael Peled. "Framing Narrative." Review of Ian Reid, *Narrative Exchanges,* and Bernard Dufhuizen, *Narratives of Transmission. Poetics Today* 18 (Winter 1997): 571–88.

Ginsburg, Ruth, and Shlomith Rimmon-Kenan. "Is There a Life after Death? Theorizing Authors and Reading *Jazz.*" *Narratologies: New Perspectives and Narrative Analysis.* Ed. David Herman. Columbus: Ohio State UP, 1999. 66–87.

Godden, Richard. "Earthing *The Hamlet:* An Anti-Ratliffian Reading." *Faulkner Journal* 14 (Spring 1999): 75–117.

———. *Fictions of Labor: William Faulkner and the South's Long Revolution.* Cambridge: Cambridge UP, 1997.

Godzich, Wlad. Foreword to Pavel, *The Poetics of Plot.*

Goodman, Paul. *The Structure of Literature.* Chicago: U of Chicago P, 1954.

Graesser, Arthur C., Cheryl Bowers, Ute J. Bayen, and Xiangen Hu. "Who Said What? Who Knows What? Tracking Speakers and Knowledge in Narratives." Peer and Chatman 255–72.

Gray, Richard. *The Life of William Faulkner: A Critical Biography.* Oxford: Blackwell, 1994.

Greet, T. Y. "The Theme and Structure of Faulkner's *The Hamlet*." *PMLA* 72 (1957). Reprinted in Hoffman and Vickery 330–47.

Gregory, Eileen. "The Temerity to Revolt: Mink Snopes and the Dispossessed in *The Mansion*." *Mississippi Quarterly* 29 (Summer 1976): 401–21.

Gresset, Michel. "Faulkner's Voice." Honnighausen, *Faulkner's Discourse* 184–94.

Guerard, Albert J. *The Triumph of the Novel: Dickens, Dostoevsky, Faulkner*. New York: Oxford UP, 1976.

Gwynn, Frederick L., and Joseph L. Blotner, eds. *Faulkner in the University: Class Conferences at the University of Virginia, 1957–1958*. Charlottesville: U of Virginia P, 1959.

Hall, James. *The Lunatic Giant in the Drawing Room: The British and American Novel since 1930*. Bloomington: Indiana UP, 1968.

Hardy, Barbara. *The Appropriate Form*. London: U of London, Athlone P, 1964.

——. *Tellers and Listeners: The Narrative Imagination*. London: U of London, Athlone P, 1975.

——. "Towards a Poetics of Fiction: 3) An Approach through Narrative." *Novel* 2 (Fall 1968): 5–15. Reprinted in Spilka 31–40. Incorporated into *Tellers and Listeners: The Narrative Imagination*.

Harold, Brent. "The Value and Limitations of Faulkner's Fictional Method." *American Literature* 67 (1975): 212–30.

Harrington, Evans. "'A Passion Week of the Heart': Religion and Faulkner's Art." *Faulkner and Religion: Faulkner and Yoknapatawpha, 1989*. Ed. Doreen Fowler and Ann J. Abadie. Jackson: UP of Mississippi, 1991. 157–76.

Harvey, W. J. *Character and the Novel*. Ithaca: Cornell UP, 1965.

Hassan, Ihab. "The Privations of Postmodernism: Faulkner as Exemplar (A Meditation in Ten Parts)." Duvall and Abadie 1–18.

Herman, David, ed. *Narratologies: New Perspectives on Narrative Analysis*. Columbus: Ohio State UP, 1999.

——. "Scripts, Sequences, and Stories: Elements of a Post-classical Narratology." *PMLA* 112 (1997): 1046–59.

——. *Story Logic: Problems and Possibilities of Narrative*. Lincoln: U of Nebraska P, 2002.

Hite, Molly. "Modernist Design, Postmodern Paranoia: Reading *Absalom, Absalom!* with *Gravity's Rainbow*." Duvall and Abadie 57–80.

Hoffman, Frederick J., and Olga Vickery, eds. *William Faulkner: Three Decades of Criticism*. East Lansing: Michigan State UP, 1960.

Hoffmann, Gerhard. "*Absalom, Absalom!* A Postmodernist Approach." Honnighausen, *Faulkner's Discourse* 276–92.

Holloway, John. *Narrative and Structure: Exploratory Essays*. Cambridge: Cambridge UP, 1979.

Holman, C. Hugh. "*Absalom, Absalom!* The Historian as Detective." *Sewanee Review* 79 (Autumn 1971): 542–53.

Honnighausen, Lothar. *Faulkner: Masks and Metaphors*. Jackson: UP of Mississippi, 1997.

——, ed. *Faulkner's Discourse: An International Symposium*. Tubingen: Max Niemeyer Verlag, 1989.

Holmes, Edward M. *Faulkner's Twice-Told Tales: His Re-use of His Material.* The Hague: Mouton, 1966.

Hopkins, Viola. "William Faulkner's *The Hamlet:* A Study in Meaning and Form." *Accent* 15 (Spring 1955): 125–44.

Howard, Alan B. "Huck Finn in the House of Usher: The Comic and Grotesque Worlds of *The Hamlet.*" *Southern Review* (U of Adelaide) 5 (June 1972): 125–46.

Hunter, Edwin R. *William Faulkner: Narrative Practice and Prose Style.* Washington, DC: Windhover Press, 1973.

James, Henry. *The Art of the Novel.* Ed. R. P. Blackmur. New York: Scribner, 1934.

———. *The Future of the Novel: Essays on the Art of Fiction.* Ed. Leon Edel. New York: Random House, 1956.

———. "The Marriages." *The Complete Tales of Henry James.* Ed. Leon Edel. Vol. 8. Philadelphia: Lippincott, 1962. 33–70.

———. *The Notebooks of Henry James.* Ed. F. O. Matthiesen and Kenneth B. Murdock. New York: Oxford UP, 1947.

Jarrell, Randall. "Stories." *A Sad Heart at the Supermarket: Essays and Fables.* New York: Atheneum, 1962. 140–59.

Johnson, Bradley A. "Constructing Female Gaze in Faulkner's 'Mountain Victory.'" *Faulkner Journal* 16 (Fall 2000/Spring 2001): 65–80.

Josipovici, Gabriel. *The World and the Book: A Study of Modern Fiction.* Stanford: Stanford UP, 1970.

Kafelnos, Emma. "Functions after Propp: Words to Talk about How We Read Narrative." *Poetics Today* 18.4 (1997): 469–94.

———. "Not (Yet) Knowing: Epistemological Effects of Deferred and Suppressed Information in Narrative." *Narratologies: New Perspectives and Narrative Analysis.* Ed. David Herman. Columbus: Ohio State UP, 1999. 33–65.

Kang, Hee. "A New Configuration of Faulkner's Feminine: Linda Snopes Kohl in *The Mansion.*" *Faulkner Journal* 8 (Fall 1992): 21–41.

Karl, Frederick R. *William Faulkner: American Writer.* New York: Weidenfeld & Nicolson, 1989.

Kartiganer, Donald M. "Faulkner Criticism: A Partial View." *Faulkner Journal* 16 (Fall 2000/Spring 2001): 81–99.

———. *The Fragile Thread: The Meaning of Form in Faulkner's Novels.* Amherst: U of Massachusetts P, 1979.

———. "*The Sound and the Fury* and Faulkner's Quest for Form." *English Literary History* 37 (December 1970): 613–40.

———. "'What I Chose to Be': Freud, Faulkner, Joe Christmas, and the Abandonment of Design." *Faulkner and Psychology: Faulkner and Yoknapatawpha, 1991.* Ed. Donald M. Kartiganer and Ann J. Abadie. Jackson: UP of Mississippi, 1994. 288–314.

Kartiganer, Donald M., and Ann J. Abadie, eds. *Faulkner and the Artist: Faulkner and Yoknapatawpha, 1993.* Jackson: UP of Mississippi, 1996.

Kearns, Michael. *Rhetorical Narratology.* Lincoln: U of Nebraska P, 1999.

Kellogg, Robert, and Robert Scholes. *The Nature of Narrative.* New York: Oxford UP, 1966.

Kenner, Hugh. *A Homemade World: The American Modernist Writers.* New York: Knopf, 1975.

Kermode, Frank. *The Art of Telling: Essays on Fiction.* Cambridge: Harvard UP, 1983.

———. "Secrets and Narrative Sequence." *Critical Inquiry* 7 (Autumn 1980): 83–101.

———. *The Sense of an Ending: Studies in the Theory of Fiction.* New York: Oxford UP, 1967.

———. "Sensing Endings." *Nineteenth Century Fiction* 33 (June 1978): 144–58.

Kidd, Millie M. "The Dialogic Perspective in William Faulkner's *The Hamlet.*" *Mississippi Quarterly* 44 (Summer 1991): 309–20.

Kinney, Arthur F. *Faulkner's Narrative Poetics: Style as Vision.* Amherst: U of Massachusetts P, 1978.

Krause, David. "Reading Bon's Letter and Faulkner's *Absalom, Absalom!*" *PMLA* 99 (1984): 225–41.

Kreiswirth, Martin. "Centers, Openings, and Endings: Some Constants" (1984). Budd and Cady 201–13.

———. "Intertexuality, Transference, and Postmodernism in *Absalom, Absalom!* The Production and Reception of Faulkner's Fictional World." Duvall and Abadie 109–23.

———. "'Paradoxical and Outrageous Discrepancy': Transgression, Auto-Intertextuality, and Faulkner's Yoknapatawpha." Kartiganer and Abadie 161–80.

———. "Plots and Counterplots: The Structure of *Light in August.*" *New Essays on Light in August.* Ed. Michael Millgate. Cambridge: Cambridge UP. 55–79.

Kroeber, Karl. *Retelling/Rereading: The Fate of Storytelling in Modern Times.* New Brunswick: Rutgers UP, 1992.

Kucich, John. "Action in the Dickens Ending: *Bleak House* and *Great Expectations.*" *Nineteenth Century Fiction* 33 (June 1978): 88–109.

Kuyk, Dirk, Jr. *Sutpen's Design: Interpreting Faulkner's* Absalom, Absalom! Charlottesville: UP of Virginia, 1990.

Lanser, Susan Sniader. *The Narrative Act: Point of View in Prose Fiction.* Princeton: Princeton UP, 1981.

Lawrence, D. H. *Studies in Classic American Literature.* 1923. New York: Viking Press, 1964.

Leaver, Florence. "The Structure of *The Hamlet.*" *Twentieth Century Literature* 1 (July 1955): 77–84.

Leitch, Thomas M. *What Stories Are: Narrative Theory and Interpretation.* University Park: Pennsylvania State UP, 1986.

Lewis, Wyndham. "William Faulkner: The Moralist with a Corn-Cob." *Men Without Art.* New York: Harcourt, Brace, 1934. 42–64.

Lisca, Peter. "*The Hamlet:* Genesis and Revisions." *Faulkner Studies* 3 (Spring 1954): 5–13.

Lockyer, Judith. *Ordered by Words: Language and Narration in the Novels of William Faulkner.* Carbondale: Southern Illinois UP, 1991.

Lodge, David. *Consciousness and the Novel: Connected Essays.* Cambridge: Harvard UP, 2002.

Lowe, N.J. *The Classical Plot and the Invention of Western Narrative.* Cambridge: Cambridge UP, 2000.

Lytle, Andrew. "*The Town:* Helen's Last Stand." *Sewanee Review* 65 (Summer 1957): 457–84.

Maclean, Marie. *Narrative as Performance: The Baudelairean Experiment.* London: Routledge, 1988.

Magny, Claude-Edmonde. "Faulkner, or Theological Inversion." *The Age of the American Novel: The Film Aesthetic of Fiction between the Two Wars.* Trans. Eleanor Hochman. 1948. New York: Frederick Ungar, 1972. 178–223.

Malraux, André. "A Preface for Faulkner's *Sanctuary.*" *La Nouvelle Revue Française* 1 Nov. 1933. Reprinted in Warren 272–74.

Marcus, Steven. "Snopes Revisited." *Partisan Review* 24 (Summer 1957). Reprinted in Hoffman and Vickery 382–91.

Margolin, Uri. "The Doer and the Deed: Action as a Basis for Characterization in Narrative." *Poetics Today* 7.2 (1986): 205–25.

Matlack, James H. "Voices of Time: Narrative Structure in *Absalom, Absalom!*" *Southern Review* 15 (April 1979): 333–54.

Matthews, John T. *The Play of Faulkner's Language.* Ithaca: Cornell UP, 1982.

McCarthy, Mary. "Characters in Fiction." *On the Contrary.* New York: Farrar, Strauss and Cudahy, 1961. 271–92.

McCole, C. J. "William Faulkner: Cretins, Coffins-worms, and Cruelty." *Lucifer at Large.* New York: Longman's, 1937. 203–28.

McMillan, John. *Games, Strategies, and Managers.* Oxford: Oxford UP, 1992.

Meriwether, James B., and Michael Millgate, eds. *Lion in the Garden: Interviews with William Faulkner 1926–1962.* New York: Random House, 1968.

Miller, J. Hillis. *Ariadne's Thread: Story Lines.* New Haven: Yale UP, 1992.

Millgate, Michael. *The Achievement of William Faulkner.* New York: Random House, 1966.

———. *Faulkner's Place.* Athens: U of Georgia P, 1997.

Minter, David. *Faulkner's Questioning Narratives: Fiction of His Major Phase, 1929–42.* Urbana: U of Illinois P, 2001.

Moore, Robert R. "Desire and Despair: Temple Drake's Self-Victimization." *Faulkner and Women: Faulkner and Yoknapatawpha, 1985.* Ed. Doreen Fowler and Ann J. Abadie. Jackson: UP of Mississippi, 1986. 112–27.

Moreland, Richard C. *Faulkner and Modernism: Rereading and Rewriting.* Madison: U of Wisconsin P, 1990.

Morris, Wesley. "Recovering the Teller in the Tale: An Unfinished Project." Kartiganer and Abadie 141–60.

Mudrick, Marvin. "Character and Event in Fiction." *Yale Review* 50 (Winter 1961): 202–18.

Oates, Joyce Carol. Letter in reply to Noel Polk. *New York Review of Books* 27 June 2002: 54.

O'Connor, Frank. *The Lonely Voice: A Study of the Short Story*. Cleveland: World Publishing Company, 1963.

O'Faolain, Sean. *The Short Story*. New York: Devin-Adair, 1951.

O'Grady, Walter. "On Plot in Modern Fiction: Hardy, James, and Conrad." *Modern Fiction Studies* 11 (Summer 1965): 107–15.

Onega, Susana, and Jose Angel Garcia Landa, eds. *Narratology: An Introduction*. London: Longman, 1996.

O'Neill, Patrick. *Fictions of Discourse: Reading Narrative Theory*. Toronto: U of Toronto P, 1994.

Pavel, Thomas. "Original Articulation: Comments on the Papers by Peter Brooks and Lucianne Frappier-Mazur." *Style* 18 (Summer 1984): 355–68.

———. *The Poetics of Plot: The Case of English Renaissance Drama*. Foreword by Wlad Godzich. Minneapolis: U of Minnesota P, 1985.

Pearson, Norman Holmes. "Faulkner's Three 'Evening Suns.'" *Yale University Library Gazette* October 1954: 61–70.

Peer, Willie Van, and Seymour Chatman, eds. *New Perspectives on Narrative Perspective*. Albany: State U of New York P, 2001.

Phelan, James. *Reading People, Reading Plots: Character, Progression and the Interpretation of Narrative*. Chicago: U of Chicago P, 1989.

———. "Why Narrators Can Be Focalizers—and Why It Matters." Peer and Chatman 51–64.

Poirier, Richard. *The Performing Self: Compositions and Decompositions in the Languages of Contemporary Life*. New York: Oxford UP, 1971.

Polk, Noel. *Children of the Dark House: Text and Context in Faulkner*. Jackson: UP of Mississippi, 1996.

———. "Idealism in *The Mansion*." *Faulkner and Idealism: Perspectives from Paris*. Ed. Michel Gresset and Patrick Samway, S.J. Jackson: UP of Mississippi, 1983. 112–26.

Porter, Michael. E. *Competitive Advantage: Creating and Sustaining Superior Performance*. New York: Free Press, 1985.

Preston, Elizabeth. "Implying Authors in *The Great Gatsby*." *Narrative* 5 (May 1997): 143–64.

Price, Martin. "The Irrelevant Detail and the Emergence of Form." *Aspects of Narrative: Selected Papers from the English Institute*. Ed. J. Hillis Miller. New York: Columbia UP, 1971. 69–91.

Proust, Marcel. *Remembrance of Things Past*. Trans. C. K. Scott Moncrieff. 2 vols. New York: Random House, 1932.

Rabinowitz, Peter J. *Before Reading: Narrative Conventions and the Politics of Interpretation*. Ithaca: Cornell UP, 1987.

Rabkin, Eric, "Spatial Form and Plot." *Critical Inquiry* 4 (Winter 1977): 253–70.

Railey, Kevin. *Natural Aristocracy: History, Ideology, and the Production of William Faulkner*. Tuscaloosa: U of Alabama P, 1999.

Rankin, Elizabeth B. "Chasing Spotted Horses: The Quest for Human Dignity in Faulkner's Snopes Trilogy." *Faulkner: The Unappeased Imagination*. Ed. Glenn O. Carey. Troy, NY: Whitston, 1980. 139–56.

Reed, Joseph W., Jr. *Faulkner's Narrative.* New Haven: Yale UP, 1973.

Reid, Ian. *Narrative Exchanges.* London: Routledge, 1992.

Richardson, Brian. *Unlikely Stories: Causality and the Nature of Modern Narrative.* Newark: U of Delaware P, 1997.

Rimmon-Kenan, Shlomith. *Narrative Fiction: Contemporary Poetics.* 2nd ed. 1983. London: Routledge, 2002.

Roberts, Diane. *Faulkner and Southern Womanhood.* Athens: U of Georgia P, 1994.

Robinson, Owen. "Monuments and Footprints: The Mythology of Flem Snopes." *Faulkner Journal* 17 (Fall 2001): 69–87.

Rogers, David. "A Masculinity of Faded Blue: V. K. Ratliff and Faulkner's Creation of Transportational Space." *Faulkner Journal* 16 (Fall 1999/Spring 2000): 125–68.

Ronen, Ruth. *Possible Worlds in Literary Theory.* Cambridge: Cambridge UP, 1994.

Ross, Stephen M. *Fiction's Inexhaustible Voice: Speech and Writing in Faulkner.* Athens: U of Georgia P, 1989.

Ruppersberg, Hugh Michael. "The Narrative Structure of Faulkner's *Requiem for a Nun.*" *Mississippi Quarterly* 31 (Summer 1978): 387–406.

Ryan, Heberden W. "Behind Closed Doors: The Unknowable and the Unknowing in *Absalom, Absalom!*" *Mississippi Quarterly* 45 (Summer 1991): 295–312.

Ryan, Marie-Laure. *Possible Worlds, Artificial Intelligence, and Narrative Theory.* Bloomington: Indiana UP, 1991.

Sartre, Jean-Paul. "Time in Faulkner: *The Sound and the Fury.*" *Literary and Philosophical Essays.* Trans. Annette Michaelson. London: Rider, 1955. Reprinted in Warren 87–93.

Schreibner, Evelyn Jaffe. "What's Love Got to Do with It? Desire and Subjectivity in Faulkner's Snopes Trilogy." *Faulkner Journal* 9 (Fall 1993/Spring 1994): 83–98.

Shearman, John. *Mannerism.* Harmondsworth, England: Penguin Books, 1967.

Shen, Dan. "Breaking Conventional Barriers: Transgressions of Modes of Focalization." Peer and Chatman 159–72.

Shklovsky, Victor. "Sterne's *Tristram Shandy:* Stylistic Commentary." *Russian Formalist Criticism: Four Essays.* Ed. Lee T. Lemon and Marion J. Reis. Lincoln: U of Nebraska P, 1965. 25–57.

Singal, Daniel J. *William Faulkner: The Making of a Modernist.* Chapel Hill: U of North Carolina P, 1997.

Skei, Hans H. *Reading Faulkner's Best Short Stories.* Columbia: U of South Carolina P, 1999.

Slatoff, Walter J. "The Edge of Order: The Pattern of Faulkner's Rhetoric." *Twentieth Century Literature* 3 (October 1957): 107–27. Reprinted in Hoffman and Vickery 173–98.

———. *Quest for Failure: A Study of William Faulkner.* Ithaca, NY: Cornell UP, 1960.

Smith, Barbara Herrnstein. "Narrative Versions, Narrative Theories." *Critical Inquiry* 7 (Autumn 1980): 213–36.

Snead, James A. *Figures of Division: William Faulkner's Major Novels.* New York: Methuen, 1986.

Spilka, Mark, ed. *Towards a Poetics of Fiction: Essays from Novel: A Forum on Fiction, 1967–1976.* Bloomington: Indiana UP, 1977.

Stevenson, Robert Louis. "A Humble Remonstrance" (1884). *Selected Writings.* Ed. Saxe Commins. New York: Random House, 1947. 915–25.

Stevick, Philip. *The Chapter in Fiction: Theories of Narrative Division.* Syracuse: Syracuse UP, 1970.

Stewart, Ann Harleman. "Models of Narrative Structure." *Semiotica* 64.1–2 (1987): 83–97.

Stonum, Gary Lee. *Faulkner's Career: An Internal Literary History.* Ithaca: Cornell UP, 1979.

———. "Modernism and Its Discontents: Faulkner Studies Enter the Nineties." *Mississippi Quarterly* 44 (Summer 1991): 355–65.

Sturgess, Philip J. M. *Narrativity: Theory and Practice.* Oxford: Clarendon Press, 1992.

Swiggart, Peter. *The Art of Faulkner's Novels.* Austin: U of Texas P, 1962.

Swink, Helen, "William Faulkner: The Novelist as Oral Narrator." *Georgia Review* 26 (Summer 1972): 183–209.

Tebbetts, Terrell L. "'I'm the man here': *Go Down, Moses* and Masculine Identity." Duvall and Abadie 81–94.

Thompson, Alan R. "The Cult of Cruelty." *Bookman* 24 (Jan.–Feb. 1932): 477–87.

Tilley, Allen. *Plot Snakes and the Dynamics of Narrative Experience.* Gainesville: UP of Florida, 1992.

Todorov, Tzvetan. *The Poetics of Prose.* Trans. Richard Howard. Ithaca: Cornell UP, 1977.

———. "Structural Analysis of Literature." *Novel* 3 (Fall 1969): 70–76.

Toliver, Harold. *Animate Illusions: Explorations of Narrative Structure.* Lincoln: U of Nebraska P, 1974.

Tomashevsky, Boris. "Thematics." *Russian Formalist Criticism: Four Essays.* Ed. Lee T. Lemon and Marion J. Reis. Lincoln: U of Nebraska P, 1965. 61–95.

Towner, Theresa M. *Faulkner on the Color Line: The Later Novels.* Jackson: UP of Mississippi, 2000.

Trouard, Dawn. "Eula's Plot: An Irrigarian Reading of Faulkner's Snopes Trilogy." *Mississippi Quarterly* 42 (Summer 1989): 281–97.

Urgo, Joseph R. *Faulkner's Apocrypha: A Fable, Snopes, and the Spirit of Human Rebellion.* Jackson: UP of Mississippi, 1989.

———. "Faulkner's Real Estate: Land and Literary Speculation in *The Hamlet.*" *Mississippi Quarterly* 48 (Summer 1995): 443–57.

———. "Postvomiting: *Pylon* and the Faulknerian Spew." Duvall and Abadie 124–42.

Vickery, Olga W. *The Novels of William Faulkner.* Baton Rouge: Louisiana State UP, 1964.

Volpe, Edmond L. *A Reader's Guide to William Faulkner.* New York: Farrar, Strauss, and Giroux, 1964.

Wadlington, Warwick. *As I Lay Dying: Stories Out of Stories.* New York: Twayne, 1992.

———. *Reading Faulknerian Tragedy.* Ithaca: Cornell UP, 1987.

Walsh, Richard. "Who Is the Narrator?" *Poetics Today* 18.4 (1997): 495–513.

Warren, Robert Penn, ed. *Faulkner: A Collection of Critical Essays.* Englewood Cliffs, NJ: Prentice-Hall, 1966.

Watkins, Floyd C., and Thomas Daniel Young. "Revisions of Style in Faulkner's *The Hamlet.*" *Modern Fiction Studies* 5 (Winter 1959): 327–36.

Watson, James G. "Faulkner: Short Story Structures and Reflexive Forms." *Mosaic* 11 (Summer 1978): 127–37.

——. *The Snopes Dilemma: Faulkner's Trilogy.* Coral Gables: U of Miami P, 1970.

——. *William Faulkner: Self-Presentation and Performance.* Austin: U of Texas P, 2000.

Watt, Ian. "The First Paragraph of *The Ambassadors:* An Explication." *Essays in Criticism* 10 (July 1960): 251–74.

Weinstein, Philip M., ed. *The Cambridge Companion to Faulkner.* Cambridge: Cambridge UP, 1995.

——. *Faulkner's Subject: A Cosmos No One Owns.* Cambridge: Cambridge UP, 1992.

——. "Postmodern Intimations: Musing on Invisibility: William Faulkner, Richard Wright, and Ralph Ellison." Duvall and Abadie 19–39.

——. "Precarious Sanctuaries: Protection and Exposure in Faulkner's Fiction." *Studies in American Fiction* 6 (1978): 173–91.

Welty, Eudora. "In Yoknapatawpha." Review of *Intruder in the Dust,* by William Faulkner. *Hudson Review* 1 (Winter 1949): 596–98. Reprinted in *The Eye of the Story: Selected Essays and Reviews.* New York: Random House, 1978. 207–11.

——. *Three Papers on Fiction.* Northampton, MA: Smith College, 1962.

Wilson, R. Rawdon. *In Palamedes' Shadow: Exploration in Play, Game, and Narrative Theory.* Boston: Northeastern UP, 1990.

Wilson, Raymond J., III. "Imitative Flem Snopes and Faulkner's Causal Sequence in *The Town.*" *Twentieth Century Literature* 26 (Winter 1980): 432–44.

Zender, Karl. F. *Faulkner and the Politics of Reading.* Baton Rouge: Louisiana State UP, 2002.

Zoellner, Robert H. "Faulkner's Prose Style in *Absalom, Absalom!*" *American Literature* 30 (January 1959): 486–502.

Appendix

Pagination Cross-Reference

The Faulkner Journal now specifies that its submissions make use of the "corrected" texts of Faulkner's novels, on the grounds that these are the "best available texts" (e.g. *Faulkner Journal,* Spring 2002, 193). Whether or not the "corrections" are accepted as authoritative, it is certainly true that these are often the *only* texts currently in print. As a convenience to the common reader, this table displays for the quotations used in this book the corresponding page numbers in the "corrected" texts or repaginated texts currently published by Random House. The relevant texts cited here are as follows:

AA	*Absalom, Absalom! The Corrected Text.* New York: Vintage International, 1990.
H	*The Hamlet. The Corrected Text.* New York: Vintage International, 1991.
Wild Palms	*If I forget Thee, Jerusalem [The Wild Palms].* New York: Vintage International, 1995.
Intruder	*Intruder in the Dust.* New York: Vintage International, 1995.
LIA	*Light in August. The Corrected Text.* New York: Vintage International, 1990.
Sanctuary	*Sanctuary. The Corrected Text.* New York: Vintage International, 1993.
SF	*The Sound and the Fury. The Corrected Text.* New York: Vintage International, 1993.
Unvanquished	*The Unvanquished. The Corrected Text.* New York: Vintage International, 1991.

Page	Citations
10	*LIA* 417
11	*LIA* 429, 432
17	*AA* 241, *Intruder* 18, 27, 71, *AA* 212, 265, *H* 345
18	*SF* 104, 158
19	*SF* 150–51, 19, 57, 149, 112, 148, 78, 116, 336, 261, 108
20	*SF* 116, 335–36, 176, 95, 173, 116
21	*SF* 137, 261, 147, 78, 178, 31, 29, 29, 58, 299–300

22	*SF* 299, 335, 124
23	*SF* 174, 44, 200, 202
25	*SF* 79
27	*AA* 14, 61, 87, 96, 80, 69, 106, 117, 115
28	*AA* 139, 175, 178, 285
29	*AA* 215, 4, 276
30	*AA* 268
31	*AA* 225, 289
32	*AA* 220
65	*H* 77, 14–20
66	*H* 220, 176, 60, 92
67	*H* 190, 397, 75, 31, 60–61, 63–64, 65–67, 68
68	*H* 68–73, 73–74, 74, 80, 63, 64, 98, 99, 26, 79, 91
69	*H* 94, 97
70	*H* 101, 400
71	*H* 131, 164, 174, 179, 181
72	*H* 182–216, 216, 217, 217, 216, 217, 219
73	*H* 217, 219, 223, 226
74	*H* 218–19, 272, 268, 241–86, 101, 100, 174–78, 80–5, 291
75	*H* 368–69, 354, 289
77	*H* 355, 299–406, 173–74, 7, 305, 306
78	*H* 331–32, 343, 358, 372
79	*H* 380, 389, 97, 390, 393
80	*H* 397, 405, 93, 94, 403
81	*H* 164
82	*H* 131
83	*H* 30
84	*H* 76–79
85	*H* 75, 77, 77, 78
86	*H* 76, 76, 78, 79, 78, 79
87	*H* 79, 161, 162, 291–92, 292–94
88	*H* 66, *Intruder* 18–25, 214–15, 232–33, 193, *H* 39, 74, 74
89	*H* 182, 166–70, 167, 167, 168, 168
90	*H* 169, 170
91	*H* 170, 170
95	*H* 240
96	*H* 241, 241, 241
97	*H* 79, 166, 176
98	*H* 180, 240
119	*H* 169
131	*H* 49, 51
142	*LIA* 105
164	*H* 371
165	*H* 261–65, 263, 263
166	*H* 263, 262

Index